D0874125

Cluster-Based Industrial Development

Also by Tetsushi Sonobe and Keijiro Otsuka

CLUSTER-BASED INDUSTRIAL DEVELOPMENT: AN EAST ASIAN MODEL

Cluster-Based Industrial Development

A Comparative Study of Asia and Africa

Tetsushi Sonobe
and
Keijiro Otsuka

palgrave
macmillan

First published 2011 by
PALGRAVE MACMILLAN

Palgrave Macmillan in the UK is an imprint of Macmillan Publishers Limited, registered in England, company number 785998, of Houndmills, Basingstoke, Hampshire RG21 6XS.

Palgrave Macmillan in the US is a division of St Martin's Press LLC, 175 Fifth Avenue, New York, NY 10010.

Palgrave Macmillan is the global academic imprint of the above companies and has companies and representatives throughout the world.

Palgrave® and Macmillan® are registered trademarks in the United States, the United Kingdom, Europe and other countries.

ISBN: 978–0–230–28018–2 hardback

This book is printed on paper suitable for recycling and made from fully managed and sustained forest sources. Logging, pulping and manufacturing processes are expected to conform to the environmental regulations of the country of origin.

A catalogue record for this book is available from the British Library.

A catalog record for this book is available from the Library of Congress.

10 9 8 7 6 5 4 3 2 1
20 19 18 17 16 15 14 13 12 11

Printed and bound in Great Britain by
CPI Antony Rowe, Chippenham and Eastbourne

Contents

Illustrations

Tables

Figures

Preface

We began our inquiry into the process of cluster-based industrial development in Japan, Taiwan, and China in December 1998, in order to explore why so many clusters in the region have managed to grow successfully. We clearly recognized that a proper understanding of the process by which industrial clusters develop would provide a clue towards designing appropriate policies to facilitate industrialization in developing countries. After completing the eight case studies of successful cluster development in the three East Asian countries, we published our previous book, entitled *Cluster-Based Industrial Development: An East Asia Model* (2006), pointing to the striking similarities in the patterns of industrial development across the eight cases in East Asia. In the preface, we stated: "We are not sure if we have really formulated the East Asian model, because our research on industrial development in other regions is far from adequate.......... It is our ultimate aim to establish empirical regularity on cluster-based industrial development through careful case studies across a variety of settings."

Subsequently, we have conducted additional case studies in the garment and rolled steel products industries near Hanoi, Vietnam; the garment industry in Dhaka, Bangladesh; the electrical fittings industry in Sargodha, Pakistan; the garment and metalworking industries in Nairobi, Kenya; the garment, leather shoe, and metalworking industries in Addis Ababa, Ethiopia; the metalworking industry in Kumasi, Ghana; and the garment industry in Dar Es Salaam, Tanzania. We also attempted to conduct case studies of the garment cluster in Delhi, the metalworking cluster in Colombo, and a few other clusters in Asia, even though we failed to collect useful data. One major aim was to identify the similarities and dissimilarities in the patterns of development among the East Asian, other Asian, and African cases. In particular, we were curious to ascertain why some industrial clusters grow fast while others do not.

We find that, while the process of the formation of industrial clusters is surprisingly similar across all the cases we have studied thus far, the difference in the industry's fate lies in the success or failure of introducing innovations following the formation of an industrial cluster consisting of a large number of enterprises producing low-quality products. We also find that managerial human capital, as well as gaining technological and managerial knowledge from advanced countries, is the key to success in innovations.

The purpose of this book is to present a "progress report" of our research on cluster-based industrial development based on our eight case studies in Asia and Africa. We would like to emphasize that there are more similarities than dissimilarities in the development pattern between the Asian and African cases. It is particularly encouraging to find that the leather shoe industry in Ethiopia has not only grown spectacularly fast, like many of the clustered industries in East Asia, but also follows what we call the "East Asian Model of Industrial Development," in which competent entrepreneurs achieve innovations based on technological and managerial knowledge transferred from abroad. The implication is that if we provide appropriate knowledge to potential entrepreneurs in industrial clusters, including those stagnant clusters in sub-Saharan Africa, such industrial clusters are likely to begin growing.

As previously noted, this book still represents a progress report, because, although clear policy implications are derived from our case studies, they have not been rigorously tested. In fact, we have been conducting experiments whereby we provide management training to selected enterprise managers for several weeks in our study sites in Ghana, Kenya, Ethiopia, Tanzania, and Vietnam, in collaboration with the World Bank and Japan International Cooperation Agency. Since the impacts of such training programs cannot be realized immediately, we expect that a few more years will be required to confirm (or disconfirm) the expected impacts.

We are heavily indebted to our former PhD students who have graduated from the National Graduate Institute for Policy Studies (GRIPS). In particular, we would like to express our sincerest gratitude to Vu Hoang Nam, John Akoten, Babur Wasim, and Khondoker Abdul Mottaleb. Two case studies in Vietnam, reported in Chapters 2 and 4, are based on Nam, Sonobe, and Otsuka (2009, 2010); two case studies in Kenya, reported in Chapters 3 and 5, draw on Akoten and Otsuka (2007) and Sonobe, Akoten, and Otsuka (2009), respectively; and a case study discussed in Chapter 7 is based on Sonobe, Akoten, and Otsuka (2010). Furthermore, the PhD dissertations of Khondoler Abdul Mottaleb, entitled "Human Capital and Industrial Development: The Case of the Garment Industry in Bangladesh," and Babur Wasim, entitled "Cluster-based Industrial Development: The Case of Electrical Fittings Cluster in Sargodha, Pakistan," provided invaluable input for Chapters 6 and 8, respectively. Obviously this book could not have been completed without the excellent studies of these former students, and we would like to thank them wholeheartedly.

We are also grateful to our colleagues at the Foundation for Advanced Studies on International Development and GRIPS: Jonna Estudillo, Tatsuo Hatta, Yujiro Hayami, Kei Kajisa, Kaliappa Kalirajan, Yukichi Mano, Tomoya Matsumoto, Yukio Sugano, and Takashi Yamano. In particular, we greatly appreciate the strong encouragement of Prof. Hayami to continue our research on cluster-based industrial development. In addition, we received useful comments from many researchers on various occasions. We would like to thank Olu Ajakaiye, Arne Bigsten, Marcel Fafchamps, Masahisa Fujita, Mulu Gebreeyesus, Koichi Hamada, Alain de Janvry, Khalid Nadvi, John Page, Mark Rosenzweig, Scott Rozelle, Betty Sadoulet, Hubert Schmitz, T. Paul Schultz, Wans Söderbom, John Strauss, Francis Teal, Chris Udry, Yutaka Yoshino, Marilou Uy, Eiji Yamamura, and Xiaobo Zhang; Paul Kandasamy, who carefully edited the manuscript; Mayuko Tanaka, who provided excellent editorial support; and Kengo Igei, who prepared the combined references. We would like to express our deepest appreciation.

Finally, we are also grateful for the financial support provided by the 21st Century Centers of Excellence (COE) Program and the Global COE Program of the Japan Society for the Promotion of Science.

TETSUSHI SONOBE AND KEIJIRO OTSUKA

May 2010

1
Introduction: The Scope and Significance of the Study

1.1   Why focus on industrial clusters?

Widespread and persistent poverty in the majority of developing countries is one of the most serious issues currently facing the world. In order
to reduce poverty, ample employment opportunities must be created for
the poor. To achieve this, the development of labor-intensive industries
is the key, as agriculture can provide only limited employment opportunities and the service sector can only become the leading sector in
the later stage of economic development. Indeed, although the Green
Revolution in Asia increased grain production dramatically, it had mod-
est effects on labor demand (David and Otsuka, 1994). As a result, it was
increased employment opportunities in the non-agricultural sector,
rather than in agriculture, that directly contributed to poverty reduction in Asia (Otsuka et al., 2009). In our observation, the service sector cannot be an engine of growth in low-income economies, because
major innovations in this sector are knowledge-intensive and labor-
saving, which is not appropriate for unskilled labor-abundant low-wage
economies. Consequently, the central question is how to promote the
development of labor-intensive industries in such countries.

The commonly accepted neoclassical presumption is that "industrial policy" does not work, and thus governments have to do little to
promote industrial development beyond the provision of infrastructure such as roads, electricity, and communication systems. This presumption is incorrect, however, because there are several important
sources of market failure that governments can address. First, transaction costs between manufacturing enterprises (e.g., assemblers and
parts suppliers) and between such enterprises and traders are known to
be high, particularly in developing countries. Asymmetric information

and imperfect contract enforcement may result in adverse selection, cheating, and hold-ups, thus negatively affecting the functioning of the market (e.g., Akerlof, 1970; Williamson, 1985; Hart and Moore, 1990). Second, innovative knowledge spills over, as is emphasized in the endogenous growth literature (e.g., Romer, 1986). Such knowledge is often tacit and, hence, not patentable or tradable, so the markets would not work in this case. The result is underinvestment in the creation of new productive ideas. Third, in the recent literature, the importance of managerial capital and management practices to firm performance is being re-evaluated (Bloom and Van Reenen, 2007, 2010; Bruhn et al., 2010; Syverson, 2010).[1] Sonobe and Otsuka (2006) revealed that entrepreneurs' managerial human capital plays a critical role in industrial development by affecting innovation. As with ordinary human capital, investment in managerial human capital is likely to be socially suboptimal due to lack of access to finance. This problem is exacerbated by information spillovers, which thwart the incentive to innovate (Arrow, 1962). Thus, there is clearly room for government intervention to promote industrial development through the correction of such market failures.[2]

In our observations, most, if not all, of the indigenously developed industries in low-income countries are cluster-based, in which a number of small and medium enterprises producing similar and related products are located in a small neighborhood. Huang and Bocchi (2008) and Schmitz and Nadvi (1999), as well as many other studies, report that there are a large number of industrial clusters in East and South Asia and Latin America. Even in sub-Saharan Africa (SSA), such industrial clusters are ubiquitous (e.g., McCormick, 1999). Examples are the shoe, garment, furniture, woodwork, and metalwork clusters. Since the majority of enterprises in the indigenously developed industrial clusters are unregistered informal enterprises, their presence is grossly underestimated. Such clusters attract enterprises as they reduce the transaction costs between manufacturing enterprises and between manufacturers and traders.[3] Indeed, within the cluster, asymmetric information about the trustworthiness of potential trading partners is not as serious as outside the cluster, because people in the cluster become well acquainted and regularly exchange information about the personality and conduct of other entrepreneurs and traders within the same cluster. Under such conditions, dishonest behavior is likely to be detected and heavily punished, and thus the temptation to behave dishonestly tends to be suppressed. As a result, market transactions are promoted. Given this scenario, the government may support the formation of industrial clusters by investing in industrial zones and marketplaces, as has been done actively by various levels of government in China (Sonobe et al., 2002, 2004; Ding, 2007; Ruan and Zhang, 2009).

Information spillover or imitation is rampant in industrial clusters. Visual inspection and reverse engineering of the new products of rival enterprises, poaching knowledgeable workers from rivals, and the acquisition of confidential technological information from a rival's parts suppliers are common methods of imitation. Patent protection of technological information is effective only for a limited set of knowledge. Moreover, managerial knowledge, which is at least as important as technological knowledge, cannot be patented. As a result, the social return to creating and introducing new knowledge, which encompasses the development of new superior products, production methods, marketing channels, and internal management systems, exceeds the private return, resulting in a socially suboptimal level of investment in new innovative knowledge, if left to free market forces. Thus, governmental support for innovation may be warranted, as in the case of the Industrial Technology Research Institute in Taiwan, which facilitated the import of foreign technologies by means of adaptive research and training (Hong and Gee, 1993). Note that "innovation" here refers to "imitative innovation" or "improvement," not to the "innovation" that leads to creative destruction in the sense of Schumpeter (1950).

In order for an enterprise to grow, its manager must be an entrepreneur, who constantly strives for new innovations. To become a dynamic entrepreneur, the manager must invest in his or her managerial human capital; however, insufficient financial resources may preclude this. Even if the manager possesses sufficient resources, he or she may not know where to invest or what to learn. Moreover, to the extent that new knowledge can be imitated by others, the private return to human capital investment may be miniscule compared with the social return. Indeed, we found that the majority of small entrepreneurs in SSA operate their businesses without realizing whether they are making profits or losses, because they do not keep records of the costs of and revenues from their various production activities. It seems to us that gross underinvestment in managerial human capital is a major constraint on efficient enterprise management in low-income countries. Here, too, there is ample room for productive support by the government.

Although not unique to the development of industrial clusters, another area where the government can potentially play a critical role is the provision of low-interest loans, due to the malfunctioning of credit markets (e.g., Beck et al., 2009; Karlan and Morduch, 2009). While we agree with this basic argument, we would also like to point out that successfully grown enterprises were rarely dependent on subsidized credit in East Asia, particularly in the early stage of development when low-quality products are produced (Sonobe and Otsuka, 2006). In addition, there is always the risk of providing cheap credit to non-innovative and non-promising enterprises. We believe that a socially productive credit policy should provide credit only to those enterprises that have established a record of successful innovations.

In sum, the facts that so many industries in developing countries are clustered, even though government does not provide any support, and that there are potentially useful roles to be played by the government warrant careful empirical studies of cluster-based industrial development.

1.2   Causes of growing and stagnating clusters

Why has SSA largely failed to develop dynamically growing industrial clusters? Is it possible to promote industrial development in this region? If so, what is the appropriate development strategy? These were the issues we raised when we completed our earlier research project on cluster-based industrial development in East Asia, which compares the growth experience of eight industrial clusters in Japan, Taiwan, and China (Sonobe and Otsuka, 2006). The surprising result of our East Asian study is that there are large similarities in the pattern of *successful* cluster-based industrial development across industries and across the three East Asian countries, which is summarized in Table 1.1.

If the production method is simple but it is not easy to sell the product, as in the case of the garment and shoe industries, it is likely to be traders who establish new enterprises to initiate a new industry. Taking advantage of their experience in commercial activities in other industries, they undertake production in the suburbs of large cities or villages not too far away from large cities, as the access to large markets is critically important.[4] If the production method is complicated, engineers tend to be the new entrepreneurs who play a critical role in initiating a new industry. Since they tend to reside in cities and their suburbs, this type of industries tends to be born in urbanized areas. By and large these pioneering entrepreneurs imitate foreign technologies; but the imitation is not a simple task, as the materials, parts, and skilled workers available in advanced countries are often unavailable in developing countries. Thus, a pioneer of new industry makes a great deal of effort to establish new production methods. Once these are established, the

Table 1.1 An endogenous model of cluster-based industrial development

Phase	Prior experience of managers	Education	Innovation, imitation, and productivity growth	Institutions
Initiation	Traders/ engineers	Low	Imitation of foreign technology, production of low-quality products	Internal production of parts, components, and final products
Quantity expansion	Spin-offs and entry from various fields	Mixed	Entry of a number of followers, imitation of imitated technologies, and stagnant productivity	Gradual development of market transactions, and formation of industrial cluster
Quality improvement	Second generation of founders and newcomers with new ideas	Very high	Multifaceted innovations, exit of non-innovative enterprises, and increasing productivity and export	Reputation and brand names, direct sales, subcontracts or vertical integration, and emergence of large enterprises

pioneer receives sizable entrepreneurial profits, despite the low quality of the products, because of high demand for such products by poor consumers.

In our observations, following the initiation of a new profitable business by a pioneer, a swarm of imitators, who produce the same low-quality products by using the same low-quality inputs as the pioneer, enter the industry and sell their products on the same local markets. In this way, an industrial cluster is formed, as is illustrated in Figure 1.1. Because of the "excessive" entry of new enterprises, however, the supply of products exceeds the demand, resulting in lower product prices and declining profitability in this quantity expansion phase. This triggers competition based around improvement in the quality of the products. It is important to note that, although productivity growth is slow in

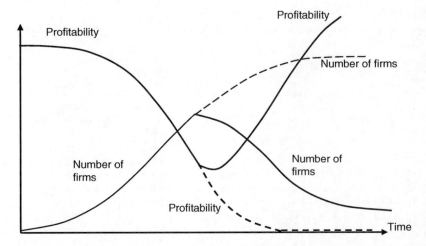

Figure 1.1   An illustration of development patterns of industrial clusters in terms of changing profitability and the number of firms

the quantity expansion phase, the expansion of market size induces the division of labor between assemblers and parts suppliers (Stigler, 1951; Ruan and Zhang, 2009), and attracts traders, engineers, and designers. The availability of such human resources sets the stage for innovations, which are nothing but "recombination of existing resources," to use the expression of Schumpeter (1912).

The success of the quality improvement requires the use of high-quality parts and materials, and the employment of more experienced and skilled workers, so that the cost of production increases. More often than not, however, consumers do not immediately perceive the quality improvement, so that the new products cannot command high prices in the market. Thus, how to convey the quality information to consumers is the key issue that the innovative entrepreneur must resolve. Commonly the establishment of brand names and the development of new direct marketing channels, such as operation of their own shops and direct sales to wholesalers, supermarkets, and department stores, are critical development strategies. The establishment of trust-based long-term subcontracting relationships with parts suppliers also becomes important, as the new products often require differentiated parts and components, which embody new ideas. In addition, stricter control of product quality and monitoring of workers must be implemented. Successful quality improvement leads to the dramatic development of the industry, with a smaller number of much larger enterprises, partly because non-innovative enterprises are forced to exit and partly because innovative enterprises expand their scale of operation (see solid curves in Figure 1.1). Once these multifaceted improvements of production methods and enterprise management are carried out successfully, large innovative enterprises emerge, and they often export their improved products to high-income countries.

We called this development pattern the "East Asian Model of Cluster-Based Industrial Development" (Sonobe and Otsuka, 2006). A question arises, however, as to whether such a development pattern is really unique to East Asia. Therefore, we have since undertaken case studies of village-based garment and steel bar clusters in Vietnam, of the spectacularly developed and exceedingly large garment cluster in Bangladesh, and of the steadily growing electrical fittings cluster in Pakistan. Although differences exist in the development pattern among the four cases and between these cases and those in East Asia studied earlier, the similarities are much more striking. Thus, we concede that the "East Asian Model" is a misnomer.

To our surprise, there are a large number of industrial clusters formed by micro, small, and medium-size enterprises in SSA, even though most of them fail to grow.[5] We conducted case studies of the small-scale garment cluster and metalwork cluster in Nairobi, Kenya, and of the export-oriented garment cluster supported by the government and the rapidly growing leather shoe cluster in Addis Ababa, Ethiopia. A clear similarity between Asia and Africa is found in the pattern of cluster formation. In both Asia and SSA, the cluster is formed by the massive entry of imitators, including spin-offs.

A major dissimilarity between Asia and SSA is observed in the occurrence or absence of multifaceted innovations. In contrast to Asia, multifaceted improvements seldom take place in SSA. Thus, as indicated by the dotted curves in Figure 1.1, the number of enterprises continues to increase and, hence, the profitability continues to decline. In this respect, the industrial clusters in Asia have an advantage over those in SSA, because the former can learn a great deal from the experience of successfully grown clusters in neighboring countries. The leather shoe cluster in Ethiopia is exceptional. It has been growing rapidly due to the introduction of multifaceted improvements in the quality of products, marketing, and internal management – a development pattern similar to the "East Asian Model." This case vividly illustrates that the same pattern of cluster development seen in Asia is possible in SSA.

1.3 In search of key growth drivers

The ultimate purpose of this study is to identify the essential determinants of the occurrence or absence of multifaceted innovations or improvements, which are the engine of the sustained growth of industrial clusters, with a view to drawing implications for designing effective industrial development policies. In order to carry out such innovations, managerial human capital, which is represented by the schooling and work experience of enterprise managers, plays a critical role in Japan, Taiwan, and China. Often important, also, is the experience of managers in marketing business as traders or as staff of the marketing division of a large enterprise, because marketing knowledge is an integral part of managerial human capital. Thus, we would like to test the following hypotheses, based on the case studies from outside these three East Asian countries:

Hypothesis 1:

The managerial human capital of enterprise managers is the major determinant of successful multifaceted innovations.

Traders, particularly local traders, contribute to the quantity expansion of industrial clusters by reducing marketing costs for clustered enterprises. In addition, as discussed earlier, improved marketing is a prerequisite for the successful quality improvement of products, because consumers do not immediately perceive the quality improvement. Thus, in China and Japan, successful entrepreneurs themselves were often traders, who are adept at marketing (Sonobe and Otsuka, 2006).

Urban and foreign traders often contribute new production methods, improved marketing knowledge, and high-quality parts and materials, thereby assisting multifaceted innovation in industrial clusters. Thus, it is worth testing the following hypothesis.

Hypothesis 2:

Traders play a critical role, not only in facilitating marketing of low-quality products during the quantity expansion phase, but also in assisting the production of upgraded products and supply of high-quality parts and materials, thereby improving the performance of enterprises in an industrial cluster.

Note, however, that as quality improvement proceeds further the role of traders tends to decline due to the increasing efforts at marketing by large, successfully innovative enterprises, according to the experience of Northeast Asia (Sonobe and Otsuka, 2006).

One advantage of low-income countries is the ample possibility of imitating technological and managerial knowledge from abroad. Although concrete statistical evidence is scarce, there is no question that all the high-performing countries in East Asia, including Japan and China, have grown rapidly based on such imitation of more advanced countries (Hamada et al., 2010). Thus, we would like to postulate the following hypothesis.

Hypothesis 3:

The key to successful multifaceted innovation is successful international knowledge transfer.

Under what conditions, then, are potential entrepreneurs motivated to undertake multifaceted innovations? As previously mentioned, according to Sonobe and Otsuka (2006), the rapidly increasing supply of low-quality products by a large number of clustered enterprises leads to lower product prices and declining profits, factors that stimulate the potential entrepreneurs to undertake multifaceted innovations. Aside from the reduction in product prices due to enhanced domestic competition, the prices of manufactured products in many developing countries have fallen because of the massive import of cheap Chinese products, what may be termed the China shock. The question is whether such an exogenously created reduction in product prices due to the China shock also leads to the stimulation of multifaceted innovations. The answer may vary from case to case. We found two cases in which the China shock has stimulated multifaceted innovations: the electrical fittings industry in Pakistan and the leather shoe industry in Ethiopia. In accordance with Hypotheses 1 to 3, we postulate that managerial human capital, traders, and knowledge transfer from advanced countries play important roles in realizing these multifaceted innovations. In contrast, the garment cluster in Nairobi, which has failed to innovate, has been unable to compete with the imported Chinese products. We believe that this failure can be attributed to weak managerial human capital, trading experience, and knowledge transfer.

If multifaceted innovations are the key to success in industrial development, governmental support for industrial development without concurrent support for such innovations is bound to fail. More specifically, we would like to argue that the provision of subsidies and other support measures without support for innovation will not lead to the successful development of clustered enterprises. This implies that support for the accumulation of managerial human capital leads to the successful development of clusters.

While Hypotheses 1 to 3, formulated in this chapter, represent fundamental propositions in this study, we will also specify more directly testable specific hypotheses in subsequent chapters. Our strategy is to prove or disprove Hypotheses 1 to 3 by implementing rigorous tests of a large number of specific hypotheses.

1.4   Scope of the study

First of all, in Part I of this book we would like to demonstrate the importance of reducing the cost of transaction between manufacturers and traders in the development of an industrial cluster by undertaking case studies of garment clusters in Vietnam and Kenya. It is shown that overseas Vietnamese traders facilitated the export of garment products from the cluster in northern Vietnam, which critically affected the enterprise performance, whereas bulk purchase of products by petty traders assisted the expansion of the size of garment enterprises in Kenya. These are supportive of Hypothesis 2 and consistent with the earlier findings by Sonobe and Otsuka (2006) that the development of industrial clusters whose products are easy to produce but difficult to sell, such as the garment industry, is trader-led.

Second, in Part II, we would like to show the importance of managerial human capital by examining the cases of a metal bar cluster in Vietnam and a metalwork cluster in Kenya. It is demonstrated that the schooling and work experience of enterprise managers, including prior experience of trading, are key determinants of upgrading products, marketing, and enterprise management, which supports Hypothesis 1. It is also important to note that some of the former micro informal enterprises have moved to industrial zones and become formal and larger enterprises in Kenya, after succeeding with multifaceted innovations. It is, therefore, a mistake to assume that micro and small enterprises in SSA never become large.

In Part III, we would like to highlight the importance of multifaceted innovations in the face of fierce competition from the flood of cheap Chinese products in the context of the electrical fittings industry in Pakistan and the leather shoe cluster in Ethiopia. We show that China Shock can be overcome by multifaceted innovations based on technology transfers from advanced countries, which is consistent with Hypothesis 3.

Finally, in Part IV, we will examine the consequences of contrasting industrial development strategies, namely the strategy of supporting innovation by introducing production and management knowledge from abroad in the garment cluster in Bangladesh and the policy of providing financial support and preferential treatment with no emphasis on innovations in the garment cluster in Ethiopia. The results are supportive of our arguments for the critical importance of the strategy of supporting investment in the accumulation of managerial human capital and learning technology and management from abroad.

Thus, based on our case studies, a clear policy implication emerges. Support for investment in the managerial human capital of enterprise managers should be provided so as to facilitate the absorption of technological and managerial knowledge from abroad and to strengthen the marketing ability of the enterprises. In addition, we would like to argue that the government should support cluster-based industrial development by constructing such key infrastructures as industrial zones and marketplaces and also by improving access to credit for innovative enterprises, which are able to allocate such credit to truly profitable investment projects.

Part I

The Role of Traders in Cluster Development

2
Overseas Vietnamese Traders in a Garment Cluster in Vietnam

As was hypothesized in Chapter 1, traders play a critically important role in the development of industrial clusters (see Hypothesis 2). Also important is the managerial human capital of enterprise managers, which is conducive to multifaceted innovations (see Hypothesis 1). The purpose of Part I (Chapters 2 and 3) is to test these two hypotheses based on case studies of garment clusters in Vietnam and Kenya. Special emphasis is placed on the role of traders, as this has seldom been proven statistically.

Historically Vietnam has developed a large number of village-based industrial clusters formed by small and medium enterprises. They create ample job opportunities and thereby contribute to economic growth and poverty reduction. Recently, modern industrial clusters have rapidly emerged from traditional villages where time-honored products, such as silk and agricultural tools, have long been produced (JICA, 2004; see also Chapter 4). The case study of these village-based industrial clusters provides a good opportunity to trace the development process of industrial clusters and to identify the factors affecting their transformation from traditional to modern sectors. To our knowledge, however, no rigorous empirical study on the development of industrial clusters in Vietnam has been attempted. A major question is to what extent traders, and enterprise managers who are former traders, contribute to the transformation process.

This chapter reports the results of our case study of a garment cluster named Laphu village in northern Vietnam. In its early stage of development, only household production was carried out, on a small scale, using mainly family labor. The households received putting-out contracts from cooperatives and state-owned enterprises, in which materials and designs were provided by the contractors. The major products used to be low-quality, simple, and homogeneous woolen knitwear sold to the domestic market. In the late 1990s, however, leading households began to shift to a more technically complicated category of products and to upgrade themselves to registered companies with higher levels of vertical integration. We hypothesize that vertical integration and the reduced use of the putting-out system represent a response to the increasing transaction costs of higher-quality products. We also hypothesize that such changes are brought about by the ex-traders and overseas Vietnamese traders. These hypotheses are tested with the survey data that we collected from 136 knitwear enterprises in Laphu village.

The organization of this chapter is as follows. Section 2.1 presents the historical background and characteristics of the production system in Laphu village. Section 2.2 describes changing characteristics of our sample enterprises over time. Section 2.3 estimates regression functions, explaining the size of enterprises in terms of revenue and value added. Finally, the major findings and policy implications are offered in Section 2.4.

2.1 Historical background and the production system

2.1.1 Tradition of knitwear production

Laphu, a one-village commune, is about 10 km to the west of the center of Hatay province.[1] From Hatay goods can be easily transported to many big inland cities, such as Hanoi and Quangninh, and to Haiphong, a port city, for export. The village is located on a main road starting from the center of Hatay province. The village is a famous industrial cluster where a large number of small and privately owned enterprises produce knitwear products.

Villagers have long experience of garment production. Before 1945, many villagers worked at French garment factories in Hanoi. In the 1960s, they worked at two state-owned garment enterprises (SOEs) established in the current center of Hatay province to produce mainly towels and socks for export to the Soviet Union. In the 1970s, two cooperatives were set up in the village and the two SOEs contracted out garment production to these cooperatives. In fact, these SOEs and cooperatives have had significant influence on the production of garments in the village, since the villagers have not only learned production methods but also acquired machines from them. The learning effect from SOEs is, thus, similar to the case of the garment sector (Murakami et al., 1994; Liu and Otsuka, 1998) and the case of the machine tool industry (Murakami et al., 1996) in China, where township and village enterprises (TVEs) learned technical and managerial expertise from SOEs. Private production at that time was prohibited by the government, but a few households produced garments illegally.

In 1991, the cooperatives in the village were closed because the SOEs stopped contracting out following the collapse of the Soviet Union market. The knitting machines of the cooperatives were given to their members. In addition, *doimoi* (reform) policies in 1986 liberalized the domestic market and encouraged private production. As a result, garment production by households began to emerge. In the beginning, some households produced collars of shirts and light coats to order from producers in Hanoi. Others produced low-quality woolen gloves and socks, which were simple and homogeneous, to sell in the domestic market. A few households could sell their products to Vietnamese migrants or *Vietkieu*, who came back occasionally or regularly from Russia for business.[2] By that time, woolen products were sold to these *Vietkieu* through local traders in Hanoi, who also provided material to Laphu. It is clear that both local and overseas traders contributed to the marketing of products manufactured in Laphu. The *Vietkieu* packed the products in their hand luggage to carry with them and sell in the low-end market in Russia.

Laphu gradually became known by a greater number of traders for its woolen knitwear. As a result, traders from Hanoi and other provinces in Vietnam started visiting Laphu to buy products. According to our interviews with traders in Hanoi, they used to buy knitwear from small producers with limited production capacity scattered around Hanoi before they turned to Laphu, whose production capacity was so large that much larger orders could be fulfilled in a shorter time period.

Laphu became well known, not only by traders from many provinces of Vietnam but also to many *Vietkieu*. The *Vietkieu* who had relatives in Laphu were the first to come directly to Laphu to buy products, and the others followed suit. Later, exporting products directly to these *Vietkieu* became an important marketing channel. Moreover, after the collapse of Soviet Union, many of these *Vietkieu* migrated to other countries in Eastern Europe. As a result, the export market for the products of Laphu has been expanded. According to the managers in Laphu, finding reliable domestic and foreign customers has become increasingly important. Thus, managers who have relatives engaged in trading garments in foreign countries use this advantage to export their products. The community relationship seems to have been used as the major instrument of contract enforcement. Probably this explains why producers prefer to sell products to their relatives (Hayami, 2006).

Managers in Laphu, however, could not have increased their export volume and expanded markets without improvement in the quality of products. As more traders came and their orders increased, the number of households producing woolen knitwear increased, reducing the output price and, hence, the profitability of producing standard products in Laphu. In the late 1990s, leading enterprises began to shift to producing more complicated categories of products. According to the managers in Laphu, the most difficult products that require the highest quality wool are sweaters, followed by caps, and then trousers, handkerchiefs, gloves, and socks.

2.1.2   The production system

There are three types of enterprises connected with one another in the production system: (1) registered companies; (2) unregistered workshops; and (3) subcontractors. The first two groups produce finished products while the last group only produces parts.[3] This study focuses on registered companies and unregistered workshops, which are called enterprises, in relation to backward linkages with subcontractors and forward linkages with buyers (Figure 2.1).

A typical production process consists of the following steps: first, wool is knitted into parts; second, inspected parts are fabricated into semi-finished products; third, semi-finished products are ironed and decorated; and fourth, finished products are packed and ready to be marketed. Subcontractors are households who specialize in either knitting or fabricating. According to a local government official, there are about 60 subcontractors specializing in fabricating, and all of them are located in the village. They have only five to ten fabricating machines on average and hire workers from surrounding villages. These subcontractors receive putting-out orders from unregistered workshops. Sometimes they receive orders directly from registered companies in the busy season from March to September. Since their size is small, a subcontractor seldom receives putting-out orders from more than one workshop or company at a time.

According to the leader of the village communist party, approximately 500–700 subcontractors in the village and 5,000 subcontractors in nearby villages are producing parts. These knitting subcontractors mainly use automatic knitting machines to produce parts for trousers, while those in the nearby villages use hand-driven machines to produce parts for sweaters, caps, and others. Small knitting subcontractors with one to two workers receive putting-out orders only from unregistered workshops, while large knitting subcontractors with 15 to 18

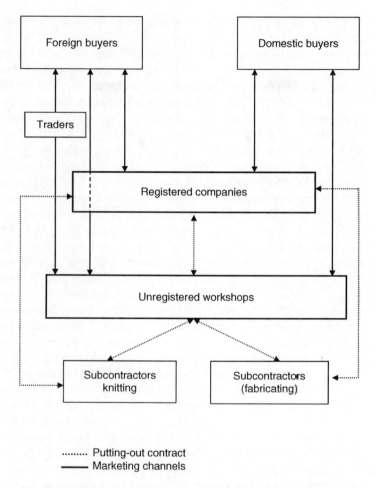

Figure 2.1 Production relationship among enterprises in a garment cluster in Vietnam

workers often receive putting-out orders directly from registered companies.[4]

It was not until 1995 that knitting spread from Laphu to the nearby villages. In 1995, some knitting households in Laphu began to sell their old machines to their workers from the nearby villages, allowing deferred payment. We gathered that half of the knitting machines used in the surrounding villages came from enterprises in Laphu. Thus, a large proportion of knitting is now shifted to households in other villages.

Putting-out contracts between subcontractors and unregistered workshops or registered companies are not made in writing. They are usually long-term and based on trust. Recommendation from old subcontractors is needed for a household to become a new subcontractor. Subcontractors do not have to deposit money when receiving material from their contractors. This is possible due to repeated and intense interaction. They visit their contractors frequently to get orders and discuss with them about designs, sizes, shapes, colors, and weight of sample products. The payment to subcontractors is on the piece-rate basis. To our surprise, a large part of the payment is made only once, at the end of the year.

While subcontractors are located both in and outside Laphu, unregistered workshops are all located within the village. There are three different marketing channels for unregistered workshops: receiving putting-out contracts from registered companies; selling to the domestic market; and selling to the foreign market. They produce final products if selling to the domestic and foreign market, while leaving the packing process to registered companies if they receive putting-out orders from them. In relation to subcontractors, workshops give putting-out orders; in relation to registered companies, workshops receive putting-out orders. This putting-out system is similar to the subcontracting system in Japan in terms of multiple layers of subcontractors (Hayami and Godo, 2005), but different from the system of TVEs in the garment sector of China, where the TVEs received subcontracting orders but did not contract out to households (Liu and Otsuka, 1998). The putting-out system in Laphu is also similar to that in Modena, Italy, where family labor is still crucial but the role of hired full-time labor has become greater (Lazerson, 1995).

Some unregistered workshops are as large as some registered companies in terms of sales revenue. They often have relatives working as traders overseas. Despite the fact that unregistered workshops cannot by law directly import material and export products, they tend to sell their products directly to these traders, with some help from registered companies, which are responsible for paperwork such as dealing with customs offices and payment through companies' foreign bank accounts. The smaller workshops export their products only through traders located in Hanoi. The relationship between these smaller workshops and traders is one of arm's length transactions.

Registered companies are the largest enterprises and have production relations with all other enterprises. They have putting-out contracts mainly with unregistered workshops, since companies can save transaction costs by dealing with a smaller number of workshops rather than dealing directly with many small subcontractors. As mentioned above, registered companies help unregistered workshops export their products, but only several registered companies in our sample offer this service. Registered companies sell their products directly to foreign and domestic buyers and import materials, mainly wool, from China through Chinese traders based in Hanoi.

At the beginning of each year, the registered companies put out materials to unregistered workshops and subcontractors after getting some deposit money from workshops and subcontractors. This credittying contract ensures that the companies, workshops and subcontractors will work with each other for that year at least. All the parties can shift to other partners in the next year if they are not satisfied with the business result in the previous year. The commonly delayed payment from registered companies to unregistered workshops and subcontractors amounts to credit advancement from the latter to the former. This occurs because foreign traders make payments only after Christmas. In this way, the high level of trust among managers in Laphu contributes significantly to the saving of working capital for registered companies.

2.2   Characteristics of sample enterprises

We conducted a survey in Laphu in the summer of 2006. The commune government office has a complete list of registered companies but not unregistered workshops. Therefore, we decided to ask hamlet leaders about the names of managers of unregistered workshops in their hamlets to prepare our own list for the survey. In total, we were able to identify 142 enterprises including registered companies and unregistered workshops in Laphu and we decided to conduct a census survey. We started with a preliminary survey of 20 enterprises and then conducted a formal survey. After the formal survey, we eliminated six enterprises from the sample because their production and cost data were either incomplete or highly suspicious. Thus, the sample actually used in the analysis consists of 136 enterprises, of which 19 are registered companies and 117 are unregistered workshops. We collected recall data on production and costs, marketing, and production organization in 2000 and 2005 to identify the changing characteristics of the garment cluster in Laphu. Because three of these subcontractors had not been upgraded to workshops or companies until 2005, we omitted these subcontractors from the analysis for 2000.[5]

2.2.1   General characteristics

Enterprises were established as subcontractors, unregistered workshops, or registered companies from the beginning (Table 2.1). In 2005, there were 136 enterprises, of which 66 had been formed as unregistered workshops from the beginning and 10 had been established as registered companies from the beginning. By the end of 2005, the 60 former subcontractors had been upgraded to unregistered workshops and nine former unregistered workshops to registered companies. It is extremely important to recognize that family production units can become workshops and that informal workshops can become formal sector companies in the process of cluster development. It can be seen from Table 2.1 that a greater number of new enterprises were set up before 2000 than after 2000. The entry of new subcontractors was particularly active in the early period, but it then gradually declined and was followed by the entry of new unregistered workshops, and more recently by registered companies. Since 2001, eight new registered companies, whose managers are all returned overseas Vietnamese, have entered the industry. This vividly indicates that traders play a critical role in cluster-based industrial development.

As shown in Table 2.2, despite the increase in the average size of enterprises, they employed only 27 workers in 2005. In contrast to the increase in the average number of workers per enterprise, the average quantity of production decreased slightly. Nevertheless, real value added and real revenue showed a remarkable increase, resulting in a significant increase in the real value added per piece, which was about 1.5 times higher in 2005 than in 2000. This observation indicates that there has been a shift of production to higher-priced and higher value added products.

Table 2.1   Types of new enterprises at the time of entry in a garment cluster in Vietnam[a]

	1984–1995	1996–2000	2001–2005
Registered company	1	1	8
Unregistered workshop	27	35	4
Subcontractor	46	14	0
Total	74	50	12

[a]All 60 enterprises that used to be subcontractors have been upgraded to workshops or companies, and nine enterprises that used to be unregistered workshops have been upgraded to companies in 2005.

Table 2.2   General information about employment and production in a garment cluster in Vietnam[a]

	2000	2005
Number of workers	15.5	27.4
Production quantity (hundred thousand pieces)	2.8	2.7
Real revenue (billion VND)	3.3	4.5
Real value added (billion VND)[b]	0.8	1.4
Real value added per piece (thousand VND)[b]	3.1	5.4
Number of enterprises	121	136

[a]Average per enterprise (real value added, real value added per piece and real revenue are deflated by price index of garments from the General Statistics Office of Vietnam, base year 1995).
[b]Value added = sales – material costs – subcontracting cost – energy cost.

2.2.2   Importance of human capital and traders

Table 2.3 presents characteristics of managers at the time of entry in different periods, including years of schooling, previous occupation, and proportion of managers who have at least one relative engaged in trading of garments abroad. Compared with the period before 1996, average education of managers decreased in the period 1996–2000 but then increased significantly after 2000. This may be because, in the early period when production was new, only educated people were able to start businesses, whereas, when the production of homogeneous products was known to everybody, less educated managers were able to enter the industry. When there was a shift to quality competition, however, only highly educated people were able to enter the business. The proportion of managers who used to be marketing specialists also showed a remarkable increase in the period after 2000. Managers who used to be marketing specialists are either traders in Vietnam, traders abroad or *Vietkieu*, or other marketing specialists who have worked in other enterprises before establishing their own business. In addition, the proportion of managers who have at least one relative engaged in trading of garments abroad increased over time. These observations indicate that managerial human capital, proxied by years of schooling and marketing experience, and close contact between managers and traders, represented by having relatives engaged in trading of garments abroad, have increased over time.

Table 2.4 examines the size of enterprises, measured by the number of employees, revenue, and value added, and their behaviors, proxied by export and sweater revenues, categorized by characteristics of

Table 2.3   General information about managers at the time of entry in a garment cluster in Vietnam

	1984–1995	1996–2000	2001–2005
Average years of schooling	10.3	9.8	11.2
Average age	34.5	38.3	37.2
Previous occupation as marketing specialist (%)	17.6	18.0	58.3
Having relatives abroad (1 if yes, 0 if no)	0.22	0.16	0.42
Number of new entrants	74	50	12

Table 2.4   Performance of enterprises by characteristics of managers in a garment cluster in Vietnam 2005[a]

	Years of schooling			Having any relative abroad		Used to be a marketing specialist	
	Less than 10	10–12	More than 12	No	Yes	No	Yes
Number of employees	11.2	30.0	153.3	11.9	82.2	9.9	69.9
Real revenue (billion VND)	1.6	4.6	21.4	1.9	13.5	1.7	11.1
Real value added (billion VND)	0.5	1.2	7.6	0.6	4.1	0.6	3.3
Real export revenue (billion VND)	0.3	2.2	18.7	0.4	11.1	0.7	10.5
Real sweater revenue (billion VND)	1.3	1.7	20	1.4	9.3	1.2	7.9
Number of enterprises	71	57	8	106	30	106	30

[a]Average per enterprise (deflated by price index of garments from the General Statistics Office of Vietnam, base year 1995).

managers in 2005.[6] There is a large gap in enterprise size between managers who have completed more than 10 years of schooling and those with fewer than 10 years of schooling. The gap is even larger for managers who have attained at least 13 years of schooling, indicating that the education of managers plays a critical role in determining the size of enterprises. The same conclusion applies to the role of personal relationships with export traders. Managers who have at least one relative engaged in trading of garments abroad perform far better than those who have none. This is possibly because relatives abroad are a source of market information, and transaction costs incurred in selling products to relatives are lower. In addition, the performance of managers who used to be marketing specialists also outweighed that of other managers. The table also shows that highly educated managers, managers who have relatives abroad, and managers who used to be marketing specialists tend to be more active in exportation and in producing sweaters, the high-quality products. The finding of the critically important roles of formal schooling and marketing expertise in the performance of enterprises is similar to the findings in the garment cluster in Bingo in Japan (Yamamura et al., 2003), in Jili in China (Sonobe et al., 2002), and in Bangladesh (Mottaleb, 2007; Chapter 8), and the findings in low-voltage electric appliances in Wenzhou in China (Sonobe et al., 2004).

As the ability to respond to changing opportunities is enhanced by schooling and training (Schultz, 1975) and efficiencies of transactions among parties are enhanced by mutual trust based on strong social networks (Hayami and Godo, 2005), managerial human capital of enterprise managers and their contacts with overseas Vietnamese traders are expected to play increasingly important roles in determining the size and performance of enterprises.

All these arguments may be summarized by the following hypothesis:

Hypothesis 2-1: In a knitwear village industry, managerial human capital of the managers and their personal ties with overseas Vietnamese traders, *Vietkieu*, lead to large-scale operation of production units.

2.2.3 Changes in marketing channels and quality of products

Table 2.5 exhibits the proportions of revenue of products marketed through different marketing channels. The proportion of revenue from exporting products (or the propensity to export) increased at the expense of the other marketing channels, especially the revenue from putting-out orders from registered companies. The increased importance of the export was due not only to the recent entry of large registered companies that export most of their products but also to the increased export of existing enterprises.

Assuming that the quality of products is measured by product prices, and material cost and value added per piece, Table 2.6 shows the relevant data by major marketing channel, using the data of enterprises exclusively selling to the domestic market and exclusively selling to the

Table 2.5   Changes in marketing channels in a garment cluster in Vietnam (%)[a]

	2000	2005
Receiving putting-out orders from registered companies	26.5	16.2
Selling to domestic market	40.6	39.9
Selling to foreign market	32.8	43.9
Total	100	100

[a]Average percentage of total sales revenue per enterprise.

Table 2.6   Price, material cost, and value added per piece of the product by marketing channel in a garment cluster in Vietnam[a]

	2000	2005
Domestic market[b]		
Real average price (thousand VND)	9.1	14.6
Material costs per piece (thousand VND)	5.5	8.4
Real value added per piece (thousand VND)	1.7	3.7
Number of enterprises	21	22
Foreign market[c]		
Real average price (thousand VND)	16.9	24.4
Material costs per piece (thousand VND)	10.1	13.3
Real value added per piece (thousand VND)	4.0	7.1
Number of enterprises	17	24

[a]Average per enterprise.
[b]From the sample of enterprises that sell only to the domestic market.
[c]From the sample of enterprises that sell only to the foreign market.

foreign market. It is clear that the quality of the products sold to the domestic market was significantly lower than for those sold to the foreign market. This finding suggests that the lower-quality products were transacted in the domestic market, while the higher-quality products are exported. Similar findings are also reported by the study of the shoe cluster in India (Knorringa, 1999) and the garment cluster in China (Sonobe et al., 2002).

According to the managers in Laphu, sweaters are the most difficult products to produce, since the production of sweaters requires higher-quality materials, more advanced knitting machines, and more time to produce a piece. As shown in Table 2.7, there was a sharp decline in the production of trousers over time, while the production of sweaters increased rapidly. The quantity of exported sweaters in 2005 has more than doubled since 2000. A similar shift in product composition also occurred in the domestic market. This shift reflects the trend towards producing higher-quality products in Laphu.

In addition, the average real price of sweaters has increased from 2000 to 2005. The rate of increase in the domestic price has been greater than that in the export price. According to local traders, Laphu was once known as a village producing low-quality and simple knitwear products. The quality of products sold to the domestic market, however, has recently been greatly improved to meet the demand of wealthier customers in large cities. At the same time, products exported by Laphu have to increasingly compete with Chinese products in the international markets.[7]

The theory of contracts implies that the upgrading of product quality would have an impact on the mode of transaction (Klein and Leffler, 1981). With product quality being upgraded, anonymous market transactions are no longer efficient, because visual inspection alone cannot be relied upon to check the quality of sophisticated products. Instead, face-to-face and long-term direct transactions between local manufacturers and traders coming from urban areas have to be developed (Humphrey and Schmitz, 1998). The fact that sweaters are increasingly exported and that the price of sweaters for export has always been higher than the price of domestic sweaters, as shown in Table 2.7, may indicate that the ability to export largely determines the enterprise size. In other words, we believe that, as the quality of the products is improved, the propensity to export becomes an important determinant of the enterprise size.

Table 2.7 Production quantity and real price by marketing channel in a garment cluster in Vietnam[a]

		Quantity (thousand pieces)		Price (thousand VND)	
		2000	2005	2000	2005
Domestic market	Sweater	15.8	18.0	19.9	25.9
	Trouser	11.6	7.1	5.9	7.2
Foreign market	Sweater	22.8	51.4	33.8	38.3
	Trouser	102.7	56.1	8.7	9.6

[a]Average per enterprise, and prices are deflated by price index of garment products from the General Statistics Office of Vietnam, base year 1995.

Thus, it seems reasonable to postulate the following hypothesis:

Hypothesis 2-2: In an export-oriented village industry, managerial human capital of the managers and their personal ties with overseas Vietnamese traders, *Vietkieu*, contribute to upgrading and increased exports of products.

2.2.4   Changes in production organization

The putting-out system has been developed among enterprises from an early stage. It is interesting to ask whether the putting-out system changed when the cluster shifted to the "quality improvement" phase. According to the managers in Laphu, the putting-out system in the early stage was considered superior to the vertically integrated production system because the former helps subcontracting enterprises save working capital, as contractors provide materials. Moreover, the putting-out system allows mobilization of a cheap rural labor force. However, a manager of a big company, which was established as early as other pioneer enterprises in Laphu, pointed out two shortcomings of the putting-out system. The first was the difficulty in meeting the delivery time of orders. Some of his subcontractors delivered unsatisfactory products only the day before the deadline to send the ordered products to customers. Some others simply could not meet the deadline. The second, and probably more severe, problem is rampant imitation in the village. He complained that he could not protect new knowledge embodied in samples of products if the samples were given to his subcontractors.

Table 2.8 shows indicators of changes in the subcontracting system. Value added ratio is defined as the ratio of value added to revenue, which, according to Adelman (1955), can be taken as a measure of vertical integration. Over time, the value added ratio has increased, suggesting that the production structure of enterprises has been gradually moving towards vertical integration. This is consistent with an increasing capital–labor ratio, measured by the deflated resale value of

Table 2.8   Capital–labor ratio, value added ratio, and subcontracting ratio in a garment cluster in Vietnam[a]

	2000	2005
Capital–labor ratio	1.94	3.21
Value added ratio (value added / revenue)	0.26	0.32
Ratio of subcontracting cost to revenue	0.34	0.25
Number of enterprises	121	136

[a]Average per enterprise.

machines to a number of workers. Moreover, the ratio of subcontracting cost to revenue, which is a direct measure of the extent of vertical disintegration, decreased over time, implying that subcontracting has been reduced and replaced by internal production. These observations indicate that, in response to the difficulty in controlling the quality of products and enforcing the delivery date, enterprises tended to shift to internal production. Registered companies have increased the proportion of internal production, especially for high-quality products, samples of new products, and key parts of products that are technically difficult to produce and require high-quality materials, such as the front part of sweaters. Unregistered workshops have increased the proportion of internal production by undertaking finishing processes such as fabricating, ironing, and packaging. The shift of the production system towards vertical integration is similar to the case of garment production in Bangladesh (see Chapter 8).

Becker and Murphy (1992) argue that the major constraint on the division of labor among firms is high transaction costs due to communication breakdowns, principal-agent conflicts, and holdup problems. When the managers in Laphu improved the quality of products, the transaction costs increased and the production system changed towards vertical integration. In addition, the improvement in the quality of products expanded the market and, therefore, increased the enterprise size. If these arguments hold, vertical integration and the expansion of the enterprise size should be associated positively. We examine this point by testing the following hypothesis:

Hypothesis 2-3: In an export-oriented village industry, managerial human capital of the managers and their personal ties with overseas Vietnamese traders, *Vietkieu*, facilitate the vertically integrated production system, in order to produce high-quality products.

2.3 Estimation methods and results

Two sets of regression functions are estimated in this section. First, the reduced-form regression functions of the determinants of the enterprise size in terms of value added and sales revenue and of the determinants of behaviors of enterprises, measured by export sales revenue and sweater sales revenue, are estimated separately for 2000 and 2005. Separate estimations are made to test the validity of our arguments that the roles of managerial human capital and migrant Vietnamese traders have become more important in more recent years. Second, in order to examine the impact of export and vertical integration on the enterprise size, we employ two-stage least square estimation methods (2SLS).

2.3.1   Determinants of the size and behaviors of enterprises

We estimated the following reduced-form regression functions under the assumption that value added and total sales revenue are good indicators of the enterprise size:

$$\text{Size}_i = \alpha_0 + \alpha_1(\text{Schooling of manager})_i + \alpha_2(\text{Marketing specialist dummy})_i + \alpha_3(\text{Years of operation})_i + \alpha_4(\text{Years of prior experience})_i + \alpha_5(\text{Age of manager})_i + \alpha_6(\text{Father dummy})_i + \alpha_7(\text{Relative dummy})_i + \alpha_8(\text{Subcontractor dummy})_i + e_i,$$

where subscript i refers to the i-th enterprise and e_i is an error term. Value added and total sales revenue are indicators of *Size*. Marketing specialist dummy is unity if the manager used to be a trader or work in the marketing section of another enterprise before establishing his own business, and it is zero otherwise. Prior experience means any experience related to the production of garments having been acquired by the manager before establishing his enterprise. Father dummy is unity if the father of the manager has worked in the garment industry, and it is zero otherwise. Relative abroad dummy is unity if the manager has at least one relative engaged in trading of garments abroad, and it is zero otherwise. Subcontractor dummy is unity if the enterprise used to be a subcontractor, and it is zero otherwise. We would expect the coefficients of the right-hand side variables to change significantly over time; in particular, α_1, α_2, and α_7 will be positive and become larger. In contrast, α_4 and α_6 will be positive but become smaller over time. In addition, we also regress export revenue and sweater revenue on the same set of independent variables.

The estimation results are shown in Table 2.9. For the regressions of value added and total sales revenue, we use the Ordinary Least Square (OLS) estimation method with heteroskedasticity-robust standard errors. Findings in columns (1)–(4) support Hypothesis 2-1. Specifically, the coefficients of manager's years of schooling are positive and highly significant at the 1 percent level. Moreover, these coefficients become larger over time. For example, one more year of schooling increased total sales revenue by 0.8 billion VND in 2000, while it increased total sales revenue by 1.19 billion VND in 2005. The coefficients of manager's years of schooling in the value added function increased even faster, from 0.19 in 2000 to 0.43 in 2005. This suggests that the managerial

Table 2.9 Determinants of the enterprise size in a garment cluster in Vietnam[a]

	Value added (OLS)		Total revenue (OLS)		Export revenue (Tobit)		Sweater revenue (Tobit)	
	2000	2005	2000	2005	2000	2005	2000	2005
	(1)	(2)	(3)	(4)	(5)	(6)	(7)	(8)
Manager's years of schooling	0.19**	0.43**	0.80**	1.19**	1.26**	1.80**	0.70**	1.15**
	(3.38)	(2.60)	(3.43)	(2.81)	(3.72)	(4.47)	(4.43)	(5.15)
Marketing specialist dummy	0.63*	0.89*	2.88*	4.02**	4.02**	6.25**	2.29**	3.82**
	(1.93)	(1.97)	(2.21)	(2.68)	(2.39)	(2.92)	(2.50)	(2.92)
Operation year	0.06	0.01	0.24	0.04	0.81**	0.05	−0.19	−0.1
	(1.30)	(0.15)	(1.34)	(0.23)	(3.10)	(0.17)	(−1.34)	(−0.57)
Manager's experience year	0.68**	0.13	2.62**	0.28	2.49**	0.31	−0.33	0.02
	(3.07)	(1.18)	(3.08)	(0.87)	(2.59)	(0.76)	(−0.60)	(0.09)
Manager's age	−0.02	0.03	−0.09	0.03	−0.27**	−0.01	−0.12**	−0.02
	(−1.34)	(1.32)	(−1.44)	(0.57)	(−2.80)	(−0.05)	(−2.63)	(−0.29)
Father dummy	0.55**	0.32	2.10**	0.62	2.90*	0.37	0.82	−0.55
	(2.58)	(0.67)	(2.52)	(0.49)	(2.12)	(0.21)	(1.11)	(−0.54)
Relative abroad dummy	0.82**	1.25**	3.48**	4.93**	5.84**	7.60**	0.91	2.84*
	(3.35)	(2.36)	(3.46)	(3.64)	(3.78)	(3.52)	(1.01)	(2.10)
Subcontractor dummy	−0.16	−0.02	−0.57	0.45	0.04	0.82	0.88	0.58
	(−1.20)	(−0.05)	(−1.10)	(0.61)	(0.03)	(0.47)	(1.29)	(0.59)
Constant	−1.08*	−4.85**	−4.51*	−11.90**	−11.81**	−23.62**	−1.25	−8.93**
	(−1.82)	(−2.64)	(−1.95)	(−2.46)	(−2.42)	(−3.80)	(−0.50)	(−2.59)
Number of enterprises	121	136	121	136	121	136	121	136
R-squared	0.66	0.49	0.68	0.59				

[a] Numbers in parentheses are t-statistics calculated on heteroskedasticity-robust standard errors for regressions of value added and total revenue and z-statistics for regressions of export revenue and sweater revenue. **Significant at the 1% level, *at the 5% level (one-sided test).

human capital becomes increasingly important in determining the size of enterprises over time. In addition, the coefficients of marketing specialist dummy in both the value added and total sales revenue functions are significantly positive and increasing over time. This finding suggests that the contribution of marketing knowledge of enterprise managers to the enterprise sizes has become increasingly important.

A similar tendency is also found in the coefficients of the relative abroad dummy. These findings suggest that, in addition to the managerial human capital, personal contact with the export traders contributes significantly to an increase in the size of enterprises, which supports Hypothesis 2-1. These findings are similar to the case of garment producers in Kenya (Chapter 3). Moreover, in these regressions, the coefficients of manager's prior experience and father dummy are positive and highly significant in 2000 but not significant in 2005. These results may reflect that managers' specific production experience and help from their fathers in the garment business are important in determining the enterprise sizes only in the early year. The general ability of managers to collect and decode information and social relationships conducive to developing cooperation between enterprises and traders, however, has become more important for enterprise management over time.

We are also interested in the determinants of export revenue and revenue from the production of high-value products such as sweaters. Therefore, we estimated the export revenue and sweater revenue functions using one-limit Tobit regression, because some enterprises do not export or do not produce sweaters. In columns (3) to (8) of Table 2.9, the determinants of total revenue, export revenue, and sweater revenue are compared. In the export revenue regressions, the estimated coefficients of manager's years of schooling, marketing specialist dummy, and relative abroad dummy are similar to those in the total revenue regression; that is, they are positive and significant, and their magnitudes increase over time, suggesting that managers with larger managerial human capital and closer contacts with export traders are leading the new trend towards increased exportation, rendering clear support for Hypothesis 2-2. The magnitudes of these coefficients, however, are higher in the export revenue regression than in the total revenue regression, which indicates that these managers have concentrated more on exporting than on domestic sales. In fact, the regressions of domestic revenue and revenue from receiving putting-out orders, which are not reported in the table, show that they do not depend significantly on the managerial human capital and the personal relationship with the export traders.

The coefficients of managers' age are negative in the export revenue regression and significant in 2000, suggesting that young managers were more active in exporting. The coefficients of operation year are positive, but significant only in 2000. This means that the specific experience of managers was important in 2000, but it lost that importance in 2005. The coefficients of manager's experience year and father dummy are positive, and only significant in 2000. Compared with the coefficients in the total revenue functions, these coefficients are roughly the same in magnitude. Thus, these findings suggest that it is the managerial human capital and the personal relationship with the export traders that play increasingly important roles in determining exportation and consequently the size of enterprises. These findings support Hypotheses 2-1 and 2-2.

In the sweater revenue functions in columns (7) and (8), the coefficients of manager's years of schooling, marketing specialist dummy, and relative abroad dummy are positive and significant in both years (except the coefficient of relative abroad dummy in 2000). The magnitudes of these coefficients increased over time, indicating the increased importance of the managerial human capital and the role played by the export traders in the production of high-quality products. The role of the export traders in sweater revenue, however, is not as clear as its effect on export revenue, since the coefficients of the relative abroad dummy in the sweater revenue functions are only significant in 2005 and their magnitudes are smaller than in the total revenue functions. The magnitudes of the coefficients of manager's years of schooling and marketing specialist dummy in the sweater revenue functions are not much different from those in the total revenue functions. This confirms the validity of Hypothesis 2-2 that managers endowed with relevant ability, knowledge, and personal trust tend to produce higher-quality products, thus contributing to the expansion of their enterprises. In addition, we estimated the functions of revenue from other technically simpler products, which are not reported here, and found that revenue from other products does not depend on managerial human capital or relationship with the export traders.

2.3.2 Determinants of changes in the marketing and production organization and their effects on the enterprise size

While managerial human capital and personal relationships with overseas traders have a positive and significant effect on the size of enterprises, a remaining question is how they increase the size of enterprises. There are two prominently emerging trends that affect the size of enterprises in Laphu: (1) increasing exportation of products and (2) increasing integration of production. Therefore, we examine whether the expansion of exports and the increase in internal production increase the enterprise size. Thus, we estimate a structural equation model in which human capital and the kinship relation with overseas traders contribute to the increase in the enterprise size through their effects on the ratio of export revenue to sales revenue and the ratio of subcontracting cost to sales revenue.

The estimates of these ratios are reported in Table 2.10. Since these ratios are censored and range between zero and unity, we apply the two-limit Tobit models for both regressions. In the export ratio regression, the coefficient of schooling is positive but not significant in 2000, while it is positive and significant in 2005 at the 5 percent significance level (one-tailed test). The coefficients of the relative abroad dummy are

Table 2.10 Determinants of export ratio and subcontracting cost ratio in a garment cluster in Vietnam (Tobit model)[a]

	Export ratio		Subcontracting cost/revenue	
	2000	2005	2000	2005
Manager's years of schooling	0.11	0.09*	−1.59	0.25
	(1.61)	(1.69)	(−1.50)	(0.41)
Marketing specialist dummy	0.37	0.56*	−13.29*	−6.81*
	(1.12)	(2.20)	(−2.14)	(−1.89)
Operation year	0.15**	0.02	−1.55*	−0.77
	(2.74)	(0.47)	(−1.73)	(−1.62)
Manager's experience year	0.07	0.13*	2.70	−0.24
	(0.28)	(1.92)	(0.71)	(−0.35)
Manager's age	−0.04*	−0.01	0.27	0.01
	(−2.21)	(−1.08)	(0.88)	(0.04)
Father dummy	0.36	0.25	−2.83	−1.64
	(1.36)	(1.15)	(−0.58)	(−0.59)
Relative abroad dummy	0.97**	0.78**	−7.75	−6.89*
	(3.09)	(2.96)	(−1.28)	(−1.84)
Subcontractor dummy	0.09	0.04	−0.44	12.73**
	(0.37)	(0.20)	(−0.10)	(4.83)
Constant	−1.02	−0.83	53.76**	27.77**
	(−1.09)	(−1.10)	(3.28)	(2.95)
Number of enterprises	121	136	121	136
Pseudo R-squared	0.25	0.26	0.03	0.04

[a]Numbers in parentheses are *z*-statistics. **Significant at the 1% level, *at the 5% level (one-sided test).

positive and highly significant at the 1percent level but their magnitudes and significance slightly decreased in 2005. This may indicate that in the early period having relatives abroad was an important advantage, while in the later period education of managers becomes essential in order to export products. In addition, the coefficients of operation year are positive and highly significant in 2000 but not significant in 2005, while the opposite is true for coefficients of both marketing specialists and years of prior experience. This may imply that prior experience and "on the job" experience can be substitutable.

In the subcontracting cost ratio regression, the coefficients of schooling are, unexpectedly, not significant, whereas the coefficients of having relatives abroad are not significant in 2000 but negative and significant in 2005. This means that better access to the export market contributes significantly to the change in the production organization towards vertical integration. The coefficients of marketing specialist dummy and operation year are significantly negative (except that the coefficient of operation year in 2005 is not significant) and their absolute value decreased over time. This would mean that the importance of the specific experience of managers in changing production organization declined in the later period. Thus, Hypothesis 2-3 is only weakly supported. Another interesting finding is that the coefficient of subcontractor dummy variable is not significant in 2000 but positive and highly significant in 2005. This may be taken to imply that managers who used to be subcontractors prefer to subcontract more as they know better how to control subcontractors.

Table 2.11 reports the results of the 2SLS estimation of determinants of the enterprise size with two endogenous explanatory variables: ratio of export sales revenue to total sales revenue (export ratio) and ratio of subcontracting cost to total sales revenue. We use four exogenous variables as instrumental variables (IVs): marketing specialist dummy, years of prior experience, relative dummy, and subcontractor dummy. These four variables are expected to affect the enterprise size indirectly through their effects on export and vertically integrated production.[8]

We regress both ln(total revenue) and ln(value added) on the same sets of variables for 2000 and 2005 separately.[9] There are common findings in both regressions for sales revenue and value added. First, the coefficients of export ratio are positive and increasing over time. These coefficients are not significant in 2000 but highly significant in 2005. This finding may indicate that in the early year selling products to the domestic market and/or receiving putting-out contracts from contractors were important marketing channels. In the later year, however,

Table 2.11 Impact of changes in marketing channel and production organization on the size of enterprise in a garment cluster in Vietnam (2SLS model)[a]

	ln(total revenue)		ln(value added)	
	2000	2005	2000	2005
Export ratio (instrumented)	1.91	2.10**	1.65	2.01**
	(1.55)	(5.43)	(1.32)	(5.35)
Subcontracting cost / revenue (instrumented)	−2.19	−2.27*	−2.50	−0.51*
	(−0.61)	(−1.83)	(−0.67)	(−2.24)
Manager's years of schooling	0.14**	0.11**	0.14**	0.11**
	(2.96)	(3.26)	(2.56)	(2.59)
Operation year	0.01	0.01	0.01	−0.01
	(0.11)	(0.55)	(0.19)	(−0.18)
Manager's age	−0.01	−0.01	−0.01	−0.01
	(−0.27)	(−0.60)	(−0.13)	(−0.35)
Father dummy	0.45**	0.11	0.51**	0.06
	(2.64)	(0.59)	(3.03)	(0.27)
Constant	−1.09	−0.49	4.73*	5.24**
	(−0.51)	(−0.65)	(2.11)	(6.76)
Joint significance tests on instruments				
F-stat of IVs on export ratio	7.15	12.27	7.15	12.27
F-stat of IVs on subcontracting cost ratio	3.20	8.75	3.20	8.75
Over-identification test: Chi-squared	2.42 [q=2]	0.39 [q=2]	1.21 [q=2]	0.50 [q=2]
R-squared	0.60	0.56	0.53	0.50
Number of enterprises	121	136	121	136

[a]Numbers in parentheses are *t*-values calculated on heteroskedasticity-robust standard errors. **Significant at the 1% level, *at the 5% level (one-sided test).

when the quality of products has been improved, improvement in the marketing channel towards exportation has become critically important for the expansion in the size of enterprises.

Second, the coefficients of subcontracting cost ratio are negative in both years but significant only in 2005. This means that in the early year internal production was not important for the expansion in the size of enterprises, because subcontracting still played an important role. As exporting products becomes a crucial marketing channel, higher-quality products must be produced and, therefore, reducing production through subcontracts has become critically important for enterprise size. Additionally, the results from Table 2.11 show that the father dummy variables are positive in both value added and total revenue functions but only significant in 2000, implying that the effect of learning from managers' fathers declined over time.

The findings in Tables 2.10 and 2.11 indicate that highly educated managers tend to innovate more by changing the marketing channel towards exporting and the production organization towards vertical integration, thereby contributing significantly to the increase in enterprise size. The final point we would like emphasize is that the coefficients of schooling are still positive and significant in both value added and total sale regression functions in Table 2.11. This suggests that schooling of managers also has a positive effect on enterprise size through other causal relations. We are, however, unable to explore them in this study because of the limitations of including more endogenous variables in the regressions due to the lack of good instrumental variables.

2.4   Concluding remarks

Recent studies have emphasized the importance of upgrading product quality and increasing exportation for cluster-based industrial development (Humphrey and Schmitz, 1996; Schmitz and Nadvi, 1999; Bigsten et al., 2004; Sonobe and Otsuka, 2006). Our analysis of the knitwear cluster in northern Vietnam fully supports this view. Specifically, in the "quality-improvement" phase, the increase in the exports significantly contributes to the expansion of the enterprise size, while in the early stage export was less important. This indicates that in the later stage, when the quality of products is improved, expanding markets beyond the domestic market becomes of utmost importance to improve the enterprise performance.

In addition, concurring with a series of studies of the industrial clusters in other countries in East Asia by Sonobe and Otsuka (2006), our analysis also indicates that the formal schooling of managers is the key to the development of enterprises in the Laphu cluster. Moreover, the personal relationship with traders abroad plays a critical role in transforming the industrial cluster, because it reduces the transaction cost, so that migrant traders can significantly contribute to the development of industrial clusters. Thus, the managerial human capital of enterprise managers and the contribution of overseas traders are the keys to the success of the cluster development in Laphu. These findings strongly support Hypotheses 1 and 2 postulated in Chapter 1.

From the statistical analysis, we also found that the increase in vertical integration over time contributed to the increase in the size of enterprises. In other words, in the early stage when the quality of products was not high and they could be visually inspected, the subcontracting system was efficient and, hence, widespread. Nevertheless, in the "quality-improvement" phase, in order to improve the quality of products and reduce transaction costs, it becomes more efficient for enterprises to increase in-house production. The increase in internal production does not merely guarantee the protection of confidential know-how, but, more importantly, secures the high quality of products in which it is difficult to detect defects.

In order for this industry to grow further, the expansion of marketing channels beyond the circle of relatives is essential. Also, the fact that the products are exported mainly to Eastern Europe indicates either weak marketing capacity or inferior quality of products or both. Therefore, it seems that there is a role to be played by the public sector in further development of the garment industry studied in this chapter. In order to test the validity of this proposition, we plan to offer management training programs to entrepreneurs in Laphu in 2010 to enhance their managerial human capital, including their ability to export.

3
Petty Traders in a Garment Cluster in Kenya

While Chapter 2 explored the impact of overseas Vietnamese traders on the performance of garment enterprises in Northern Vietnam, this chapter provides an in-depth analysis to uncover the role of petty traders in the performance of garment enterprises in Nairobi. As was specified in Hypothesis 2 in Chapter 1, traders are important in the development of industries because they disseminate market information, which tends to be scarce, particularly among a large number of micro and small enterprises (MSEs). Not only do traders provide vital information on products and designs demanded by consumers (Knorringa, 1999), they also introduce new information on improved products and production methods (Hayami and Kawagoe, 1993). Traders are attracted to clusters because the cost of searching and negotiating between traders and producers tends to be low in clusters due to the concentration and competition of a large number of producers in a small area (e.g., Levy, 1991; Sonobe et al., 2002, 2004; Yamamura et al., 2003). Consequently, enterprises located in industrial clusters are generally more market-oriented in terms of inter-enterprise transactions and more profitable than other enterprises.

There is no doubt that traders are important in enterprise performance. Yet, much less is known about the impact of dealing in stable and bulky transactions on the performance of manufacturing enterprises. The purpose of this chapter is to explore the mechanism that drives differences in performance among enterprises and to assess and quantify the impact of transactions with traders on enterprise performance using the case study of Nairobi's clustered micro and small garment producers. These producers are located in three major clusters and operate small shops in the marketplaces. In the early 1970s, when the two clusters were established by the Nairobi City

Council, enterprises were retailing second-hand clothes. However, according to McCormick et al., (1994), the first turning point came in the late 1970s when businesses turned from retailing secondhand clothes to making new clothing. These traders-turned-producers were tailors, and much of their material supply came directly from customers.

Owing to the advantage of clusters in facilitating technological spillovers in the form of imitations, easy accessibility to desired skilled labor, transaction of parts and materials at low costs with other firms (Marshall, 1920), and accessibility to market (McCormick et al., 1997), it may have dawned on many Nairobian prospective entrepreneurs that initiating and operating a business in a cluster was advantageous. With the increased demand for stalls or shops in the cluster, it became necessary for the City Council to establish a third cluster in the suburbs of Nairobi in 1980, which attracted new and existing tailors who formerly used to operate from their houses. In the early- to mid-1990s, the three clusters, particularly the two original ones, underwent a second turning point: some tailors had developed over time to become mini-manufacturers with the influx of traders from Nairobi, surrounding towns, and the neighboring countries such as Tanzania and Uganda. Indeed at the time of the survey in 2003, the two original clusters consisted of both mini-manufacturers with factory-like operation and tailors relying on family members engaged in garment production within their shops. In the third cluster, located away from the city center, all the producers were tailors.

The central question that this chapter addresses is: what is the underlying mechanism that explains the transformation process from tailors to mini-manufacturers? The answer to this question may lie in a comparison of the operation and performance of tailors and mini-manufacturers, which will demonstrate that producers receiving bulk orders from traders operate workshops outside the marketplace, produce large quantities of a small number of products, and use high-speed electric sewing machines.

The rest of the chapter is organized as follows. Section 3.1 explains the characteristics of the three garment clusters in Nairobi, whereas Section 3.2 describes the survey data and the characteristics of sample enterprises. Empirical methodologies to test the validity of specific empirical hypotheses are shown and followed by an examination of the regression results in Section 3.3. Finally, Section 3.4 concludes with major findings, and suggests policy implications and future directions for research.

3.1 Garment clusters in Nairobi

As shown in Figure 3.1, the study sites consist of three garment-producing marketplaces. Following Bigsten et al., (2000), we define micro firms as enterprises consisting of one to four employees and small firms as those with 5–15 employees. Two clusters, Gikomba and Uhuru, hereafter the urban (URB) and semi-urban (SEM) marketplaces, respectively, are near the city center and were built in 1974 by the Nairobi City Council. The other cluster, Kariobangi or the suburban (SUB) marketplace, was more recently built in 1980 by the City Council; it is relatively far away and is situated between two large slums. These clusters can be called "marketplaces" because garment producers sell their products at their shops housed in crowded commercial buildings. Producers may be classified as "tailors" or "mini-manufacturers" depending on the location of their workshop: the former have workshops inside the marketplace (which we refer to as "inside workshop"), whereas the latter have factory-like workshops outside the marketplace ("outside workshop").[1] The former sell their products primarily to consumers, while the latter sell them primarily to traders.

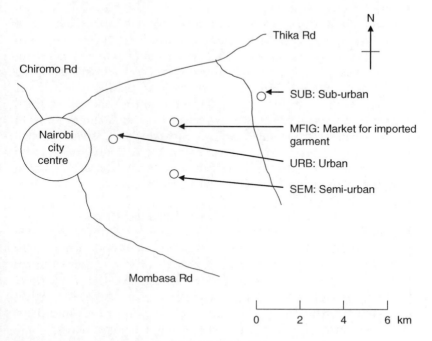

Figure 3.1 Location of the study sites in Nairobi

The URB is located about 2 km southeast of the city center and consists of three large two-storey concrete blocks with 243 stalls in total. One block was damaged in two fires in 2000 and 2002, resulting in huge losses. This calamity notwithstanding, some producers managed to revive their businesses. There are a few producers who engage in transactions of standardized products with traders, while the majority of producers are tailors, producing non-standardized garments directly for consumers. Due to the congested neighborhood, most producers have workshops inside the marketplace, employing a high fraction of casual workers who receive piece-rate wages. Being close to the city, URB is congested, with many small traders selling second-hand and new apparel outside the marketplace. The URB is also located near the public transport terminus from which buses to distant cities are available, making it cheaper to transport garment products from this cluster.

The SEM is the largest marketplace, with five large two-storey concrete blocks, composed of 405 stalls. It is situated about 6 km southeast of the city center. The cluster was dormant in the 1970s and 1980s after its inception, but with the introduction of electricity in the marketplace in 1989 more garment producers joined the cluster. Estimates in 1989 reveal the number of garment producers to be 361, with an average of 3.5 workers per producer (McCormick and Kinyanjui, 2000). Many producers working for traders make a relatively small number of standardized products in large quantities in workshops located outside. In the early- to mid-1990s SEM producers were able to attract traders who came from distant areas, including neighboring countries such as Uganda, Tanzania, and Somalia. The SEM, which is more dynamic in terms of producer–trader transactions than other marketplaces, is less crowded but easily accessible by a wide class of customers, including traders who make bulk purchases. Besides, many workshops have increasingly been established outside the SEM, partly due to the availability of space in its neighborhood.

Situated about 10 km to the northeast of Nairobi city center, the SUB consists of 720 stalls of varying sizes (McCormick and Kinyanjui, 2000). Access to the SUB is poor because of the bad roads and inconvenient transportation systems. Out of the 720 stalls or shops, about 120 are garment producers. A few producers own specialized electric machines that perform such tasks as buttonhole sewing, overlock, and embroidery. Almost without exception, the major customers are consumers. That means that the presence of traders who purchase garments in bulk and, hence, lead to the production of a large quantity of standardized goods is seriously lacking. It seems that the SUB has grown slowly probably because of its inability to attract traders.

Each of the three marketplaces seems to enjoy some Marshallian externalities (Marshall, 1920). These include the low cost of purchasing inputs owing to the presence of specialized retailers selling many varieties of cloth, buttons, thread, and zips; the availability of a pool of skilled workers from which additional workers can be drawn when needed; and technological spillovers, as imitations of garment designs are easy within and across the marketplaces. Further, some producers have developed a new organizational structure by locating their workshops outside marketplaces, which may be termed "innovation" or "new combination" in the sense of Schumpeter (1912). As will be demonstrated, this innovation is crucial for firm performance.

In addition to the above sites, a marketplace for imported garments (the Eastleigh, or MFIG) was visited to obtain additional information on the increasing importance of imported clothes from China. The MFIG, mainly inhabited by Kenyans of Somali origin, including refugees, is located about 6 km to the east of the city center. As will be explained later, this marketplace was unimportant until the early 1990s, when liberalization of the product markets in Kenya was still underway. However, it has become more active since the late 1990s and provides a tough challenge to domestic garment producers.

3.2 Characteristics of sample enterprises

3.2.1 Data collection

The data to be used in the analyses come from a survey of micro and small garment firms located in three garment clusters in Nairobi, namely the SEM, URB, and SUB. Since the majority of micro and small garment producers in Kenya are concentrated in these three clusters, a randomly drawn sample from these clusters can be regarded as a representative sample of the whole MSE-based garment sector in Kenya.

We initially conducted an informal survey of garment enterprises in the three clusters in May 2002 to identify the major analytical issues. Subsequently we prepared a questionnaire, which was pretested in March 2003, to capture details about the founder, marketing channels, and major characteristics of garment production. Based on the pretesting, we revised the questionnaire and conducted a formal survey in May to July 2003, in which a stratified random sample of 225 garment producers (109 from the SEM, 58 each from the URB and the SUB) was chosen and respondents interviewed. Among other information, the survey collected data on employment, material costs, production, proportion of sales to traders, and workshop location in April 2003, as well as recall data on basic information in 1995.[2] Although recall data for 1995 are less accurate, we consider it useful to obtain benchmark information on the size of enterprise operation in the past. Further interviews involving a random sample of 26 traders from the SEM, 15 from the URB, and 44 from the MFIG (i.e., the marketplace for imported garments,[3] located within Nairobi city) were conducted, and information such as the proportion of garment products that traders purchased from different marketplaces in 1995 and 2003 was collected. Note that the year 1995 is the year that Kenya's real GDP growth rate recovered to 1 percent, resulting in the creation of new jobs from both incoming and existing firms (Daniels and Mead, 1998).

3.2.2 Characteristics of managers

Table 3.1 presents the characteristics of managers by marketplace. As indicated in this table, managers at the SEM and URB tend to be more educated and older than those at the SUB. Over a third of the producers in the first two marketplaces have had formal training in garment production, at institutions such as polytechnics and colleges, and their previous occupations were also in the garment business. As a result, the SEM and URB are likely to outperform the SUB, leading to more dense industrial clusters in the former two locations. Indeed, the SEM is the largest and the SUB is the smallest cluster among the three. Although the performance of producers inside the clusters and those totally outside cannot be compared, as the latter are too few, it is instructive to compare the performance of producers among the three contrasting clusters in order to conjecture the role of clusters in industrial development.

Table 3.1 Characteristics of managers by marketplace in garment clusters in Kenya[a]

	SEM	URB	SUB
Education (years)	9.6	9.1	7.0
Age (years)	40.2	42.7	38.7
Training in garments (%)	40	36	22
Previous occupation in same business (%)	38	38	19
Sample size	109	58	58

[a]SEM: semi-urban; URB: urban; SUB: suburban.

3.2.3 Major characteristics of enterprises

According to Table 3.2, which shows the importance of traders and outside workshops, the main business customers for producers in both the SEM and URB were traders, although their relative importance decreased from 1995 to 2003. Note that these traders are "petty" traders who come to the marketplaces by bus and carry purchased garment products in sacks. In the case of the SUB, sales to traders were relatively low and remained so even in 2003. The ratio of mini-manufacturers in the first two clusters rose over time, indicating the increasing importance of mini-manufacturers. Although the recall data from 1990 would be subject to errors, there is a strong indication that the ratio of mini-manufacturers rose sharply at the SEM and steadily at the URB from 1990 to 1995. In 2003, half of SEM producers and about a third of URB producers were mini-manufacturers.

Except for the SUB, which did not register any outside workshops, the foregoing discussion suggests that clusters that develop internal capabilities attract more traders. Unlike firms at the SEM and URB, which tend to have factory-like operations, the SUB firms are smaller in size and are wholly family-based. The fact that sales to traders are more important in more developed clusters indicates that the formation of dense and large clusters attracts traders by lowering the transaction costs, as argued by Sonobe et al., (2002). Furthermore, the observation that there are many mini-manufacturers in the SEM, some in the URB, and none in the SUB, suggests that both the absence of transactions with traders and the limited availability of space are important barriers to the growth of clusters. Finally, note that, according to our informal interviews, transactions between producers and traders intensified from

Table 3.2 Importance of traders and outside workshop in garment clusters in Kenya[a]

		SEM	URB	SUB
Sales to traders (%)	1995	75	76	12
	2003	64	72	10
Outside workshop (%)	1990	26	20	0
	1995	43	28	0
	2003	50	31	0
Sample enterprises existing in 1990		53	37	22
Sample size for 1995 and 2003		109	58	58

[a]SEM: semi-urban; URB: urban; SUB: suburban.

the early 1990s onwards, with a higher participation of foreign traders from neighboring countries such as Tanzania and Uganda, which stimulated the establishment of the outside workshop.

3.2.4   Characteristics of mini-manufacturers and tailors

The comparison of enterprise characteristics by the type of producer shown in Table 3.3 suggests the better performance of mini-manufacturers over tailors in 2003. The former are likely to be Kikuyu, who are the majority ethnic group. The Kikuyus participate in large numbers in various economic sectors, including garment-making, perhaps suggesting that they are more aggressive and enterprising in business ventures than other tribes. The mini-manufacturers have significantly higher sales ratios to traders, are relatively more educated, make products with fewer designs, and use product labels longer than tailors. The use of product labels is one of the means that firms use to counteract the effect of quality uncertainty, which may lead to undesirable social outcomes such as the disappearance of high-quality products from the markets (e.g., Akerlof, 1970). The production of high-quality products requires the use of electric sewing machines and such specialized machines as embroidery machines, which are relatively expensive. Thus, mini-manufacturers have a relatively higher ratio of electric machines and produce larger quantities of standardized products such as uniforms using materials sourced cheaply from wholesalers. Consequently, they enjoy higher revenue per product, are more profitable as measured by the gross profit (i.e., sales revenue net of material and labor costs, including imputed costs of family labor, derived from the highest wage paid among workers), and are able to pay higher wages to workers who tend to be more productive.[4] Therefore, transaction with traders culminates in higher production efficiency as measured by the relative total factor productivity (TFP) index for mini-manufacturers (109 percent) than for tailors (87 percent), defined as the ratio of TFP index of a firm to that of an "average" firm,[5] and higher returns on capital for mini-manufacturers (6.99 percent) than for tailors (2.98 percent), which is measured by the ratio of gross profit to the resale value of sewing machines and other equipment. All the statistical data, summarized in Table 3.3, are consistent with our prior expectations. However, controlling for various characteristics in an empirical framework is indispensable in testing for the validity of these expectations.

Also, note that the number of workers is significantly larger for the mini-manufacturers than for tailors, not only in 2003 but also in 1995, suggesting the superior performance of the former over the latter. Although

Table 3.3 Characteristics of enterprises by mini-manufacturer and tailor in garment clusters in Kenya in 2003

	Mini-manufacturer	Tailor	*t*-stat[a]
Characteristics of manager and workers			
Majority ethnic group (%)	84	61	−3.55
Proportion of related workers (%)	20	15	−1.17
Schooling of manager (years)	9.49	8.12	−3.67
Previous occupation in garments (%)	40	30	−1.51
Employment			
Hourly wage (Kshs)	18.52	14.62	−3.61
Labor hours (1,000 per firm per year)	12.6	7.8	−5.30
No. of workers in 2003	4.5	2.8	−5.51
No. of workers in 1995	7.2	3.7	−5.88
Production, sales, and profitability			
Sales to traders (%)	74	38	−6.64
Product designs (no.)	5.44	7.33	2.15
Product labeling (years of use)	4.75	1.78	−4.20
Proportion in value of electric machines	0.76	0.61	−3.53
Materials from wholesalers (%)	68	55	−2.20
Sales revenue per year (Kshs, 1,000)[b]	1,572	764	−3.88
Sales revenue per product per year (Kshs, 1,000)[b]	1,177	414	−5.55
Gross profit per year (Kshs, 1,000)[b,c]	299	190	−2.00
Return on capital (%) [d]	6.99	2.98	−5.82
Relative TFP index (%)[e]	109	87	−5.56
Sample size	73	152	

[a] *t*-statistic for difference in means.
[b] Sales and gross profit are in current year prices. 1 US $ = Kenya shilling (Kshs) 75.70 (as at July 2003).
[c] Gross profit is defined as sales revenue net of material and labor costs, including imputed cost of family labor, derived from the highest wage paid among workers.
[d] Return on capital (%) is the ratio of profit to the resale value of sewing machines and other equipment.
[e] Relative TFP index (%) is the ratio of firm *i*'s TFP index to that of an "average" firm.

the data on the number of workers in 1995 may be subject to recall errors, it seems clear that the size of operation has generally declined since 1995. In fact, McCormick et al., (1997) observe a declining trend in the employment size of similar firms in the early 1990s. Although unreported, the same tendency is observed for sales revenue. We show employment data in 1995 because we use it in a series of regression analyses as a variable representing predetermined level of firm size.[6]

3.2.5   Impact of the "China shock"

The reason for the reduction in firm size over time may be understood by examining Table 3.4, which shows the proportion of purchases made by traders from five sources in 1995 and 2003. The data were obtained by asking 85 randomly selected traders to state the ratio of their purchases at each marketplace they visited. The three market-places experienced reduced sales to traders, especially in the late 1990s, as traders chose to buy more products from the MFIG.

Except for purchases from Indian and African wholesalers located downtown, these traders did not report any purchases from other sources including producers outside the marketplaces, indicating that the traders were attracted to the three marketplaces and the market-place for imported products due to the low cost of transactions. It is clear that in 1995 the most important marketplace to traders was the SEM (36 percent), followed by the URB (30 percent). The SUB (0 per-cent) was least attractive to traders, and it remained so even in 2003. While almost all marketplaces registered reduced sales to traders, the MFIG quadrupled its share of sales, rising from 12 percent in 1995 to 59 percent in 2003. Its dramatically increased importance reflects the competitive price and quality of imported garment products from China, which pose a great challenge to garment producers in Kenya. Despite this challenge, about a third of all enterprises expanded, while fewer than half contracted in sales from 1995 to 2003. For most firms, the reduction in sales led to such measures as the disposal of excess fixed inputs such as old sewing machines and replacing the wage work-ers with related workers, such as close friends and family members, who receive low or no explicit wages, at least in the short run. Indeed, from the sample, the proportion of related workers more than doubled between 1995 and 2003.

Table 3.4   Percentage of purchases made by traders across locations over time in garment clusters in Kenya[a]

Year	SEM	URB	SUB	MFIG	Indian/African Wholesalers	Total
1995	36	30	0	12	23	100
2003	14	20	0	59	7	100

[a]Computed from a random survey of 85 traders. SEM: semi-urban; URB: urban; SUB: suburban; MFIG: Market for imported garments (the Eastleigh).

3.3 Estimation methods and results

In the previous section, various enterprise characteristics were compared without setting other variables constant. In this section, we attempt to isolate the impact of each variable econometrically with a view to testing two hypotheses specified below. How these hypotheses are related is illustrated in Figure 3.2.

3.3.1 Determinants of the proportion of sales to traders

Since traders are interested in bulky transactions with producers who can produce large quantities of homogeneous products without cheating, it seems sensible to postulate the following hypothesis:

Hypothesis 3-1: Producers who are endowed with managerial human capital, and trustworthy, attract traders for bulky transactions.

The characteristics of these producers can be examined by estimating the following reduced-form equation:

$$\text{Trader}_i = \alpha_0 + \alpha_1 \text{FC}_i + \alpha_2 \text{TR}_i + \alpha_3 \text{SE}_i + \alpha_4 \text{MHK}_i + \alpha_5 \text{LOC}_i + \varepsilon_{1i}, \qquad (3.1)$$

where

Trader = the percentage of sales to traders at the time of the survey for producer i;

FC = A vector of firm characteristics including operation years of the firm or firm age (in years) and size (the number of workers including the owner) in 1995;

TR = a set of variables relating to trust and reputation, such as the number of years a product label has been in use, the number of relatives in the garment sector and its squared term, and membership in the majority ethnic group;

SE = proprietor's socio-economic characteristics other than human capital, such as age (years), gender, place of birth, and marital status;

MHK = proprietor's managerial human capital variable, which is proxied by the level of education (years), previous occupation in the garment sector, and formal training in garment-making;

LOC = firm location dummy variables for SUB and URB (with SEM being the default), capturing such factors as the level and state of physical infrastructure and insecurity;[7]

α_j ($j=0,\ldots,5$) = parameters to be estimated; and

ε_1 = disturbance term.

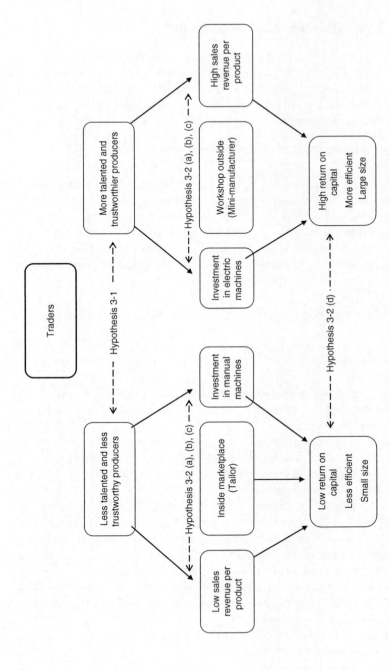

Figure 3.2 An illustration of the operation and performance of garment enterprise in Nairobi

In estimating equation (3.1), we use the two-limit Tobit model because the dependent variable is censored at zero from below and unity from above. We use logarithm for continuous variables.[8] For "size," we use employment in 1995, as it can be regarded as predetermined.

To test Hypothesis 3-1, we examine whether trustworthy and educated proprietors endowed with high levels of both human and social capital succeed in making sales to traders. Thus, the duration of product label use, the number of relatives in the garment business, membership in the majority ethnic group, and education are expected to have positive and significant effects.

3.3.2 Determinants of outside workshop, machine use and revenue per product

Once producers are engaged in bulky transactions of homogeneous products, it will become profitable for them to initiate workshop production while using high-speed electric machines, in order to enjoy scale economies. Thus, we would like to postulate the following hypothesis:

Hypothesis 3-2: Producers who enter into sales contracts with traders (a) choose an outside workshop (*WKS*), (b) decide to use a high ratio of electric machines (*ElKratio*), and (c) choose to make fewer product designs, with the aim of raising sales revenue, which may be captured by log revenue per product (*Lnrevpp*), (d) thereby resulting in highly efficient and profitable operations.

These choices are assumed to be made simultaneously. In modeling the regression functions to identify the determinants of these choices and performance with a view to testing Hypothesis 3-2, the following equation is estimated:

$$Z_{1i} = \beta_0 + \beta_1 Trader_i + \beta_2 FC_i + \beta_3 TR_i + \beta_4 SE_i$$
$$+ \beta_5 HK_i + \beta_6 LOC_i + \varepsilon_{2i}, \tag{3.2}$$

where Z_{1i} is a vector of dependent variables (i.e., *WKS*, *ElKratio*, and *Lnrevpp*). Regressors include *Trader* as well as those variables used in (3.1). Note that *Trader* is endogenous in equation (3.2). To avoid the endogeneity problem, a suitable instrument that is correlated with *Trader* but not with the error term should be identified. From the data, the number of relatives in the garment business and its squared term serve this purpose, because, while producers with more relatives are likely to register higher sales to traders due to better connection with traders, having relatives *per se* does not influence the decision and performance of a firm. In examining factors influencing workshop location, a two-step technique developed by Rivers and Vuong (1988), which serves as a test of endogeneity, is used. In this approach, residuals predicted in the first step regression (i.e., equation (3.1)) are used as a new regressor in equation (3.2). If *Trader* is associated with the outside workshop, as 3-1(a) argues, then the effect of *Trader* should be positive and significant. In addition, firm age and proprietor age may have positive and significant effects, if experience is conducive to the management of outside workshops.

Hypothesis 3-2(b) seeks to find whether producers dealing in sales transactions with traders use a high ratio of electric machines to produce large quantities of high-quality standardized products. In other words, the hypothesis seeks to determine whether the variable *Trader* has a positive and significant effect on *ElKratio*, the ratio of electric machines used by a producer. Since this ratio ranges from zero to one, a two-step procedure designed for Tobit models advanced by Smith and Blundell (1986) that is analogous to the Rivers–Vuong (1988) method is adopted. It is expected that the effect of *Trader* will be positive and significant. Moreover, firm size and managerial human capital are expected to have positive and significant impacts on the ratio of electric machines, since it is efficient to use electric machines to produce large quantities of products, while managerial human capital may be useful in their operation and maintenance. Similarly, in testing Hypothesis 3-2(c) that producers engaged in sales transactions with traders as captured by *Trader* enjoy high revenue per product, the two-stage least squares (2SLS) technique is applied to determine the impact of *Trader* on *Lnrevpp*. If the last part of Hypothesis 3-2 is valid, *Trader* should have a positive and significant impact on the log of revenue per product.

3.3.3   Determinants of the return on capital and production efficiency

As stated above, transactions with traders are likely to alter the mode of operation of producers by encouraging them to use outside workshops and a high ratio of high-speed machines. Producers engaging in sales transactions with traders are also likely to achieve high revenue per product. So Hypothesis 3-2(d) postulates that producers who depend on traders are likely to be more profitable and efficient than those who rely on consumers. Then, sales transactions with traders culminate in producers being more profitable, as indicated by the higher returns on capital (ROC), and more efficient, as measured by the higher TFP index.

In other words, the dependent variables in equation (3.2) as well as manager and firm characteristics should enter each of the two performance indicator functions, as follows:

$$Z_{2i} = f(Lnrevpp, WKS, ElKratio, Trader, \text{manager and firm characteristics}) \tag{3.3}$$

where Z_{2i} is a vector of the dependent variables, TFP index and *ROC*.

Note that *Lnrevpp*, *WKS*, *ElKratio* and *Trader* are endogenous. As shown in Figure 3.2, although transactions with traders are expected to have an indirect impact on *ROC* (or TFP), *ElKratio*, *WKS*, and *Lnrevpp* will have direct effects on *ROC* (or TFP). Given the paucity of exogenous variables, it is not feasible to endogenize all of these variables. Thus, we estimate the "semi-reduced" form equation in which the predicted value of *Trader* is used as an explanatory variable. Specifically, the following semi-reduced form equation is estimated:

$$Z_{3i} = \delta_0 + \delta_1 Trader_i + \delta_2 FC_i + \delta_3 TR_i + \delta_4 SE_i + \delta_5 HK_i + \delta_6 LOC_i + \varepsilon_{3i} \tag{3.4}$$

where Z_{3i} denotes a vector of the dependent variables, relative TFP index (%), and return on capital (*ROC*), while the rest of the variables remain the same as those listed in (3.1).

Hypothesis 3-2(d) argues that producers selling to traders are more profitable, which may be measured by *ROC*, the return on capital or the gross profit divided by the resale value of machineries, than those who do not. It is expected that *Trader* will enter positively and significantly in the *ROC* equation. Producers with many years of formal education are also expected to register high *ROC* because of their better management skills.

Hypothesis 3-2(d) alternatively postulates that firms that rely on traders are more efficient than an average firm in the use of inputs, which may be reflected in high TFP indexes. This suggests that firms with entrepreneurs engaged in factory-like operations have superior managerial human capital that is manifested in high profits. For such firms, education is indispensable for making proper business management decisions. Thus, *Trader*, the duration of product label use, and managerial human capital are expected to have positive and significant impacts on TFP, which is also consistent with Hypotheses 1 and 2 postulated in Chapter 1.

3.3.4   Transaction with traders

Table 3.5 shows the determinants of transaction with traders, with the dependent variable being the current percentage of sales to traders.[9] It is clear that the number of relatives in the same business, education, and duration of product label use increase significantly with sales to traders. This is consistent with Hypothesis 3-1 that competent and dependable producers with strong social networks attract traders. This suggests that traders look for educated managers capable of making high quality products that can be distinguished from poor products through labeling. However, the impact of relatives on sales to traders increases at a decreasing rate, peaking when the number of relatives is 13. In terms of marginal effect, an increase in the number of relatives in the same business by one person increases sales to traders by 7.5 percentage points,

Table 3.5 Tobit estimates of the importance of traders in garment clusters in Kenya[a]

	Coefficient	*t*-statistic	Marginal effect[b]
Ln (employment in 1995)	−1.51**[c]	−3.95	−0.94
Ln (firm age, years)	−5.42	−0.66	−3.37
Duration of product labeling, years	0.98*	1.71	0.61
Outside workshop	14.84*	2.41	10.79
Male	−0.18	−0.03	−0.13
Married	6.77	0.64	4.92
Ethnic majority	22.16**	3.13	16.11
Birth in Nairobi	10.68	0.66	7.77
Ln (manager's age, years)	0.90	0.06	0.56
Ln (education, years)	21.35**	2.61	13.30
Previous occupation in same business	7.72	1.35	5.61
Training in garment-making dummy	4.37	0.74	3.18
Suburban (SUB)[c]	−79.64**	−8.21	−57.90
Urban (URB)	3.95	0.60	2.87
Relatives in same business	13.03**	4.65	8.12
(relatives in same business)^2	−0.50*	−1.71	−0.31
Constant	−9.86	−0.16	
Log likelihood value	−719.47		
Pseudo R-squared	0.14		
Sample size	225		

[a]Dependent variable is the percentage of sales to traders. **Significant at the 1%, *at the 5% level.
[b]The marginal effect gives the partial effect of each regressor (evaluated at the mean) conditional on the dependent variable being positive. It is obtained by multiplying each coefficient by an appropriate adjustment factor for continuous or binary variables.
[c]Base category: Semi-urban (SEM).

an increase in the duration of product labeling by 1 year increases sales to traders by 0.6 percentage points, while a 1 percent increase in schooling years increases sales to traders by about 13 percentage points.[10] This suggests that education has a large impact on sales to traders. Further, there is strong evidence that producers belonging to the majority ethnic group enjoy higher sales ratios.[11] The effect of firm size is negative, indicating that a 1 percent increase in firm size in 1995 lowers current sales to traders by about 0.9 percent. This suggests that, although the larger firms can deliver in bulk to traders, it was not the large firms in 1995 that have successfully developed contractual relationships with traders as of 2003. The SUB makes far lower sales to traders than the SEM, probably because its isolation works to its disadvantage due to high transaction costs, as Weijland (1999) predicts. Indeed, Sonobe et al., (2002) note that remoteness is associated with larger transaction costs of garment products with traders in China. Except for ethnicity, other socio-economic factors of managers have no significant impact on sales to traders.

3.3.5 Outside workshop, electric machines, and revenue per product

The first three columns of Table 3.6 present Tobit estimates of factors that determine the choice of outside workshop, the ratio of electric machines used, and revenue per product. In terms of the workshop location, there is evidence that producers working with traders are more likely to have outside workshops, as indicated by the significant coefficient of *Trader* in column 1 of Table 3.6. This means that firms tend to choose outside workshops if they are contacted by traders. This is consistent with Hypothesis 3-2(a), which states that sales transactions with traders encourage producers to locate their workshops outside the cluster. The tendency of producers to use outside workshops is a reflection of their desire to make standardized products in large quantities. The age of the proprietor and firm age, which are proxies for experience, increase the probability of owning an outside workshop. Married managers are more likely to own outside workshops, possibly because they overcome credit constraints by pooling resources with spouses and can thereby expand production.[12] Relative to the SEM, producers in the SUB do not have outside workshops because they have virtually no sales transactions with traders. On the other hand, producers in the URB are not likely to use an outside workshop because of space constraints in its neighborhood. This is consistent with McCormick et al's., (1997) observation that space constraints are

Table 3.6 Determinants of outside workshop, ratio of electric machines, revenue per product, return on capital, and efficiency in garment clusters In Kenya[a]

	(1) WKS Coefficient	(2) ElKratio Coefficient	(3) Lnrevpp Coefficient	(4) ROC Coefficient	(5) TFP Index Coefficient
Trader	0.01**[b]	0.04**	0.02**	0.06*	0.39**
	(2.94)	(5.51)	(3.65)	(2.90)	(7.82)
Residual	−0.32	−0.03	−0.01	−0.20	−0.17
	(−0.45)	(−1.49)	(−1.21)	(−1.35)	(−1.23)
Ln (employment in 1995)	−0.01	0.06	0.26*	−0.29	−1.64
	(−0.59)	(1.44)	(2.90)	(−0.40)	(−0.52)
Ln (firm age, years)	0.69**	−0.04	0.04	0.56	3.42**
	(3.01)	(−0.73)	(0.22)	(2.36)	(9.66)
Duration of product labeling, years	0.001	0.002	0.01**	0.02	0.64*
	(0.86)	(0.84)	(2.93)	(0.35)	(2.86)
Outside workshop	0.83**	−0.02	0.01	1.62**	5.06
	(5.67)	(−0.83)	(0.07)	(8.79)	(1.73)
Male	0.01	0.02	−0.03	1.07**	4.08
	(0.72)	(0.36)	(−0.11)	(2.92)	(0.69)
Married	0.09**	0.26**	0.56**	2.42**	11.04**
	(3.46)	(3.42)	(2.97)	(2.95)	(2.98)
Ethnic majority	0.003	−0.03	0.14	−0.01	0.49
	(0.08)	(−1.70)	(1.33)	(−0.03)	(0.17)
Birth in Nairobi	−0.03	0.05	1.41**	1.21	1.30
	(−1.03)	(0.75)	(3.87)	(1.04)	(0.16)

	(1)	(2)	(3)	(4)	(5)
Ln (manager's age, years)	0.41**	0.26**	0.24	1.73	11.66
	(3.93)	(8.73)	(0.39)	(0.88)	(0.94)
Ln (education, years)	−0.002	0.12**	0.21	3.84**	18.33**
	(−0.10)	(2.94)	(1.68)	(4.76)	(7.43)
Previous occupation in same business	−0.03	0.09**	0.11	0.35	−2.70
	(−0.45)	(7.26)	(1.86)	(0.39)	(−0.61)
Training in garment-making dummy	−0.01	0.06	−0.05	−0.03	0.35
	(−0.86)	(1.53)	(−0.50)	(−0.15)	(0.26)
Suburban (SUB)	−0.11**	0.22	0.60	1.72	10.47
	(−6.08)	(1.53)	(1.53)	(0.92)	(1.37)
Urban (URB)	−0.06*	−0.01	−0.62**	−1.81**	−9.84**
	(−4.44)	(−0.51)	(−8.69)	(−6.68)	(−6.93)
Constant	0.34**	−1.09**	9.41**	−17.89	−29.75
	(4.02)	(−7.28)	(3.66)	(−2.18)	(−0.55)
R-squared	0.77	0.26	0.15	0.34	0.35
Sample size	225	225	225	225	225

aDependent variable is (1) workshop location dummy (=1 if outside marketplace), (2) ratio in value of electric machines to total capital, (3) log of revenue per product, (4) return on capital, i.e., ratio of profit to resale value of sewing machines and other equipment, and (5) TFP (%) is the ratio of firm i's TFP index to that of an "average" firm. The estimates for equations (1) and (2) are based on the Rivers–Vuong (1988) and Smith–Blundell (1986) two-step approaches, respectively, while equations (3), (4), and (5) are based on 2SLS. Numbers in parentheses just below the coefficients are t- or z-statistics. **Significant at the 1% level, *at the 5% level.

a limiting factor for the growth of MSEs, especially those operating market stalls in Nairobi.

Column 2 in Table 3.6 presents the determinants of the ratio of electric machines used. Consistent with Hypothesis 3-2(b), the results suggest that *Trader* increases the proportion of electric machines used. The same is true of proprietor age, education, and previous occupation in the same sector. Thus, more experienced managers with better capacity to produce large volumes of products tend to invest in more electric machines. Married managers employ more electric machines, presumably because they can pool resources with spouses to install efficient machines. The location dummies are insignificant, suggesting the lack of locational advantage.

The estimation result using the two-stage least squares (2SLS) method, shown in column 3 of Table 3.6, suggests that sales transactions with traders as indicated by *Trader* have a positive and significant impact on revenue per product: a 50 percent increase in sales to traders increases revenue by 1 percent (equivalent to Kshs 4,140 per product per year for a tailor). This result is consistent with Hypothesis 3-2(c). Firm size and the duration of product labeling enter significantly and positively as well. Managers born in Nairobi city seem to obtain higher revenue per product, perhaps indicating their better management ability due to greater exposure to education and training facilities. Indeed, it appears that birth partly captures the effect of human capital on revenue, since education and training are insignificant. In terms of location, the SEM tends to have higher revenue per product than the URB, again pointing to the SEM's intensive producer–trader interactions. Lastly, revenue per product does not seem to differ by ethnicity or gender.

The results in columns 1 through 3 support the first half of Hypothesis 3-2, that producer–trader transactions are positively associated with the use of outside workshops, higher ratio of electric machines, and higher revenue per garment product.

3.3.6   Return on capital and production efficiency

Hypothesis 3-2(d) seeks to establish that management by producers who work with traders is more profitable than others. This is confirmed by the positive and highly significant coefficient of *Trader* in column 4 of Table 3.6. Consistent with Hypothesis 1 specified in chapter 1, there is strong evidence that the managerial human capital in the form of education increases profits. The finding by Daniels and Mead (1998) that MSEs owned by women earn less income than men in Kenya seems to be supported as well in column 4, which suggests that women managers earn 1.07 percent less return on capital. Women managers may be unable to reap higher return on capital due to household demands that do not allow them to devote sufficient time to their business, but not necessarily due to any disadvantage in accessing credit (Akoten et al., 2006). Finally, the URB appears to suffer low returns relative to the SEM for two possible reasons. First, "power interruption and inaccessibility to electricity" is among the most severe constraints facing urban enterprises, as claimed by 100 percent of MSEs in urban areas (CBS et al., 1999: 71). Second, the prevalence of relatively high insecurity at the URB may hamper investment in more productive technologies.

The last part of Hypothesis 3-2 also argues that producers relying on traders are more productive than others. Column 5 of Table 3.6 reports the determinants of productivity, with the dependent variable being the ratio of firm *i*'s TFP index relative to that of an "average" firm. The highly and positively significant coefficient of *Trader* as observed from the table clearly attests to the validity of the hypothesis that producer–trader transactions increase productivity. As expected, the use of product labeling as a proxy for quality increases productivity. Likewise, better-educated managers are more productive, since they are likely to combine inputs in production more efficiently, while firm age, a proxy for experience, increases efficiency as well, due presumably to the positive effect of learning-by-doing. In other words, management experience constitutes a part of the managerial human capital. That education increases efficiency is consistent with the finding of Burki and Terrell (1998) and our Hypothesis 1. Another important finding is that married managers are more efficient, which suggests that couples are more likely to combine and manage their household and business tasks more efficiently. In terms of enterprise location, firms located at the URB are less productive than firms operating at the SEM.

3.4   Concluding remarks

In general, traders who enter into sales transactions with managers working in the MSE sector in Kenya tend to operate differently from those in Asia, who are usually rich and engage in voluminous interlinked contracts characterized by the provision of materials and credit as well as the guaranteed purchase of finished products. For instance, in the putting-out system in the Philippines, urban-based traders (or contractors) design cloth and give materials and credit to rural subcontractors, who use cheap rural labor to produce the final product. The contractors then pay for the finished garments and ship them to urban areas or overseas markets from which they obtain fresh orders (Kikuchi, 1998; Sonobe and Briones, 2001). The same pattern is reported for Japan (Itoh and Tanimoto, 1998) as well as in industrial clusters such as those in the Emilia Romagna region of Northern Italy (Rabellotti, 1995) and in the Sinos Valley in Brazil (Schmitz, 1995).[13] In the case of Kenya, it is yet to be seen whether relational contracting will develop in future. However, although they are small and poor, the activity of Kenya's petty garment traders has a large impact on the transformation of tailors to mini-manufacturers, as this study demonstrated.

It was found in this chapter that trustworthy and educated producers with strong social networks attract traders. These producers manufacture large quantities of more standardized products in outside workshops, enabling them to enjoy higher production efficiency. In contrast, producers who produce small quantities of less standardized products from inside shops tend to work for consumers directly. Also, firms relying on traders and those run by older, married, well-educated, and experienced managers use a higher fraction of electric machines, thereby generating higher returns on capital.

Barriers to the performance of small- and medium-sized producers are discussed in Schmitz (1982) and McCormick et al., (1997). These include imperfect credit markets, difficulties in accessing raw materials, and weak demand. The establishment of the marketplace by the local government enhances market access not only in Kenya but also in China (Sonobe et al., 2002, 2004). The low cost of transactions with traders seems to be a particularly important condition for improved performance and the transformation of cluster-based firms in Kenya, where markets are not well developed. This may explain partly why indigenous African enterprises tend to be family-based and too small to be efficient compared with factory-based modern enterprises, which enjoy transactions at relatively developed marketing sectors (e.g., Ramachandran and Shah, 1999). Thus, indigenous manufacturing enterprises in Africa may not achieve high profits and efficiency unless marketing problems are addressed.

To sum up, both Chapters 2 and 3 provided clear evidence that traders play a critical role in improving production efficiency of clustered enterprises. This clearly supports Hypothesis 2 specified in Chapter 1. In all likelihood, this finding implies that the establishment of improved marketing systems is the key to successful cluster-based industrial development. The analyses in Chapters 2 and 3 also confirm the critical importance of managerial human capital in improving management efficiency, which is consistent with Hypothesis 1. To the extent that the acquisition of marketing knowledge, information, and skills by innovative enterprises has spillover effects, social return to the acquisition of managerial ability exceeds the private return. Herein lies a potential role to be played by the public sector, which may provide training programs on management to enterprise managers.

Part II
The Role of Managerial Human Capital in the Upgrading Process

4
The Product Ladder in the Steel Bar Industry in Vietnam

Managerial ability of enterprise managers, which we call managerial human capital in this study, is expected to play a critical role in carrying out multifaceted innovations, as formulated in Hypothesis 1 in Chapter 1. The purpose of Part II (Chapters 4 and 5) is to substantiate this hypothesis based on the case studies of a steel bar cluster in northern Vietnam and a metalwork cluster in Nairobi, Kenya. Particularly noteworthy is the fact that the steel bar cluster in Vietnam is a village-based, rural industry, which can be found in Asia but not in SSA.

At the outset, we would like to point out that in developing countries the majority of the poor reside in the rural areas. To reduce poverty, the promotion of small and medium enterprises (SMEs) in the rural economy has been a major agenda of these countries, because SMEs create employment opportunities for the poor (Humphrey and Schmitz, 1996; Hayami, 1998; Otsuka et al., 2009). The success of the overall economic development and the poverty reduction in China can be attributed to the successful development of the township and village enterprises (TVEs) in the 1980s and 1990s, which vividly demonstrates the importance of the development of SMEs (e.g., Heston and Sicular, 2008). The question of whether other transition economies such as Vietnam can be as successful as China, therefore, needs to be investigated.

There are a large number of village-based industrial clusters consisting of household enterprises and SMEs in the rural areas of Vietnam, especially in the northern region (JICA, 2004; Chapter 2). These clusters are often located within the boundaries of villages, where extended families have lived together over generations. Many of them produce traditional products such as silk and bamboo furniture by hand or by using simple machines. These products can be called Z-goods in the sense of Hymer and Resnick (1969). Some other villages have been transformed to become modern industrial clusters where modern technology and machines are used to produce what Ranis and Stewart (1993) would call modern Z-goods. Aside from Chapter 2 of this book, however, the transformation process of these village-based industrial clusters has not been carefully investigated.

This chapter presents another case study of a village-based industrial cluster in northern Vietnam, where modern iron and steel products are increasingly produced. Similarly to other village-based industrial clusters in Vietnam, the development of this cluster was greatly influenced by state-owned enterprises (SOEs) located near the village and a cooperative in the village. By receiving subcontracting orders from the SOEs through the cooperative, the households in the village acquired machines, technology, and know-how in management and marketing to produce new and modern products. In this respect, the development of the village enterprises is similar to that of the collective TVEs in the suburbs of Shanghai and Jiangsu province in China (Murakami et al., 1994, 1996). Another important and perhaps unique aspect of the development of the village industry in northern Vietnam is the dense family ties between proprietors of the enterprises and their family members, including parents and siblings, who originally founded their businesses. Such family ties generate social capital for the proprietors, which appears to influence the proprietors' decisions on what to produce and how to improve product quality, production organization, and marketing channels.

Based on survey data collected from 204 enterprises, this chapter focuses on the determinants of the improvement in product lines, product quality, material procurement, product marketing, labor management, and the overall performance of the enterprises. To produce modern and higher-quality products, it is necessary for the enterprises to acquire higher-quality materials. Because it is difficult to check the quality of new materials and improved products by visual inspection, the enterprises have gradually shifted from anonymous transactions with local traders in the local market to long-term direct transactions with outside traders. Additionally, the management of labor has been improved by strengthening the relationship with foremen. In line with Hypothesis 1 specified in Chapter 1, we postulate that the proprietor's general human capital, acquired by formal education, and experience in marketing and management play a key role in the improvement in products, production organization, marketing channels, and performance of the enterprise. We also hypothesize that the proprietor's social capital, measured by family ties with fathers, fathers-in-law, blood siblings, and siblings-in-law facilitates the multifaceted improvements and performance of the enterprise.

This chapter is organized as follows. After briefly describing the historical background of iron and steel production as well as the marketing and production organization in the study village, Section 4.1 advances testable hypotheses. Section 4.2 explains our sampling method and the characteristics of the sample enterprises, which is followed by the regression analysis in Section 4.3. Finally, the major findings are summarized and policy implications are discussed in Section 4.4.

4.1 Historical background and hypotheses

4.1.1 Tradition of iron and steel production

The study village is called Dahoi. It is located in a province surrounded by big cities such as Haiphong, a port city through which iron plates are imported and scrap metal is procured, and Quangninh, where charcoal is produced. Many of the SOEs that have influenced the production of steel products in the village are located in these cities. For example, Thainguyen Iron and Steel SOE, which is located about 80 km northwest of the village and used to have monopoly power in the iron and steel product market and monopsony power in the material and labor markets for steel production, was the source of knowledge for new products in the village. These SOEs also provided the village with access to materials, machines, skilled labor, management know-how, and market information.

Historically, Dahoi used to be a village of blacksmiths that dates back 400 years. For most of its history, the village had produced simple agricultural tools. In the early 20th century, the disruption in colonial trade provided the village with an opportunity to supply the domestic market with such products as shovels and hoes, which had previously been imported (DiGregorio, 2001). During the war against the French in the 1950s, the village produced weapons such as daggers and bayonets.

In 1958, a cooperative was established in the village, and 55 households became members. Nearby SOEs contracted out the production of agricultural tools and parts of weapons to the cooperative, just as SOEs did to the TVEs in China (Murakami et al., 1994, 1996; Liu and Otsuka, 1998). By becoming members of the cooperative and by working closely with the SOEs, the village households gained technical knowledge and market information. Until the early 1980s, household production was not officially forbidden but private commercial activities across district boundaries were subject to confiscation. By 1985, the cooperative in the village was closed since the products of the SOEs could not compete with imported products from China, and the SOEs stopped contracting out to the cooperative. Since then, all the production in the village has been undertaken by household enterprises.

The *Doi Moi* (renovation) policies, which were implemented in 1986 to promote the private sector and liberalize the domestic market, brought favorable conditions for household production in the village. A remarkable change began when one villager set up a household enterprise to produce wire rods in 1986. Previously, wire rods had been produced only by Thainguyen Iron and Steel SOE. Through visits to this SOE, this villager successfully imitated the production method of the wire rods, and even lowered the production cost by using cut billets as material. Cut billets are thin strips of cheap scrap iron plates that were cut by manually operated shears. The wire rods produced in the village were initially crude, but cheap, so they could meet the demand of the poor in Vietnam. Wire rods are used directly in house construction or processed into various types of products such as nails and spikes. The production of the wire rods was soon imitated by other household enterprises in the village. Demand for the cut billets, therefore, increased substantially. The techniques of cutting the scrap iron plates into the cut billets were also quickly diffused. As a result, the village enterprises specialized in producing either wire rods or cut billets, and turned from independent into specialized and interdependent production units.

In the early 1990s, the village enterprises started producing square and round steel bars, which are more modern than wire rods and are used for house construction. The square and round bars are reinforced steel bars produced by using cast billets imported from Russia or produced by Thainguyen Iron and Steel SOE. By visiting this SOE to procure the cast billets, the villagers learnt the technology and started to produce them by melting scrap metal with chemical substances. Later on, cheap electrical arc furnaces imported from China became available and the supply of electricity improved, allowing a number of villagers to enter the foundry sector.

In 1997, the villager who was the first to produce the wire rods observed a decline in his profit and decided to produce angle iron, which is U or V-shaped construction steel. Angle iron is the most technically difficult product due to the precision of the angles required. The production of angle iron requires cast billets of higher quality and machines that are more advanced than others. By the late 1990s, all the different types of products that are currently produced had been introduced into the village. The village has gradually become famous for its construction steel products and attracted a large number of traders who supply the materials to and purchase the finished products from the village.

4.1.2 Marketing and production organization

The specialization and division of labor among the enterprises in the village is illustrated in Figure 4.1. The village enterprises specialize in producing either cut billets, wire rods, cast billets, square and round bars, or angle iron,[1] to list the products in order from the simplest and least modern to the most sophisticated and modern items. Indeed, the production of these products forms a product ladder, up which the village enterprises have been moving. For instance, many of the village enterprises have changed their product lines from cut billets to wire rods or from cast billets to angle iron.

The enterprises that produce finished steel products, that is, wire rods, square and round bars, and angle iron, procure intermediate products, that is, cut or cast billets, from other enterprises in the village. Those that produce cut billets procure used iron plates from Haiphong province. The used iron plates are offcuts imported from ship-building sites abroad or scrap plates supplied from ship-dismantling sites within the country. In the past, there were several local traders of these iron plates in the village. Now, however, due to the recent improvement in the road

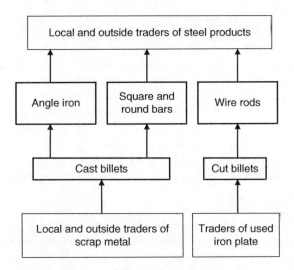

Figure 4.1 Marketing channels and production organization in a steel bar cluster in Vietnam

network that connects the village and Haiphong province, the proprietors themselves travel to buy these iron plates.

The enterprises that produce cast billets procure scrap metal as material from local and outside traders. The local traders bring the scrap metal to a local market in the village, where anonymous spot transactions take place. It is time-consuming and difficult for the proprietors to check the quality of the scrap metal sold at the local market. In fact, the scrap metal sold by the local traders may be "lemons" containing substances other than metal. In contrast, the outside traders sell scrap metal directly to the enterprises that cast billets, and maintain longstanding relationships with these customers to avoid the problem of lemons. As a result, the scrap metal transacted by the local traders is of lower quality, whereas that transacted by the outside traders is of higher quality.

The village enterprises that produce the finished products deal with both local and outside traders. The local traders, including petty traders and shops in the village, transact with the proprietors of the enterprises at an anonymous market. In contrast, the outside traders directly place orders for large quantities of products. The outside traders and their customers usually have a long-term relationship based on mutual trust. The quality of the products that are transacted directly by the outside traders is higher than the quality of those that are transacted through the local market by the local traders, which is consistent with the observations in China by Sonobe et al. (2002, 2004). Although we do not focus on the role of traders in this chapter, there is no question that they are important, as in the cases reported in Chapters 2 and 3.

Except for those producing cut billets, enterprises organize hired workers as a team supervised by a foreman. There is only one foreman in an enterprise at any time. The foreman assumes important roles not only as a supervisor but also as a technician, because he is in charge of technical issues such as adjusting the temperature to melt the metal, the quantity of chemicals mixed into the melted metal, and the machines. The proprietors and the foremen are not tied by any formally written labor contract, but rather by informal agreements between them.

4.1.3   Testable hypotheses

Many of these village enterprises have upgraded their product lines from less modern to more modern products, since the production of the latter provides them with more profitable opportunities. To the extent that education is valuable in order to be able to adjust to these new opportunities (Schultz, 1975), it is expected that the formal education of the proprietors is a key factor that affects the proprietor's decision to produce more modern products.

In addition to the increase in production of more modern products, the quality of products has improved remarkably. When the quality of products improves, transaction costs among material suppliers, producers, and traders tend to increase because of the increasing difficulty in checking the quality in advance. In order to reduce the transaction costs and guarantee the on-time delivery of products free from defects, it is more effective to directly procure high-quality materials from and sell the improved products to the outside traders than to transact anonymously through the traders in the local markets. The proprietors in Dahoi have indeed attempted to do so. Moreover, they have improved the management of labor by strengthening relationships with the foremen. Since the foremen are knowledgeable about production, they are often poached by other enterprises. Thus, it is important for the proprietors to strengthen their relationships with the foremen by providing incentives such as bonuses in addition to their wages to entice them to stay longer. Such decisions may be made by the proprietors who are more educated.

Indeed, a strong link between formal education and innovations has been found in cluster-based industrial development in East Asia (e.g., Sonobe and Otsuka, 2006, as well as in Chapters 2 and 3). Therefore, regarding the roles of general human capital acquired by formal education, it seems reasonable to postulate the following hypothesis:

Hypothesis 4-1 on the role of general human capital (GHC): A more educated proprietor tends to produce a more modern and higher-quality product, to increase long-term direct transactions with outside traders, to have a longer-term contract with the foreman, and to achieve better performance than others.

In former socialist countries such as Vietnam, commercial activities and private businesses used to be depressed. As a result, marketing and management expertise is scarce in rural areas, and, accordingly, the value of experience in marketing and management is high in village industries. For example, the specific human capital that a proprietor has acquired by experience in marketing will help him or her obtain material at low costs and market products at high prices. To the extent that long-term direct transactions with outside traders are more profitable than anonymous spot transactions with local traders, we expect that proprietors with prior experience in marketing will procure material from outside traders and sell products to them while maintaining long-term relationships with them. Similarly, the specific human capital related to management is expected to play an important role, mainly in labor management, inventory control, accounting, and other managerial tasks within enterprises. Among these managerial tasks, maintaining a good relationship with the foreman is of particular importance in view of the important contribution of the foreman to the operation of the enterprise. Both types of prior experience will lead to better business results in general, by shifting down the marginal cost curve or shifting up the marginal revenue curve or both. Regarding the specific human capital of the proprietors, we would like to advance the following hypothesis:

Hypothesis 4-2 on the role of specific human capital (SHC): The proprietor's marketing experience and management experience allow him or her to make direct and long-term transactions with outside traders and to enter into a long-term contract with the foreman, respectively, and both enhance enterprise performance.

Although we distinguish between general and specific human capital in this chapter, both of them are integral parts of the managerial human capital discussed in Chapter 1.

In villages in Vietnam where extended families live together, it is a tradition that, when parents retire, they hand over their private business to the eldest son when he becomes an adult. It is interesting to observe that women in Dahoi village are capable of doing business, so that some parents transfer their businesses to their daughters if they are the eldest. Therefore, both the parents and the parents-in-law of the proprietor might affect his or her decision on what to produce. It seems, however, reasonable to expect that they would not affect his or her decision on how to innovate after the business is transferred.

The eldest child, who takes over the parents' business, is supposed to help his younger siblings by employing them as workers, offering financial and technical assistance, or introducing customers when they establish their own businesses later. Such strong family ties in the village are similar to what has been observed in the case of a surgical instrument cluster in Pakistan, where family ties, which include extended family, are important for the cluster's development (Nadvi, 1996). It seems reasonable to expect that these family members would affect the proprietor's decision on what to produce, how to innovate, and consequently the performance of the enterprise. We, therefore, postulate the following hypothesis:

Hypothesis 4-3 on the role of social capital (SC): The proprietor's parents and parents-in-law influence his or her decision on what to produce while his or her blood siblings and siblings-in-law influence the improvement in the product quality, the increase in the long-term direct transactions with outside traders, the duration of contract with the foreman, and the overall performance of the enterprise.

4.2   Characteristics of sample enterprises

We conducted a survey in Dahoi in the summer of 2007. According to the list of enterprises provided by the commune government office, there were 133 enterprises that produced cut billets, 39 wire rods, 118 cast billets, 42 square and round bars, and 40 angle iron.[2] Based on the list, we interviewed all the enterprises that produced wire rods, square and round bars, and angle iron. We randomly selected 42 enterprises that produced cut billets and 44 enterprises that produced cast billets. We excluded two enterprises that produced cut billets and one enterprise that produced cast billets from our sample because of the incompleteness of their information. Thus, our sample consisted of 204 enterprises. The data set contains recall information on production and costs, marketing, and production organization in 2000, 2002, 2004, and 2006.

As shown in the lower part of Table 4.1, 152 out of the 204 sample enterprises were operating in 2000. During the study period, 36 enterprises upgraded their product lines. Four enterprises changed their products from square and round bars to cast billets because they could not compete with other enterprises. The other 32 moved up the product ladder from less modern to more modern products: six changed from cut billets to wire rods; 10 changed from either cut billets or wire rods to cast billets; four changed from cut billets, wire rods, or cast billets to square and round bars; and 12 changed from cut billets, wire rods, cast billets, or square and round bars to angle iron. While moving up the product ladder, these enterprises had better overall performance than those that continued producing the same products that the movers had produced earlier.

As indicators of the overall performance of the enterprises, we use the employment size measured by the number of workers, the operation size proxied by value added,[3] and the productive efficiency proxied by labor productivity, defined as the value added per worker. Gaps in the overall performance among the enterprises producing different products are shown in the upper part of Table 4.1. Moving up the product ladder, the average number of workers, average real value added, and average labor productivity of the enterprises are greater if their products are more modern. For example, the differences in the average employment size

Table 4.1   Average size of employment and production of sample enterprises by sector in a steel bar cluster in Vietnam[a]

	Cut billets (1)	Wire rods (2)	Cast billets (3)	Square and round bars (4)	Angle iron (5)
Number of workers					
2006	10.2	21.0	16.1	27.3	36.0
2004	9.8	20.4	15.8	25.8	30.8
2002	9.6	19.1	15.7	23.3	27.2
2000	9.9	19.0	15.6	22.7	26.5
Real value added (100 million VND)					
2006	1.4	4.3	4.9	15.4	35.1
2004	1.4	3.7	4.8	12.2	25.0
2002	1.0	2.7	4.5	8.3	17.1
2000	1.0	2.0	3.4	5.8	11.4
Labor productivity (real value added/worker)					
2006	14.1	20.9	30.3	53.9	86.7
2004	14.8	18.5	29.4	46.5	77.1
2002	11.2	14.6	26.8	35.6	62.8
2000	10.4	10.8	20.7	25.3	43.5
Number of sample enterprises					
2006	40	39	43	42	40
2004	41	38	44	41	37
2002	36	36	30	41	29
2000	36	29	26	38	23

[a]Value added is deflated by the price index of steel products taken from the General Statistics Office of Vietnam (1995 = 100).

and real value added between the enterprises that produce angle iron and those that produce cut billets were about 3.5 and 25 times, respectively, in 2006. As a result, the labor productivity of the former is, on average, about six times higher than that of the latter. The former have also increased their employment size, operation size, and labor productivity faster than the latter over time. These observations indicate that the production of new and modern products has created opportunities for the village enterprises to expand their operation and improve their performance.

In addition to the upgrading of product lines, the enterprises in the village have improved the quality of products, the method of procuring materials and marketing products, and labor management. Table 4.2 presents the average real prices of products and materials. The fact that these average real prices have increased over time suggests that the village enterprises have continuously improved the quality of products to the extent that the price index of the products, which is used as a deflator, captures the general price trend. The improvement in the method of procuring materials and marketing products is reported in Table 4.3. The enterprises that produce cast billets have increased the proportion of materials procured directly from outside traders from 44.5 percent in 2000 to 65.6 percent in 2006. According to our respondents, procuring materials directly from the outside traders, with whom they have long-term relationships, ensures not only the quality but also the stable supply of materials. Table 4.3 also shows that the proportion of long-term direct sales to the outside traders of the enterprises that produce wire rods, square and round bars, and angle iron increased by about

Table 4.2 Average real unit prices of products and materials by sector in a steel bar cluster in Vietnam[a] (million VND)

	Cut billets (1)	Wire rods (2)	Cast billets (3)	Square and round bars (4)	Angle iron (5)
2006	4.9 (4.6)	5.8	4.9 (3.9)	5.9	6.4
2004	4.5 (4.2)	5.2	4.4 (3.4)	5.2	5.6
2002	3.7 (3.4)	4.3	3.7 (2.8)	4.2	4.8
2000	2.9 (2.6)	3.3	2.8 (2.1)	3.1	3.6

[a]Unit prices of product and material are deflated by the price index of steel products taken from the General Statistics Office of Vietnam (1995 = 100).
Numbers in parentheses are average real unit prices of materials.

Table 4.3 Percentage of long-term direct procurement of materials from and long-term direct sales of products to outside traders by sector in a steel bar cluster in Vietnam (%)

	Sales of products	Procurement of materials	Sales of products	
	Wire rods (1)	Cast billets (2)	Square and round bars (3)	Angle iron (4)
2006	11.1	65.6	68.0	67.3
2004	10.7	59.7	59.2	57.5
2002	9.4	51.4	46.3	49.6
2000	7.1	44.5	41.4	42.7

1.5 times from 2000 to 2006. In 2006, the percentages of the long-term direct sales of the enterprises that produce square and round bars and angle iron were around 68 percent, while the percentage of those that produce wire rods was only 11 percent. These observations indicate that long-term direct sales to the outside traders were critically important for the enterprises whose products are more modern.

Table 4.4 presents the average working years of a foreman, measured as the number of years since the enterprise has started producing a particular product divided by the number of foremen employed during that time. The average working years have increased during the study period, indicating that the village enterprises have strengthened the relationships with the foremen. The average working years are longer for the enterprises whose products are more modern, suggesting the importance of the longer-term employment of foremen in the production of modern products. Thus, Tables 4.1 to 4.4 all indicate that the production of more modern and higher-quality products has been accompanied by improvements in material procurement, product marketing, and labor management. These improvements can be called multifaceted innovations.

Table 4.5 reports the characteristics of the sample proprietors. The average age of the proprietors and the percentage of males are similar in the five sectors. They differ, however, in formal education. Moving up the product ladder, the proprietor's average years of schooling increase. For example, on average, the proprietors who produce angle iron have 8.4 years of schooling, while those who produce cut billets have only 4.9 years. This observation supports GHC in that the more modern the products, the more important the formal education of the proprietors becomes. Although there are some exceptions, Table 4.5 indicates that the percentage of the proprietors whose parents and parents-in-law used to work in the industry is higher if the enterprises produce the

Table 4.4   Average working years of a foreman in a steel bar cluster in Vietnam[a]

	Cut billets (1)	Wire rods (2)	Cast billets (3)	Square and round bars (4)	Angle iron (5)
2006	n.a.[a]	1.2	1.8	2.0	2.2
2004	n.a.	1.0	1.6	1.9	1.9
2002	n.a.	0.8	1.6	1.7	1.7
2000	n.a.	0.7	1.3	1.5	1.2

[a]There is no foreman in the enterprises that produce cut billets.

Table 4.5 Characteristics of proprietors and enterprises by sector in a steel bar cluster in Vietnam in 2006[a]

	Cut billets (1)	Wire rods (2)	Cast billets (3)	Square and round bars (4)	Angle iron (5)
Personal:					
Schooling years	4.9	6.4	6.7	7.3	8.4
Prior experience in marketing (%)	17.5	23.1	18.6	40.5	27.5
Prior experience in production (%)	52.5	64.1	18.6	52.4	47.5
Proprietor age (years)	34.5	36.7	38.6	37.3	35.9
Gender (% male)	40.0	64.1	41.9	40.5	42.5
Family:					
Parents used to be in industry (%)	57.5	71.8	72.0	83.3	75.0
Parents-in-law used to be in industry (%)	42.5	61.5	53.5	57.1	60.0
Number of blood siblings[b]	1.1	0.7	0.9	1.1	1.2
Number of siblings-in-law[b]	0.7	1.1	0.6	0.7	0.8
Enterprise history:					
Operation year	8.7	10.9	13.3	12.6	10.9
Years of top management	8.5	10.9	13.3	11.7	10.4
Years of producing current products	8.0	6.9	5.9	7.5	6.1
Own initial investment (%)	64.1	70.8	79.1	79.8	79.8

[a]Average per proprietor and per enterprise.
[b]Who had already operated businesses before the establishment of the enterprise.

products that are more modern. The proprietors whose products are more modern also have more blood siblings who had founded their businesses before the establishment of the enterprises. These findings support the hypothesis on the role of social capital (SC). To provide concrete evidence, we attempt to estimate the effect of these proprietors' characteristics on their decision on what to produce, while controlling for their other characteristics.

As shown in Table 4.5, the percentage of proprietors who have marketing experience and the percentage of those who have production experience are surprisingly low if they produce cast billets. During the study period, four and six proprietors changed their product lines from cut billets and wire rods to cast billets, respectively. These proprietors did not have prior experience in marketing or production. They did, however, have an average of 13.4 years of experience in top management, which is 2.5 years higher than the average of the proprietors who continued producing cut billets and wire rods. These observations suggest that experience in marketing, production, and management could be substitutes for each other.

Table 4.5 further presents the difference between the operation years and the years for which the enterprises have produced the current products. The difference is negligible if the enterprises produce cut billets. The differences are, however, significant, ranging from 4.0 to 7.4 years, for the other sectors. This finding suggests that the enterprises had experience of production of less modern products before moving up the product ladder to produce more modern products. Table 4.5 also shows that the sample enterprises depended heavily on the proprietors' own capital for the initial investment, which is universally the case to our knowledge.

4.3   Estimation methods and results

4.3.1   Estimation methods

The existence of the product ladder in the village and the strategy of the enterprises to move up the ladder suggest that what they select to produce is not random. Failure to account adequately for the potential non-random sorting of the enterprises across different product categories may lead to biased estimates of the determinants of their performance. We, therefore, apply the Heckman two-step estimation method. As is clearly shown in Table 4.1, along the product ladder, the more modern the product is, the larger are the employment size, the operation size, and the labor productivity of the enterprise. Therefore, we apply the ordered probit model in the first-step estimation. Specifically, we regress the five product lines that are numbered from one to five following the order in the product ladder on a set of explanatory variables that consists of the personal and family characteristics of the proprietors and two more variables indicating the enterprise history, years of top management and percentage of own initial investment, as presented in Table 4.5. In the first step, if the proprietor's schooling is found to have a positive effect on his or her decision to produce modern products, it will lend support to Hypothesis 4-1 on GHC. If his or her experience in management and the occupation of his or her parents and parents-in-law in the iron and steel production have similar effects, Hypothesis 4-2 on SHC and Hypothesis 4-3 on SC will be supported. In the second step, we attempt to estimate the functions that explain the prices of products, the percentages of long-term direct procurement of materials from and long-term direct sales of products to the outside traders, the average working years of a foreman, the value added, and the labor productivity. The same set of explanatory variables plus inverse Mills ratios, which are computed from the first-step estimation, are used in the estimation to account for the selection bias.

The main argument we have made so far on the effects of the proprietor's human capital and social capital on the multifaceted improvements of the enterprise is based on an implicit presumption that these improvements contribute to the enterprise performance. Thus, it is desirable to estimate the effects of these improvements on the value added and labor productivity. If these effects are found to be positive, our presumption can be justified.

The application of the Heckman two-step estimation hinges on the availability of variables that affect the proprietor's decision on what to produce but do not directly affect the multifaceted improvements and performance of the enterprises, which are excluded from the second-step estimation. In Dahoi village, where many generations of villagers have been producing iron and steel products, it seems reasonable to assume that the occupation of the proprietor's parents and parents-in-law, who used to be in the industry, can serve as such identification restrictions. Indeed, when we estimate the reduced-form functions explaining the improvement in the product quality, production organization, marketing channels, and the overall performance of the enterprises, we observe that the occupation of the proprietor's parents and parents-in-law does not have any direct effect. We pool the data in 4 years and use a full set of year dummies in all the regressions.

4.3.2 Estimation results

The first column of Table 4.6 reports the results of the first-step estimation in the Heckman two-step estimation of the determinants of the value added. The effects of the proprietor's years of schooling on his or her choice of more modern products are positive and highly significant, which supports Hypothesis 4-1 on GHC. The proprietor's years of top management also have a positive and significant effect on this decision, which is consistent with Hypothesis 4-2 on SHC. Moreover, the effect of the proprietor's experience in iron and steel production on this decision is positive and significant. These observations suggest that the capable proprietors have moved up the product ladder to produce products that are more modern. The dummy variables representing the involvement of the proprietor's parents and parents-in-law in the industry have positive and significant effects on his or her decision on what to produce, which supports Hypothesis 4-3 on SC. Additionally, the effect of the number of the proprietor's blood siblings on this decision is positive and significant. These findings indicate that the family ties of the proprietor are an important determinant of the production of more modern products. Table 4.6 also reports the positive and significant effect of the proprietor's own initial investment ratio on his or her decision on what to produce. These findings suggest that the proprietors who had accumulated a larger amount of financial capital tend to produce products that are more modern.

The second to sixth columns in Table 4.6 present the results of the second-step estimation of the determinants of the value added. The proprietor's schooling and the number of the proprietor's blood siblings and siblings-in-law all have positive and significant effects on the value added of the enterprises, except for those that produce cut billets, which are the simplest products. These findings support Hypothesis 4-1 on GHC and 4-3 on SC on the effects of the proprietor's formal education and family ties on the operation size of the enterprise. Table 4.6 further reports the positive and significant effect of the proprietor's prior experience in marketing on the operation size, which is consistent with Hypothesis 4-2 on SHC that marketing expertise is scarce and, hence, valuable in the village industry.[4] The negative and significant coefficient of the inverse Mills ratio in column 2 suggests that the regression without selection-bias correction is biased.[5] Except the year 2002 dummy for the enterprises that produce cut billets, the other year dummies are positive and significant in the operation size regressions, suggesting that the village enterprises have expanded their operation sizes over time.

In addition to the examination of the determinants of the operation size, we estimate the determinants of labor productivity (Table 4.7). The effect of the proprietor's schooling on the labor productivity of the enterprises that produce cast billets, square and round bars, and angle iron is found to be positive and significant, while it is insignificant for the enterprises that produce cut billets and wire rods. These findings are consistent with Hypothesis 4-1 on GHC, suggesting that, when the enterprises produce more modern products, the proprietor's formal education is particularly important to increase the productivity. Consistent with Hypothesis 4-2 on SHC, the proprietor's years of top management have positive and significant effects on the labor productivity of all the enterprises, except those that produce cut billets.

The effect of the proprietor's marketing experience on labor productivity is positive but insignificant. This finding, together with the earlier finding of its positive impact on value added shown in Table 4.6, suggests that the proprietors who have prior experience in marketing tend to expand their operation size without improving the productivity. Table 4.7 further shows that the number of the proprietor's blood siblings and siblings-in-law has positive and significant effects on the labor productivity of the enterprises whose products are cast billets and square and round bars, which supports Hypothesis 4-3 on SC. The insignificance of the coefficients of the inverse Mills ratio suggests that selection bias is not a problem in estimating the determinants of labor productivity. The set of year dummies has similar effects on labor productivity as it does on operation size in Table 4.6, suggesting that the village enterprises had higher labor productivity in the later years.

Table 4.8 presents the results of the second-step estimation of the determinants of product prices. The effect of the proprietor's schooling on the product price, except for the price of cut billets, is positive and significant, suggesting the critical importance of the proprietor's formal education in improving the quality of modern products as advanced in Hypothesis 4-1 on GHC. Even though the real price of cut billets has increased over time, as shown in Table 4.2, the estimation results in Table 4.8 indicate that highly educated proprietors have not necessarily produced high-price cut billets. The insignificant effect of the proprietor's schooling on the operation size (in Table 4.6) and on the labor productivity (in Table 4.7) of the enterprises that produce cut billets is likely to be related to its insignificant effect on the price, as shown in Table 4.8.

Table 4.8 also reports a positive and highly significant effect of the proprietor's marketing experience on product prices, which is consistent with our argument in Hypothesis 4-2 on SHC that marketing expertise is scarce and valuable in the village. In addition, the number of the proprietor's blood siblings and siblings-in-law has positive and significant effects on the prices of such modern products as square and round bars and angle iron. This finding lends support to Hypothesis 4-3 on SC. The insignificant coefficients of the inverse Mills ratio indicate that selection bias is negligible in the estimation of the determinants of product price.

The results of the second-step estimation of the determinants of the long-term direct transactions of materials and products are presented in Table 4.9. Because these percentages are censored at zero and 100, we apply two-limit Tobit models. The effects of the proprietor's schooling on long-term direct transactions with the outside traders are positive and significant in all the regression functions. These findings are

Table 4.6 Determinants of operation size in a steel bar cluster in Vietnam (Heckman two-step model)[a]

	First-step	Second-step – ln (value added)				
	(1)	Cut billets (2)	Wire rods (3)	Cast billets (4)	Square and round bars (5)	Angle iron (6)
Years of schooling	0.205**	−0.052	0.077*	0.073*	0.107**	0.108**
	(11.47)	(−0.94)	(1.85)	(1.78)	(2.39)	(2.16)
Years of top management	0.032**	−0.002	0.027**	0.004	0.005	0.036**
	(3.44)	(−0.15)	(2.66)	(0.46)	(0.50)	(2.65)
Prior marketing experience dummy	0.065	0.210*	0.167**	0.243**	0.150**	0.282**
	(0.67)	(1.75)	(2.20)	(3.00)	(2.53)	(3.08)
Prior production experience dummy	0.154*	−0.116	0.132*	0.432**	0.128*	0.034
	(1.73)	(−1.15)	(1.77)	(4.88)	(1.69)	(0.30)
Parents dummy	0.185*					
	(1.84)					
Parents-in-law dummy	0.221**					
	(2.58)					
No. of blood siblings	0.082**	0.013	0.049*	0.103**	0.093**	0.089**
	(2.54)	(0.29)	(1.74)	(3.95)	(3.35)	(2.64)
No. of siblings-in-law	0.004	0.045	0.055**	0.084**	0.093**	0.127**
	(0.12)	(1.52)	(2.33)	(2.26)	(4.37)	(3.65)

Manager age	0.009	0.002	−0.002	−0.013**	−0.002	−0.011
	(1.44)	(0.22)	(−0.35)	(−2.79)	(−0.46)	(−1.51)
Gender (male=1)	−0.308**	0.113	−0.022	0.008	0.027	0.044
	(−3.61)	(0.93)	(−0.30)	(0.11)	(0.33)	(0.41)
Own initial investment ratio	1.608**	−0.420	0.310	−0.241	0.091	0.062
	(6.00)	(−1.01)	(0.92)	(−0.63)	(0.24)	(0.15)
Year 2006 dummy	−0.095	0.510**	0.641**	0.594**	0.905**	0.748**
	(−0.78)	(4.12)	(7.66)	(6.80)	(11.47)	(6.78)
Year 2004 dummy	−0.042	0.518**	0.496**	0.457**	0.687**	0.525**
	(−0.36)	(4.45)	(6.31)	(5.67)	(9.30)	(5.08)
Year 2002 dummy	−0.005	0.001	0.220**	0.270**	0.321**	0.260**
	(−0.04)	(0.01)	(2.86)	(3.29)	(4.49)	(2.51)
Inverse Mills ratio		−0.712**	0.052	−0.028	0.061	−0.069
		(−2.01)	(0.26)	(−0.15)	(0.28)	(−0.22)
Constant		4.142**	4.363**	5.556**	5.285**	6.135**
		(11.03)	(8.33)	(8.22)	(6.37)	(4.75)
Observations	729	153	142	143	162	129

aNumbers in parentheses are t-statistics. **Significant at the 1% level, *at the 5% level (one-sided test).

Table 4.7   Determinants of labor productivity in a steel bar cluster in Vietnam (Heckman two-step model)[a]

	ln (value added /number of workers)				
	Cut billets (1)	Wire rods (2)	Cast billets (3)	Sq. and round bars (4)	Angle iron (5)
Years of schooling	−0.040	0.066	0.072**	0.095**	0.083**
	(−0.68)	(1.51)	(2.34)	(2.40)	(2.63)
Years of top	0.014	0.022**	0.013*	0.015*	0.017**
management	(0.94)	(2.01)	(1.89)	(1.80)	(2.02)
Prior marketing	0.001	0.086	0.094	0.070	0.066
experience	(0.01)	(1.07)	(1.54)	(1.31)	(1.14)
dummy					
Prior production	−0.132	0.093	0.286**	0.069	0.051
experience	(−1.27)	(1.17)	(4.30)	(1.03)	(0.70)
dummy					
No. of blood	0.006	0.018	0.065**	0.063**	0.032
siblings	(0.13)	(0.61)	(3.31)	(2.53)	(1.50)
No. of siblings-	0.048	−0.006	0.029	0.071**	0.028
in-law	(1.58)	(−0.25)	(1.02)	(3.75)	(1.26)
Manager age	−0.002	−0.002	−0.010**	0.002	−0.001
	(−0.21)	(−0.39)	(−2.75)	(0.61)	(−0.30)
Gender (male=1)	0.202	−0.013	0.051	−0.039	−0.013
	(1.55)	(−0.16)	(0.90)	(−0.53)	(−0.20)
Own initial	−0.240	0.374	0.107	0.220	−0.147
investment ratio	(−0.54)	(1.04)	(0.37)	(0.64)	(−0.56)
Year 2006 dummy	0.415**	0.565**	0.458**	0.677**	0.529**
	(3.13)	(6.38)	(6.95)	(9.60)	(7.56)
Year 2004 dummy	0.480**	0.440**	0.387**	0.532**	0.425**
	(3.86)	(5.27)	(6.35)	(8.05)	(6.48)
Year 2002 dummy	−0.004	0.215**	0.245**	0.282**	0.268**
	(−0.03)	(2.64)	(3.95)	(4.41)	(4.07)
Inverse Mills ratio	−0.493	0.067	0.092	0.128	0.051
	(−1.28)	(0.32)	(0.65)	(0.67)	(0.25)
Constant	1.989**	1.638**	2.524**	2.034**	3.111**
	(5.16)	(2.95)	(4.95)	(2.75)	(3.79)
Observations	153	142	143	162	129

[a]Numbers in parentheses are *t*-statistics. **Significant at the 1% level, *at the 5% level (one-sided test).

consistent with Hypothesis 4-1 on GHC that the proprietor's general human capital is critically important to the multifaceted improvements of the enterprises. Also, the positive and significant effects of the proprietor's marketing experience on long-term direct transactions

Table 4.8 Determinants of product prices in a steel bar cluster in Vietnam (Heckman two-step model)[a]

	ln(product price)				
	Cut billets (1)	Wire rods (2)	Cast billets (3)	Square and round bars (4)	Angle iron (5)
Years of schooling	−0.012	0.025*	0.024*	0.021**	0.040**
	(−1.43)	(1.81)	(1.95)	(2.03)	(2.71)
Years of top	−0.002	0.003	0.001	−0.001	0.014**
management	(−1.12)	(0.97)	(0.25)	(−0.22)	(3.66)
Prior marketing	0.043**	0.096**	0.070**	0.066**	0.115**
experience dummy	(2.36)	(3.93)	(2.88)	(4.76)	(4.19)
Prior production	0.002	0.003	0.003	−0.020	0.061*
experience dummy	(0.11)	(0.14)	(0.12)	(−1.11)	(1.79)
No. of blood	0.001	0.014	0.004	0.012*	0.020*
siblings	(0.03)	(1.54)	(0.44)	(1.88)	(1.94)
No. of siblings-	0.001	0.010	0.014	0.009*	0.016
in-law	(0.34)	(1.32)	(1.29)	(1.87)	(1.55)
Manager age	−0.001	0.003	−0.001	−0.001	−0.003
	(−0.67)	(1.57)	(−0.41)	(−0.41)	(−1.29)
Gender (male=1)	0.018	−0.033	−0.008	0.016	−0.024
	(1.01)	(−1.36)	(−0.33)	(0.84)	(−0.75)
Own initial	−0.124**	0.050	0.100	−0.021	0.015
investment ratio	(−1.98)	(0.45)	(0.86)	(−0.23)	(0.68)
Year 2006 dummy	0.531**	0.539**	0.552**	0.616**	0.488**
	(28.52)	(19.72)	(20.80)	(33.61)	(14.85)
Year 2004 dummy	0.391**	0.400**	0.390**	0.450**	0.341**
	(22.36)	(15.55)	(15.91)	(26.20)	(11.04)
Year 2002 dummy	0.200**	0.221**	0.215**	0.249**	0.193**
	(11.31)	(8.77)	(8.63)	(14.96)	(6.20)
Inverse Mills ratio	−0.086	0.074	0.054	0.021	0.107
	(−1.60)	(1.15)	(0.95)	(0.42)	(1.14)
Constant	1.257**	1.034**	0.912**	1.114**	0.807**
	(22.82)	(6.05)	(4.45)	(5.78)	(2.12)
Observations	153	142	143	162	129

[a]Numbers in parentheses are t-statistics. **Significant at the 1% level, *at the 5% level (one-sided test).

with outside traders support Hypothesis 4-2 on SHC. Furthermore, it is interesting to find that the coefficients of the number of the proprietor's blood siblings and siblings-in-law are positive and highly significant in all the regression functions, except the number of siblings-in-law in the function of direct sales of wire rods. These findings

Table 4.9 Determinants of long-term direct procurement of materials from and long-term direct sales of products to outside traders in a steel bar cluster in Vietnam (Heckman two-step model; second-step: two-limit Tobit model)[a]

	Sales of products	Procurement of materials	Sales of products	
	Wire rods (1)	Cast billets (2)	Square and round bars (3)	Angle iron (4)
Years of schooling	2.062*	6.792**	3.813**	4.591**
	(1.81)	(3.12)	(2.00)	(2.17)
Years of top	0.644**	0.346	0.449	1.561**
management	(2.29)	(0.70)	(1.13)	(2.73)
Prior marketing	4.916**	20.972**	11.791**	17.958**
experience dummy	(2.41)	(4.88)	(4.66)	(4.60)
Prior production	−0.539	10.358**	9.528**	1.509
experience dummy	(−0.27)	(2.20)	(2.94)	(0.31)
No. of blood siblings	3.164**	6.247**	3.294**	5.241**
	(4.22)	(4.50)	(2.77)	(3.71)
No. of siblings-in-law	0.764	5.505**	3.636**	7.159**
	(1.20)	(2.77)	(4.00)	(4.77)
Manager age	−0.039	−0.548**	−0.403**	−0.270
	(−0.29)	(−2.25)	(−2.04)	(−0.85)
Gender (male=1)	−1.488	−5.561	−4.717	5.975
	(−0.74)	(−1.40)	(−1.34)	(1.34)
Own initial	15.320*	−0.205	−1.092	2.500
investment ratio	(1.67)	(−0.01)	(−0.07)	(0.14)
Year 2006 dummy	3.792*	28.203**	26.748**	19.896**
	(1.66)	(6.03)	(7.90)	(4.28)
Year 2004 dummy	4.278**	21.135**	17.794**	10.765**
	(1.99)	(4.89)	(5.63)	(2.48)
Year 2002 dummy	2.666	9.193**	5.040	3.488
	(1.27)	(2.10)	(1.65)	(0.80)
Inverse Mills ratio	−5.687	−18.527*	−4.191	3.157
	(−1.05)	(−1.85)	(−0.45)	(0.23)
Constant	−23.293	−1.119	9.234	−21.254
	(−1.63)	(−0.03)	(0.26)	(−0.39)
Observations	142	143	162	129

[a]Numbers in parentheses are t-statistics. **Significant at the 1% level, *at the 5% level (one-sided test).

suggest that the proprietor's family ties play an important role in the improvement in the procurement of materials and the marketing of products, as postulated in Hypothesis 4-3 on SC. Although implicit, outside traders seem to contribute to the quality important, which is

Table 4.10 Determinants of average working years of a foreman in a steel bar cluster in Vietnam (Heckman two-step model)[a]

	ln(average working years of a foreman)			
	Wire rods (1)	Cast billets (2)	Square and round bars (3)	Angle iron (4)
Years of schooling	0.030	0.106*	0.142**	0.117**
	(0.76)	(1.97)	(2.33)	(2.64)
Years of top management	0.020**	0.022*	0.024**	0.030**
	(2.07)	(1.87)	(2.10)	(2.45)
Prior marketing experience	0.102	0.027	0.078	0.148
dummy	(1.44)	(0.33)	(1.10)	(1.47)
Prior production experience	0.065	0.304**	0.122	0.091
dummy	(1.02)	(2.91)	(1.40)	(0.78)
No. of blood siblings	0.037	0.045*	0.195**	0.053
	(1.55)	(1.78)	(5.18)	(1.48)
No. of siblings-in-law	−0.007	−0.053	0.071**	0.059*
	(−0.37)	(−1.38)	(3.05)	(1.96)
Manager age	0.003	0.001	0.011*	0.005
	(0.50)	(0.10)	(1.68)	(0.63)
Gender (male=1)	0.026	−0.033	−0.001	0.005
	(0.34)	(−0.40)	(−0.01)	(0.05)
Own initial investment ratio	0.466	0.424	0.562	−0.331
	(1.31)	(0.84)	(1.07)	(−0.88)
Year 2006 dummy	0.585**	0.305**	0.249**	0.432**
	(5.76)	(3.29)	(2.32)	(4.17)
Year 2004 dummy	0.419**	0.219**	0.231**	0.332**
	(4.77)	(2.46)	(2.17)	(3.48)
Year 2002 dummy	0.262**	0.195**	0.133	0.237**
	(3.38)	(2.00)	(1.23)	(2.46)
Inverse Mills ratio	−0.199	−0.266	−0.358	0.265
	(−1.08)	(−1.14)	(−1.25)	(0.97)
Constant	−1.261**	−1.145	−2.275**	−1.479
	(−2.58)	(−1.24)	(−2.07)	(−1.26)
Observations	142	143	162	129

[a]Numbers in parentheses are *t*-statistics. **Significant at the 1% level, *at the 5% level (one-sided test).

consistent with Hypothesis 2 specified in Chapter 1. The positive and significant coefficients of the inverse Mills ratio in Column 2 suggest that it is important to correct for the selection bias in this estimation.[6] The year dummies in the later years are positive and significant, suggesting that the village enterprises have increased direct transactions over time.

Table 4.11 Panel regression of operation size in ln(value added) in a steel bar cluster in Vietnam[a]

	Wire rods		Cast billets		Square and round bars		Angle iron	
	Fixed effects	Random effects	Fixed effects	Random effects	Fixed effects	Random effects	Fixed effects	Random effects
Direct sales of products	0.288 (1.25)	0.404* (1.77)			0.575** (2.74)	0.707** (4.07)	1.025** (3.25)	1.221** (5.59)
Direct procurement of materials			0.270* (1.67)	0.456** (3.08)				
ln (average working years of a foreman)	0.043 (1.03)	0.040 (0.97)	0.174** (3.04)	0.151** (2.73)	0.001 (0.01)	0.062 (0.99)	0.173* (1.76)	0.248** (2.97)
Years of schooling		0.072** (2.98)		0.067** (2.64)	0.068 (1.05)	0.094** (4.70)	-0.151 (-1.18)	0.050** (2.66)
Years of top management (in 2006)		0.025* (1.79)		0.001 (0.13)	0.010 (0.32)	-0.002 (-0.29)	0.102 (1.62)	0.017 (1.37)
Prior marketing experience dummy		0.133 (1.02)		0.118 (0.81)		0.033 (0.32)		0.080 (0.67)
Prior production experience dummy		0.094 (0.71)		0.401** (2.94)		0.044 (0.47)		0.012 (0.10)
Parents dummy		0.036 (0.29)		0.069 (0.57)		0.066 (0.60)		0.041 (0.30)
Parents-in-law dummy		-0.053 (-0.46)		-0.004 (-0.04)		-0.033 (-0.40)		0.087 (0.92)

	(1)	(2)	(3)	(4)	(5)	(6)	(7)	(8)
No. of blood siblings	0.824**	0.024	0.467**	0.065*	0.802**	0.046	0.612**	0.039
	(19.70)	(0.50)	(7.36)	(1.82)	(9.36)	(1.29)	(4.51)	(1.18)
No. of siblings-in-law		0.044		0.050		0.053		0.031
		(1.05)		(0.82)		(1.49)		(0.70)
Manager age (in 2006)		0.001		−0.011		−0.003		−0.009
		(0.10)		(−1.39)		(−0.43)		(1.06)
Gender (male=1)		−0.003		0.001		−0.005		−0.082
		(−0.02)		(0.01)		(−0.06)		(−0.85)
Own initial investment ratio		0.216		−0.242		0.086		0.374
		(0.62)		(−0.58)		(0.26)		(0.96)
Year 2006 dummy	0.630**	0.814**	0.351**	0.425**	0.660**	0.721**	0.444**	0.488**
	(17.63)	(19.39)	(6.58)	(7.00)	(9.02)	(10.15)	(4.27)	(4.83)
Year 2004 dummy	0.630**	0.622**	0.351**	0.324**	0.660**	0.585**	0.444**	0.369**
	(17.63)	(17.29)	(6.58)	(6.27)	(9.02)	(9.49)	(4.27)	(4.48)
Year 2002 dummy	0.259**	0.256**	0.185**	0.180**	0.351**	0.312**	0.229**	0.188**
	(9.04)	(8.83)	(4.64)	(4.46)	(7.28)	(6.81)	(3.02)	(2.71)
Constant	5.314**	4.398**	5.597**	5.370**	5.588**	5.314**	7.33**	5.870**
	(167.07)	(10.32)	(77.16)	(10.63)	(19.27)	(14.13)	(10.33)	(13.37)
Observations	142	142	143	143	162	162	129	129
Hausman test: chi-square	1.76		8.83		10.86		5.22	
(p>chi-square)	0.88		0.12		0.15		0.63	

aNumbers in parentheses are t-statistics. **Significant at the 1% level, *at the 5% level (one-sided test).

89

Table 4.12 Panel regression of labor productivity in ln(value added/number of workers) in a steel bar cluster in Vietnam[a]

	Wire rods		Cast billets		Square and round bars		Angle iron	
	Fixed effects	Random effects	Fixed effects	Random effects	Fixed effects	Random effects	Fixed effects	Random effects
Direct sales of products	−0.394 (−1.49)	−0.301 (−1.14)			0.761** (3.75)	0.675** (4.14)	0.853** (3.35)	0.593** (3.67)
Direct procurement of materials			0.027 (0.17)	0.229* (1.71)				
ln (average working years of a foreman)	−0.039 (−0.81)	−0.058 (−1.21)	0.151** (2.65)	0.126* (2.44)	0.070 (0.99)	0.069 (1.18)	0.184* (2.32)	0.216** (3.36)
Years of schooling		0.060* (2.53)		0.049** (2.60)	0.069 (1.11)	0.068** (3.73)	−0.007 (0.07)	0.036** (2.74)
Years of top management (in 2006)		0.023* (1.67)		0.010 (1.23)	0.027 (0.91)	0.013* (2.09)	0.029 (0.57)	0.003 (0.32)
Prior marketing experience dummy		0.099 (0.77)		0.013 (0.12)		−0.019 (−0.21)		−0.081 (−1.01)
Prior production experience dummy		0.040 (0.30)		0.274** (2.74)		0.013 (0.16)		0.005 (0.06)
Parents dummy		0.015 (0.12)		−0.034 (−0.39)		−0.067 (−0.68)		−0.008 (−0.09)
Parents-in-law dummy		−0.050 (−0.44)		−0.001 (−0.02)		−0.026 (−0.35)		0.026 (0.41)

No. of blood siblings		0.010		0.034		0.022		0.003
		(0.22)		(1.31)		(0.69)		(0.14)
No. of siblings-in-law		-0.012		0.010		0.037		-0.026
		(-0.30)		(0.23)		(1.17)		(-0.87)
Manager age (in 2006)		0.001		-0.009		0.003		-0.002
		(0.01)		(-1.54)		(0.54)		(-0.33)
Gender (male=1)		0.045		0.081		-0.018		-0.059
		(0.36)		(1.00)		(-0.22)		(-0.91)
Own initial investment ratio		0.340		-0.008		0.013		-0.037
		(0.98)		(-0.03)		(0.11)		(-0.14)
Year 2006 dummy	0.838**	0.838**	0.421**	0.376**	0.583**	0.588**	0.301**	0.348**
	(17.54)	(17.16)	(6.66)	(6.64)	(7.05)	(8.82)	(2.75)	(4.55)
Year 2004 dummy	0.651**	0.649**	0.353**	0.322**	0.482**	0.480**	0.267**	0.301**
	(15.95)	(15.52)	(6.63)	(6.62)	(6.82)	(8.28)	(3.19)	(4.74)
Year 2002 dummy	0.317**	0.318**	0.196**	0.191**	0.301**	0.290**	0.205**	0.209**
	(9.67)	(9.39)	(4.94)	(4.88)	(6.46)	(6.65)	(3.34)	(3.77)
Constant	2.376**	1.566**	3.017**	2.736**	2.263**	2.382**	3.411**	3.436**
	(65.37)	(3.73)	(41.76)	(7.33)	(8.08)	(7.07)	(5.96)	(11.70)
Observations	142	142	143	143	162	162	129	129
Hausman test: chi-square	3.55		8.96		3.87		7.84	
(p>chi-square)	0.74		0.11		0.80		0.35	

[a]Numbers in parentheses are t-statistics. **Significant at the 1% level, *at the 5% level (one-sided test).

Table 4.10 reports the results of the second-step estimation of the determinants of the average working years of a foreman. The effects of the proprietor's schooling on the average working years of a foreman are positive and significant except for the enterprises that produce wire rods, which is consistent with Hypothesis 4-1 on GHC. Since the wire rods are the simplest among the products whose production requires foremen, the establishment of long-term relations with the foremen may not be so important. In addition, the proprietor's experience in management has a positive and significant effect on the average working years of a foreman, which supports the hypothesis on SHC.

Because improvement in labor management is likely to increase labor productivity, the positive and significant effects of the proprietor's schooling and experience in management on the average working years of a foreman are consistent with their positive and significant effects on labor productivity, presented in Table 4.7. Similarly, the insignificant effect of the proprietor's experience in marketing on the average working years of a foreman, reported in Table 4.10, is consistent with its insignificant effect on labor productivity, presented in Table 4.7. Table 4.10 also demonstrates that the number of the proprietor's blood siblings and siblings-in-law has positive and significant effects on labor management, except for the enterprises that produce wire rods. This finding supports Hypothesis 4-3 on SC. The insignificant coefficients of the inverse Mills ratio indicate that selection bias is not a problem. The set of year dummies is positive and significant, suggesting that the village enterprises' labor management has been improved since 2000.

The estimation results presented in Tables 4.6 to 4.10 all support our hypotheses. Note, however, that our interpretation of the estimation results is based on an implicit presumption that improvements in material procurement, product marketing, and labor management contribute to overall performance. To examine the validity of this presumption, we regress the overall performance of the enterprises on the variables representing the multifaceted improvements using the fixed effects and random effects estimation methods. Except for the percentage of long-term direct procurement of materials from and direct sales of products to the outside traders, the average working years of a foreman, and the proprietor's age and years of top management, the other variables are time-invariant. In each group of enterprises that produce square and round bars and angle iron, there are two enterprises whose proprietors have changed. The proprietor's age and years of top management increase together over time. We use the age and years of top management in 2006 as explanatory variables. We also include a full set of year dummies to capture any changes in the general economic conditions that may affect the performance of the enterprises.

Table 4.11 reports the estimation results of the effects of the improvement in marketing and production organization on the operation size. The result of the Hausman specification tests suggests that the individual effects are uncorrelated with the regressors in all the random effects models. In the regressions that use the random effects model, the effects of the ratios of the long-term direct procurement of materials from and the long-term direct sales of products to the outside traders on operation size are positive and significant. In addition, the average working years of a foreman has a positive and significant effect on the operation size of the enterprises that produce cast billets and angle iron. These estimation results support our presumption.

The estimation results of the effects of the multifaceted improvements on labor productivity are reported in Table 4.12. Similarly to Table 4.11, the result of the Hausman specification tests suggests that the individual effects are uncorrelated with the regressors in all the random effects models. In the random effects models, the ratios of the long-term direct procurement of materials from and the long-term direct sales of products to the outside traders has positive and significant effects on labor productivity, except for the enterprises that produce wire rods. The average working years of a foreman has a positive and significant effect on the labor productivity of the enterprises that produce cast billets and angle iron. These findings further reinforce the validity of our presumption. It is also important to note that the effects of the proprietor's schooling on the performance of the enterprises are positive and significant in the random effects models in both Tables 4.11 and 4.12, suggesting that the proprietor's formal education affects the performance of the enterprises through other channels.

4.4 Concluding remarks

This chapter explored the determinants of the transformation of village industries in northern Vietnam by investigating the case of an iron and steel village-based industrial cluster. The process of transforming the traditional village-based industrial cluster into a modern cluster is affected by the legacies of the former planned economy, including the transfer of the production technology from the SOEs to the village enterprises and the weak marketing and management ability of the proprietors due to the weak tradition of free market systems during the socialist period.

The empirical analyses support the view discussed in Chapter 1 that multifaceted minor innovations, encompassing improvements in the quality of products, marketing, and management, are critically important for the performance of enterprises. Specifically, during the transformation process, the village enterprises have changed their product lines to those that are more modern, and have improved the quality of products. This improvement in products has been accompanied by an increase in the long-term direct procurement of materials from and long-term direct sales of products to outside traders. In addition, the enterprises have tightened the relationships with their foremen. These minor innovations have contributed to the expansion of the operation size and the enhancement of labor productivity in the village enterprises.

Our empirical analyses reveal that the proprietor's general human capital, acquired by formal schooling, is the key to the success of such multifaceted minor innovations and the overall enterprise performance. No less important is the proprietor's specific human capital, acquired by experience in marketing and management. These findings clearly support Hypothesis 4-2. Moreover, the proprietor's social capital, based on strong family ties with parents and siblings, contributed to the multifaceted improvements and performance of the village enterprises. In other words, both the managerial human capital and the social capital of the proprietor are critical determinants of the successful transformation of village industry in northern Vietnam.

In our observations, new knowledge on production, marketing, and management tends to be imitated by competing enterprises, even though such knowledge is kept confidential among a circle of close family members in the village. To the extent that such knowledge spills over, private incentives to innovate are thwarted. Therefore, the public provision of new management and marketing knowledge is warranted to develop village industries in Vietnam. This is particularly important in this country because, unlike in China, the SOEs are not well developed, and nowhere else can the village enterprises learn improved production and management knowledge. Thus, how to build the managerial human capital of the proprietors is a major challenge that the Vietnamese government faces if it really wishes to transform hundreds of traditional village-based industrial clusters.

5
The Move to the Formal Sector in the Metalwork Industry in Kenya

The critical importance of managerial human capital in carrying out multifaceted innovations, including upgrading of products in Vietnam, has been reported in Chapter 4 and a large number of other case studies in other Asian countries. The question now arises as to whether managerial human capital plays a similar role in SSA. True, it has been found to be important in the leather shoe industry in Ethiopia, but whether this can be generalized to the rest of SSA is a critical question. In this chapter, we take up the case of indigenous garment industrial clusters consisting of marginal and small enterprises in Kenya, which have been largely stagnant and have suffered from the China shock.

In general, the manufacturing sector in SSA is dominated by very small and informal enterprises, and they grow only when they are young, as Collier and Gunning (1999), Tybout (2000), and Bigsten and Söderbom (2006) attest, among others. Because of the lack of growth, their job creation falls far short of what they are expected to achieve. A number of possibly serious hindrances to enterprise growth have been enumerated in the literature. For example, Sleuwaegen and Goedhuys (2002) and Bigsten et al., (2004) argue that small and informal enterprises are reluctant to become large because being large requires being formal and subject to excessive regulations. Collier and Gunning (1999) and Fisman (2001) call attention to market failures in insurance and credit markets, which would be especially serious for very small enterprises.

In their review of the literature on enterprise growth in SSA, Bigsten and Söderbom (2006, p. 260) conclude, while referring to the major findings, such as uncertainty being more detrimental to capital investment than credit constraint: "Improving our understanding of why these results are observed seems an important area for future research." Another important finding is the positive association between enterprise growth and the general human capital or formal education of the entrepreneur, which is reported by McPherson (1996), Ramachandran and Shah (1999), Mengistae (2006), and Chapter 3 in this volume. This finding is curious, because enterprises in SSA do not continue to grow. Indeed, it appears inconsistent with the accepted view of human capital articulated by Schultz (1975), which attributes the value of human capital to the ability to deal with dynamic disequilibria. How can we reconcile these two seemingly contradictory findings: the positive effect of human capital on enterprise growth and the cessation of growth after the incipient stage following the establishment of the enterprise?

This chapter attempts to answer these questions by examining enterprise data collected from our study site of Nairobi, Kenya. The area is called Kariobangi Light Industries, and was designated as an area for artisans by local government in 1989.[1] Its development dates from the early 1980s, when the workers of formal-sector factories lost jobs in consequence of the implementation of the Structural Adjustment Program (SAP) and began to establish garages and workshops along the main road. They cleared the bushes to construct roads inside the area. The current population of enterprises is about 300, and half of them are related to metalworking. They call themselves *Jua Kali* in Swahili, meaning informal-sector artisans.[2] The detailed information obtained from them through personal interviews will facilitate the interpretation of the results of our statistical analysis.

Our data set contains recall information from five years, 1998, 2000, 2002, 2005, and 2006, during which some enterprises attempted to improve their products. In the 1990s, the enterprises in the Kariobangi Light Industries produced low-quality products, and there were many enterprises producing almost the same products, because the production of such products was easy but profitable when the producers were few in number. As the entry of new enterprises continued, however, the profitability of producing low-quality products declined. Instead, improvement in the quality of products, together with the introduction of new marketing channels suitable to the improved products, became profitable, especially for educated entrepreneurs. Although we do not have direct evidence for the declining profitability of producing low-quality products and the increasing profitability of quality improvement, our regression results are consistent with this story. The effects of the education level of entrepreneurs on employment size and growth became stronger in later years than in earlier years. These results are consistent with the results of the eight case studies conducted in East Asia by Sonobe and Otsuka (2006). An interesting feature of our data is the inclusion of seven enterprises that left Kariobangi for formal industrial areas. To our knowledge, no existing study traces such leavers and compares the behavior and performance before and after becoming formal. The leavers told us that they left Kariobangi because they needed more spacious sites and that their relocation greatly facilitated marketing by improving the reputation of their enterprises.

The rest of the chapter is organized as follows. After briefly explaining our method of data collection, Section 5.1 describes major characteristics of the Kariobangi Light Industries. Section 5.2 compares the characteristics of the leavers and the remaining group, using the information on their educational and occupational backgrounds. This section also advances our hypotheses concerning the changing roles of managerial human capital in determining enterprise performance. Regression analyses are carried out in Section 5.3. Section 5.4 concludes the chapter with a summary of findings and policy implications.

5.1 Metalwork cluster in Nairobi

At the Kariobangi Light Industries, no census of the enterprises has been carried out in the past. The Kariobangi *Jua Kali* Association, however, estimated the number of manufacturing enterprises to be around 150 as of 2006.[3] There are also a number of restaurants, canteens, kiosks, stationery stores, carpenters, and other enterprises in the service sector. We decided to focus on manufacturing enterprises because manufacturing, especially metalworking, was said to be the core activity in Kariobangi. But we included hardware shops in the sample, because the production of fabricated metal products and hardware trading can be done by the same enterprises and because sheet bending and some other services can be done by both metal product enterprises and hardware shops. We also added to the sample the seven leavers, who are defined as the enterprises relocated from the Kariobangi Light Industries to the Baba Dogo Industrial Area or the Mukuru Kwa Njenga Industrial Area by the time of our survey of enterprises. The association identified 137 enterprises as satisfying our specifications. In September 2006, we attempted a survey of all these enterprises, but we could meet only workers but not entrepreneurs at 10 enterprises. Thus, the number of enterprises in the sample is 127, as shown in Table 5.1.

This table classifies the sample enterprises into six groups according to their activities. The largest group fabricates metal products, such as

Table 5.1   Number of new entrants by period and activity in a metalwork cluster in Kenya

	Until 2000	From 2001 to 2006	Total
Fabrication of metal products	27	21	48
Balances	7	2	9
Flour mills	6	2	8
Wheelbarrows	1	4	5
Other metal products	13	13	26
Casting or machining of metal parts	24	13	37
Car repairing	12	2	14
Soap making	4	2	6
Hardware retailing	3	7	9
Miscellaneous services	6	6	12
Total	76	51	127

steel windows, steel furniture, and simple machines. More than half of this group produce non-mechanical items, such as window frames, grilles, and furniture. The rest of this group produce mechanical devices, such as scale balances and flour mills. The producers of these simple machines tend to contract out the production of parts to small foundries and lathe turners located nearby. Besides such subcontracting, these parts makers produce simple repair parts for vehicles as well. Also, lathe turners repair balance scales and parts for cars and simple machines, and produce hinges, bolts, and nuts that are used by producers of steel gates and furniture. These foundries and lathe turners constitute the second group in Kariobangi. The third group, engaged in car repairing, are called garages or garage mechanics. Garages here include panel beaters. Thus, the division of labor is practiced between metal product producers, garages, and parts suppliers. Almost all of them procure materials from hardware traders. Therefore, our study site is characterized by a cluster of metalwork enterprises.

We were curious about the reason why there were soap (detergent) producers in this metalwork cluster. According to the owner of a relatively large enterprise producing soaps, her business has no linkage with metalwork, but she and her husband thought that they would suffer no harassment from government officials in the Kariobangi Light Industries because it was designated as an industrial area for *Jua Kali*. Miscellaneous services include metal and plastic recycling, battery recharging, and electroplating.

According to the leaders of the association, the entry of new enterprises was active throughout the 1990s, but it has declined or seemingly ceased since the early 2000s, despite favorable macroeconomic conditions in recent years. Such evolution of the number of new entrants may be explained by the endogenous model of cluster development explained in Section 1.2 in Chapter 1. The metal products produced in Kariobangi are obviously copies of imported products. In the 1980s and 1990s, demand for low-quality but cheap substitutes for expensive imports would have been high because such substitutes were in short supply. Noticing that the pioneers earned high profits, followers began producing copies of the original product. As the number of producers increased, parts suppliers and hardware shops emerged, and all of them would have benefited from the development of the division of labor. The proliferation of the producers of the same products would, however, have lowered the product prices and hence the profitability. According to Sonobe and Otsuka (2006), similar evolution of a number of new entrants was observed in the development processes of industrial clusters in Japan, Taiwan, and China.

The leaders of the association added another reason for the decreasing entry of new enterprises. This is the increasing congestion and worsening insecurity in Kariobangi. The congestion has been aggravated by the increased population of inhabitants in the area. While the area is designated as industrial, it now has many four- to five-storey buildings that use only the ground floor for businesses and the upper stories as apartments. The inhabitants of these apartments complain of the noises and smells coming from the workshops. The hostile attitudes of new inhabitants and the inflow of refugees from neighboring countries have resulted in security problems, which have become so serious that the association recently mobilized jobless young men into a vigilante group.

Table 5.2 presents the information on where the entrepreneurs worked before they started their own businesses in Kariobangi. As shown in column (iii), 61 entrepreneurs used to work as *Jua Kali* and 79 worked in the formal sector. There are 28 entrepreneurs who worked in both *Jua Kali* and formal sectors, and 15 had neither type of work experience. In this table, the formal sector is subdivided into four subcategories: factories owned by Indians, other foreigners, Kenyans, and the public sector. Among the seven leavers, two had been *Jua Kali* from the beginning of their careers. Four were skilled workers or middle managers at formal-sector factories, and one was a civil engineer employed by the government. More than half of the enterprises remaining in Kariobangi have work experience in the formal sector.

Table 5.2   Number of enterprises by previous workplace of entrepreneur and current location in a metalwork cluster in Kenya

	Number of Kariobangi enterprises		
	that left for formal industrial area by 2006 (leavers) (i)	staying behind (remaining group) (ii)	Total (iii)
Jua Kali sector workshops	2	59	61
Formal sector:	5	74	79
Indian ventures	0	25	25
Other foreign ventures	3	25	28
Local private factories	1	15	16
Public sector	1	9	10
Neither	0	15	15

Why did so many entrepreneurs come from the formal sector to Kariobangi to become *Jua Kali*? A push factor would be the implementation of the SAP and the consequent contraction of the formal manufacturing sector. Pull factors would be the initially high demand for cheap substitutes for imported products, which very small workshops could easily produce with inexpensive equipment while enjoying the benefits arising from the agglomeration. Fafchamps and Söderbom (2006) have developed a model in which increases in employment size make it more difficult to monitor workers and necessitate employers to offer higher wages to workers in order to discourage shirking. According to their estimates, the wage rate increases with the expansion of employment size more steeply in SSA than in Morocco. *Jua Kali* clusters such as the Kariobangi Light Industries would provide the skilled workers and middle managers of large formal-sector factories with lucrative outside opportunities, and hence contribute to wage increases in the formal sector.[4] The high wages would, in turn, weaken competitiveness of the large factories and lead to further downsizing.

Table 5.3 compares the leavers and the remaining group with respect to enterprise size for each activity type. Enterprise size is measured by the number of workers. We found it much more difficult to obtain reliable data on other measures of enterprise size, such as value added and sales revenues, which seems to be a common problem in enterprise surveys in SSA in view of the fact that many studies of enterprise growth in the region focus on employment. Among the seven leavers,

Table 5.3   Average employment size in 2006 by activity and current location in a metalwork cluster in Kenya[a]

| | Number of employees per enterprise | |
	leavers	remaining group
Fabrication of metal products	23.3	5.6
Casting or machining of metal parts	–	4.8
Car repairing	30	4.3
Soap making	26.5	13.3
Hardware trading	–	2.9
Miscellaneous services	–	3.8
Total	25.1	6.2

[a]Of the seven leavers, four fabricate metal products, one repairs cars, and two produce soap and detergents.

four are manufacturers fabricating minibus bodies, soil-block-making machines, steel furniture, and steel tanks. They employed 23.3 workers on average in 2006, whereas the fabricators remaining in Kariobangi employed only 5.6 workers on average. None of the parts suppliers had left Kariobangi for formal industrial areas by 2006. Probably, parts suppliers have less incentive to leave because their major customers are in Kariobangi. The garage that entered the formal sector employed as many as 30 workers, whereas the garages that remained informal had only 4.3 workers on average. Soap-making factories are relatively large even in Kariobangi, but the two leavers are twice their size. If all activities are combined, the mean employment size of the leavers is four times as large as that of the remaining group.

The steel tank fabricator left Kariobangi in 1992, but the other six leavers were relocated in 2002 or after (and before 2006). When the recent leavers left Kariobangi, they employed 13 workers on average, which is double the employment size of the remaining group in 2006. But, within a few years, they doubled their employment to 25.1 workers. Thus, relocation to become formal seems to facilitate enterprise growth considerably.

The leavers gave us three reasons for their relocation during our interviews with them. Firstly, the insecurity or the fear of being mugged in Kariobangi repelled prospective customers. Secondly, for prospective customers, Kariobangi and the term *Jua Kali* are synonymous with poor-quality products. Thirdly, unlike the formal industrial areas, Kariobangi has very poor infrastructure and little space for the expansion of operations. The first two reasons concern the difficulty in marketing in Kariobangi. The unreliable supply of electricity, which is included in the third reason, would discourage mechanization. Bumpy and muddy roads would make it difficult to ship high-precision products. The lack of space would directly limit enterprise growth. Relocation to a formal industrial area would sweep away these problems, even though it is costly because of moving costs and regulations, including income tax payment.

To our knowledge, such relocation of enterprises from a congested cluster to an industrial zone and concomitant change from informal to formal enterprise are seldom reported in SSA, except in the case of the shoe cluster in Ethiopia reported in Chapter 7. In Asia, however, such changes are so common that we have never paid any particular attention (see the evidence in Chapter 2). Indeed, many currently giant enterprises in Japan, Taiwan, and China used to be small-scale informal family enterprises. The important point is that it is wrong to assume that small enterprises will remain small forever; on the contrary, many of the currently large enterprises were once small but have grown large over time.

5.2   Characteristics of sample enterprises

5.2.1   Characteristics of entrepreneurs

Table 5.4 presents the data on the characteristics of entrepreneurs by enterprise type. Here the remaining enterprises are classified into those with work experience in the formal sector and those without such experience. The leavers were a little older than the others, and they were 43.6 years old on average when their enterprises were relocated to formal industrial areas. The majority of the remaining group were younger than this average age in 2006. The leavers had longer years of formal schooling and formal vocational training, longer work experience prior to starting their own businesses, and longer experiences of management thereafter. In short, they were likely to possess more abundant managerial human capital than the remaining group. In addition, four of the seven leavers had partners, who had similar occupational backgrounds and were able to help the entrepreneurs. Four entrepreneurs inherited businesses from their parents, but the vast majority of the sample entrepreneurs started their own businesses.

In our definition, formal vocational training includes technical training in mechanical engineering at a polytechnic, but it does not include

Table 5.4 Characteristics of entrepreneurs by enterprise type in a metalwork cluster in Kenya

| | | Remaining group | |
	Leavers (i)	with formal sector experience (ii)	without formal sector experience (iii)
Number of entrepreneurs	7	74	46
Average age as of 2006	45.6	41.7	36.5
Average age when left for the formal Industrial Area	43.6	–	–
Average years of general education	13.0	11.3	10.1
Average years of vocational training	2.6	1.3	0.4
Average years of prior experience in similar trades	8.7	4.5	3.0
Average years of management experience	9.3	8.3	6.3
Number of entrepreneurs with partners	4	6	1
Number of successors	1	2	1
% entrepreneurs who knew jig and fixture when started	42.9	37.8	26.1
Average number of business trips abroad	2.0	0.89	0.41

the study of mechanical engineering at a university. Instead, the latter is included in formal schooling. We include any training, whether provided at polytechnics or other institutions, in vocational training as opposed to schooling if it emphasizes practical aspects and attaches little importance to theoretical aspects. University education attaches importance to theories even in specialized courses such as mechanical engineering.

In our sample, more than 80 percent of the entrepreneurs received technical training or education at vocational schools, colleges, or universities. Moreover, as was shown in Table 5.3, the majority used to work at formal-sector factories. Judging from the educational and occupational backgrounds of the entrepreneurs, therefore, the cluster is considered to be fairly abundant in human capital specific to engineering areas.

As shown in the second row from the bottom of Table 5.4, however, only one-third of the entrepreneurs knew what jigs and fixtures were when they started their businesses. Jigs and fixtures are small devices that lathe turners make to increase the precision and efficiency of their work. They are indispensable for mass processing of high-precision parts. Fabricators may not use jigs or fixtures themselves, but they should be interested in whether the lathe turners processing parts for them use or do not use jigs and fixtures. The low percentage of entrepreneurs knowing about jigs and fixtures indicates that the engineering knowledge held by the entrepreneurs was narrow. But as of 2006, the majority of the entrepreneurs of all types and more than 70 percent of the leavers and those with experience in the formal sector knew what jigs and fixtures were, even though only a few actually used them. This increase in knowledge suggests that the entrepreneurs are increasingly interested in mass production of high-quality parts and products using lathe and other machine tools.

In our observation, the entrepreneurs become increasingly motivated to improve their product quality, as the proliferation of producers intensifies competition and lowers the profitability of producing low-quality and standard products. However, the improvement of products will not in itself increase profits unless buyers recognize and appreciate the improved quality, as is argued in Section 1.2. Thus, differentiating an enterprise's own improved products clearly from inferior products produced by other enterprises through branding and finding new marketing channels becomes critically important. The improvement of product quality may be easy for the entrepreneurs in the *Jua Kali* cluster who are experienced engineers, but it would be difficult for those who did not understand the concept of precision. Upgrading marketing methods and finding new marketing channels would be still more difficult for almost all the entrepreneurs there. If they succeed in accomplishing these improvements, then their marginal revenue curves will shift upward and they will employ a greater number of workers than before. But the expansion will make labor management more difficult than before. Thus, quality improvement will eventually require improved labor management as well.

5.2.2   Hypotheses

As Schultz (1975) argues cogently, formal schooling would assume importance when new decisions are made in a dynamic context. Thus, we contend that those entrepreneurs with higher formal education are more likely to succeed in multifaceted improvements in product quality, marketing, and management. As a result of a series of improvements, an enterprise will grow in size. In line with Hypothesis 1 specified in Chapter 1, a testable hypothesis may be postulated as follows:

Hypothesis 5-1 on the effect of general human capital (GHC) on enterprise size and growth: The effects of formal education of entrepreneurs on enterprise size and enterprise growth are positive and have increased over time in the *Jua Kali* cluster.

In our view, the recent relocation of the six leavers from the cluster to formal industrial areas is a result of the increased effects of schooling. Hypothesis 5-1 asserts that the effects of GHC increased even among the remaining enterprises. Because improvements must be multifaceted, specialized vocational training without much emphasis on theoretical thinking will not be as useful as formal schooling for enterprise growth. Thus, we conjecture that the effects of vocational training on size and growth will become weaker relative to the effects of schooling.

Turning to marketing, our hypothesis argues that progressive entrepreneurs become more motivated to market their higher-quality products to the buyers who appreciate high quality, and that more educated entrepreneurs are more likely to succeed in such marketing. We may refer to the buyers who appreciate high quality as quality-conscious customers for convenience. According to Fafchamps (2004, pp. 81–8), nearly 80 percent of enterprises in nine countries in SSA sell the whole or part of their outputs to end-users of their products, such as manufacturers and consumers, and the rest is sold to traders. Exports account for only 8 percent of their outputs. Similarly, at the Kariobangi Light Industries and a much larger cluster of metalworking enterprises in Ghana (Iddrisu and Sonobe, 2007), the most primitive but still the most common way of marketing among informal artisans and craftsmen is to wait for individual customers to come to workshops in the cluster to buy something for their own use. This marketing method accounts for 40 to 50 percent of their sales revenues.[5]

Marketing to traders, that is, wholesalers and retailers, requires products to have relatively uniform quality and to be produced in large quantities, as is emphasized in Chapter 3. A similar tendency is found among metalwork enterprises in Ghana (Iddrisu and Sonobe, 2007). In Kariobangi, however, there seems to be no consensus of opinion regarding which marketing channel is more lucrative or which requires higher-quality products. Instead, the sample entrepreneurs would agree that it is challenging and hence profitable to sell products to foreign or international companies, government and non-government organizations in Kenya or abroad. These customers are much more conscious about the quality of products than any other types of customers that the enterprises in Kariobangi have. Thus, it seems reasonable to count them as quality-conscious customers.

Table 5.5 describes trends in marketing to quality-conscious customers. Because a big order from a quality-conscious buyer may come suddenly toward the end of a year, the percentage of marketing to quality-conscious buyers for the whole year can be known only after the year has ended. Because we conducted the enterprise survey in September 2006, we could not obtain this percentage for 2006. This is why Table 5.5 compares 1998/2000 and 2005 instead of 2006. By 1998/2000, we mean the pooled data from the two years 1998 and 2000. Although we obtained recall data on employment in 1998, 2000, 2002, 2005, and 2006, about 40 percent of the sample enterprises started businesses after 2000, as was shown in Table 5.1. To increase the number of observations up to the level comparable with the later period, we took the average of the first two years in the sample. In columns (ii) and (iii), the remaining group is divided into those enterprises established in 1998 or before and those established in 1999 or later. The percentage of sales revenues from marketing to quality-conscious customers declined equally for both subgroups of the remaining enterprises, whereas it slightly increased for the leavers. Thus, the major determinant of marketing to quality-conscious customers, or improvement in marketing, is not the experience of managing an enterprise. Instead, our hypothesis on multifaceted improvements implies that the major determinant is the managerial human capital, which is formed, importantly, by formal schooling. Thus, we advance the following hypothesis:

Hypothesis 5-2 on the effect of general human capital on marketing: The effects of formal education of entrepreneurs on marketing to quality-conscious customers are positive and have increased over time in the *Jua Kali* cluster.

To test this hypothesis, we will use the percentage of sales revenues from marketing to quality-conscious buyers.[6] Table 5.5 also shows the percentage of material cost for purchasing materials directly from factories or trading houses as opposed to purchasing from hardware shops in the cluster or other merchants in Nairobi.[7] Such direct procurement was an important aspect of multifaceted improvements in the footwear industry in Ethiopia (see Chapter 7). Like marketing to quality-conscious customers, direct procurement decreased for the newly established remaining enterprises, but it increased significantly for the leavers. These observations suggest that it is difficult to accomplish multifaceted improvement in the *Jua Kali* cluster.

Table 5.5 Marketing and procurement by enterprise type in a metalwork cluster in Kenya

	Leavers (i)	Remaining group established in	
		1999 or later (ii)	before 1999 (iii)
Marketing to quality-conscious customers (% of sales revenue)			
1998/2000	51.0	10.0	9.0
2005	55.0	5.8	5.9
Direct procurement (% of material cost)			
1998/2000	31.0	42.6	22.8
2005	50.7	26.1	24.6

While we hypothesized that the entrepreneurs in the cluster would be increasingly interested in expanding their businesses, it is difficult to increase quality-conscious customers and obtain space for expansion as long as they stay in the cluster. Such growth constraints are increasingly binding as the entrepreneurs are motivated to achieve quality improvement under increasingly strong competitive pressure. Moreover, the worsening insecurity problem and the increasing congestion are highly likely to tighten the constraint on enterprise growth. The growth constraint may be expressed in the growth regression analysis as the negative effect of the current enterprise size on the subsequent growth. Since the constraint is expected to be increasingly binding, we hypothesize as follows:

Hypothesis 5-3 on the effect of enterprise size on growth: The negative effect of the current enterprise size on its subsequent growth has become stronger over time in the *Jua Kali* cluster.

If entrepreneurs have become increasingly motivated to grow and the constraint on growth has become more severe in *Jua Kali* clusters, the incidence of exodus to formal industrial areas should increase. Indeed, from 2002 to 2006, there were six such relocations out of the Kariobangi Light Industries, even though we cannot test this conjecture rigorously. Instead, we will examine by regression analysis whether the relocation and increases in marketing to high-quality buyers actually contribute to the expansion of enterprise size.

Before embarking on hypothesis testing, it is useful to glance over the trends in enterprise growth. Table 5.6 presents the data on the number

Table 5.6   Average number of employees and average annual growth rate of employment by enterprise type in a metalwork cluster in Kenya

| | | Remaining group | | | |
| | | Year established | | Years of schooling | |
	Leavers (i)	1999 or later (ii)	before 1999 (iii)	Below 11 (iv)	Above 12 (v)
Number of workers					
1998/2000	17.0	2.4	5.2	2.8	4.9
2006	25.1	4.2	6.9	3.3	7.7
Annual growth rate (%)					
1998–2002	13.8		4.7	3.0	4.4
2002–2006	17.7	13.8	1.2	3.6	9.6

of workers in 1998/2000 and 2006 and annual employment growth rate during the periods from 1998 to 2000 and from 2002 to 2006. The annual growth rate is approximated by the difference in the logarithm of the number of workers between the beginning and end of the period divided by the number of years in the period. It is shown in columns (ii) and (iii) that the old enterprises are greater and the difference in the means is statistically significant, although the table does not show test statistics. Consistently with empirical studies of enterprise growth in SSA as well as other regions, the older enterprises had a much lower growth rate than the more recently established enterprises from 2002 to 2006. In columns (iv) and (v), the remaining group is divided into those entrepreneurs who went to school for 11 years or less and those who went for 12 years or more. The enterprise size is significantly larger for the more educated entrepreneurs. According to the lower portion of the table, the more educated entrepreneurs had higher rates of enterprise growth than the less educated, and the growth accelerated particularly rapidly for the more educated entrepreneurs, which is consistent with Hypothesis 5-1. Yet, it is clear that the growth rate of the leavers is far higher than that of the remaining enterprises, which is consistent with Hypothesis 5-3.

5.3   Estimation methods and results

5.3.1   Specification

In order to test Hypotheses 5-1 and 5-3, we estimate the functions that explain the number of workers and its growth rate in the sample that excludes the leavers. Because we are interested in changes in the strength of the effect of schooling, we estimate these functions in each year or period separately to examine whether the coefficients change over time. We exclude the leavers in order to show that the importance of schooling for good enterprise performance increased even among the remaining enterprises.[8] The two functions to be estimated include such explanatory variables as the entrepreneur's years of schooling and some other characteristics shown in Table 5.4, as explanatory variables. The functions do not include all the variables shown in Table 5.4, however, in order to avoid the problems of multicollinearity and endogeneity. A strong multicollinearity is found among age, years of schooling, years of vocational training, years of prior experience, and years of management of the current business as of 2006, because the sum of the latter four is equal to the age as of 2006 minus the age of entering school, which does not vary much from observation to observation. We exclude age from the regression.

The dummy variable indicating whether the entrepreneur has work experience in the formal sector turned out to be positively and closely correlated with the years of schooling and the years of vocational training. The dummy variable indicating whether the entrepreneur knew jigs and fixtures when they started their businesses is positively and closely correlated with the years of schooling. We suspect endogeneity regarding the dummy variable indicating whether the entrepreneur has a partner, or the number of partners. The possible reason for endogeneity is that a partner stays with an enterprise because the performance of the enterprise is good. The number of business trips abroad may be endogenous because good enterprise performance may allow the entrepreneur to go abroad. These variables are excluded from the regression. Because work experience in the formal sector is excluded, the estimated effects of schooling and vocational training on enterprise size and growth include the effects of the technical or managerial knowledge that the entrepreneur acquired through working at a formal-sector factory, especially a foreign venture. This point should be kept in mind when we interpret the estimation results below.

The function that explains enterprise growth includes the same set of explanatory variables representing the characteristics of the entrepreneur. The leavers are excluded from the sample for the same reason as above. It also includes the logarithm of the number of workers in the initial year of the period. This is a conventional specification of the growth regression used in the literature of enterprise growth as well as cross-country growth comparison. The OLS estimation of this regression equation, however, is subject to the endogeneity bias arising from the correlation between the initial size and the error term. A sophisticated approach to this problem may be to employ generalized method of moment (GMM) estimators such as the Arellano and Bond (1991) estimator, which uses the lagged variables as instruments for the first difference equation. Bigsten and Gebreeyesus (2007) apply this approach to the panel data on the manufacturing enterprises in Addis Ababa. This approach, however, cannot be applied to our data because they do not include enough annual data.

Instead, we instrumented the initial enterprise size with some of the variables representing the characteristics of the entrepreneur. In other words, we use the estimation of the function that explains enterprise size as the first stage of the two-stage least square (2SLS) regression. As will be shown shortly, it turns out that years of vocational training, years of prior work experience, and years of management of the current business are good instruments for the initial enterprise size in the sense that they have significant effects on the initial size but no direct effects on the subsequent growth. The validity of the instrumental variables in this sense is checked with the first-stage F test and the over-identification test.

To test Hypothesis 5-2, we regress the fraction of sales revenues from quality-conscious customers on the same set of the explanatory variables as the enterprise size and growth regressions, using the sample that excludes the leavers. Since the fraction is censored from below at 0, we use the Tobit model specification. We also run panel fix-effects regressions to see the effect of the relocation from the cluster to a formal industrial area. Here we include the leavers in the sample. The dependent variable is the number of workers, and the main explanatory variable is the dummy variable that indicates whether the enterprise remains in the Kariobangi Light Industry or in a formal industrial area in the year. This variable is equal to 0 before the enterprise is relocated and 1 after the relocation. If the relocation is associated with an increase in the number of workers, the coefficient of this dummy will be estimated to be positive. This equation will also include the fraction of sales revenues from quality-conscious customers and the fraction of material costs procured directly from factories, to examine whether marketing to quality-conscious customers and direct procurement contribute to enterprise growth. Although the location, marketing, and procurement variables are likely to be endogenous, the fixed-model specification is expected to mitigate endogeneity biases.

5.3.2 Estimation results

Table 5.7 reports the results of the estimation of the enterprise size function. In column (i), the estimation uses the 1998/2000 pooled data while adding a year dummy on the right-hand side of the regression equation. Six dummy variables indicating activity types are also used to control for the effects common to the enterprises of the same activity type. The default for these activity-type dummies is metal product fabrication other than the production of scale balances, such as the fabrication of steel windows, steel furniture, and flour mills.

The effect of years of schooling on the enterprise size is positive in all columns. It is only marginally significant in the first two columns,

Table 5.7 Estimates of the effect of entrepreneurs' human capital on employment size in the sample excluding the leavers in a metalwork cluster in Kenya[a]

	1998/2000 (i)	2002 (ii)	2005 (iii)	2006 (iv)
Years of schooling	0.044*	0.054*	0.095**	0.126**
	(1.78)	(1.75)	(3.24)	(3.74)
Years of vocational training	0.070*	0.053	−0.015	0.006
	(1.69)	(0.98)	(−0.27)	(0.10)
Years of prior experience	0.079**	0.027	−0.005	0.008
	(4.24)	(1.47)	(−0.31)	(0.51)
Years of management	0.059**	0.073**	0.042**	0.020
	(4.70)	(5.02)	(3.06)	(1.25)
Soap-making dummy	0.542	0.785*	0.443	0.068
	(1.55)	(1.88)	(1.14)	(1.25)
Car repair dummy	0.482**	0.470*	0.148	0.022
	(2.52)	(1.98)	(0.60)	(0.08)
Parts dummy	0.499**	0.140	−0.140	−0.132
	(3.15)	(0.78)	(−0.80)	(−0.66)
Balance dummy	1.015**	0.702*	0.027	−0.014
	(4.70)	(2.46)	(0.10)	(−0.66)
Hardware dummy	0.119	−0.211	−0.302	−0.418
	(0.40)	(−0.66)	(−1.09)	(−1.32)
Misc. service dummy	0.135	0.143	−0.140	−0.080
	(0.55)	(0.54)	(−0.51)	(−0.26)
Year 2000 dummy	−0.054			
	(−0.46)			
Intercept	−0.200	−0.222	0.017	−0.236
	(−0.68)	(−0.64)	(0.05)	(−0.59)
Number of enterprises	129	97	112	113
R-squared	0.36	0.39	0.23	0.19

[a]He dependent variable is the logarithm of the number of employees. Numbers in parentheses are t-statistics. **Significant at the 1% level, *at the 5% level.

but highly significant in the last two columns. Moreover, the magnitude of the effect increased from 0.044 in 1998/2000 to 0.126 in 2006. These results strongly support Hypothesis 5-1 on the effect of general human capital. The effect of vocational training declines over time. The years of prior experience had a strong effect in 1998/2000 but lost significance in the later years. The effect of the years of management is positive and highly significant in the first three columns, but it is insignificant in column (iv). These results are highly consistent with our basic hypotheses that the incentive for quality improvement increases over time and that the quality improvement is knowledge-intensive rather than experience-intensive.

The scale balance dummy has a positive and significant effect in the first two columns, but not in the next two. This result reflects the fact that the active entry of new producers of scale balances lowered the price of the product and reduced enterprise sizes from the top level to the average level in the cluster. The estimation results tell us that similar changes took place among garages and parts suppliers. If the leavers are included in the estimation, the estimated effect of schooling becomes stronger and increases more steeply than that shown in Table 5.7. All other qualitative results remain unchanged.

Table 5.8 presents the results of the growth regressions. The first two columns cover the two periods from 1998 to 2000 and from 2000 to 2002. The data on the two periods are pooled, and unobserved fixed effects, if any, are not treated specially as in the panel fixed-effect model. Column (i) shows the OLS estimates and column (ii) shows the 2SLS estimates. Likewise, columns (iii) and (iv) show OLS and 2SLS estimates, respectively, based on the pooled data of the two periods, 2002–5 and 2005–6. The dependent variable is the annual growth rate of the number of workers during each period. In the 2SLS regressions, the initial employment size is instrumented with years of vocational training, prior work experience, and management, as mentioned earlier. These variables have jointly significant effects in the first-stage regression in both the early two periods and the later two periods, as shown toward the bottom of Table 5.8, even though only years of management had a significant effect in 2002 and 2005 according to Table 5.7. The results of the over-identification test as per Davidson and MacKinnon (1993) indicate that these instrumental variables do not have any direct effect on enterprise growth.

In the early two periods, the OLS and 2SLS estimates of the growth equation are similar, and both indicate that the years of schooling had

Table 5.8 Estimates of the effect of entrepreneurs' human capital on employment growth in the sample excluding the leavers in a metalwork cluster in Kenya[a]

	1998–2000 and 2000–2002		2002–2005 and 2005–2006	
	OLS (i)	2SLS (ii)	OLS (iii)	2SLS (iv)
Lagged log of employment[b]	−0.073** (−2.81)	−0.083* (−2.40)	−0.064* (−1.66)	−0.299** (−2.53)
Years of schooling	0.008 (1.20)	0.008 (1.19)	0.030** (2.64)	0.050** (3.30)
Years of vocational training	0.004 (0.40)		−0.001 (−0.05)	
Years of prior experience	−0.006 (−1.02)		0.004 (0.69)	
Years of management	0.001 (0.35)		−0.014** (−2.51)	
Soap-making dummy	0.264** (2.66)	0.272** (4.21)	−0.247 (−1.64)	−0.120 (−0.50)
Car repair dummy	−0.023 (−0.41)	−0.002 (−0.05)	−0.095 (−1.04)	−0.043 (−0.44)
Parts dummy	−0.060 (−1.29)	−0.043 (−0.89)	−0.041 (−0.62)	−0.053 (−0.67)
Balance dummy	−0.090 (−1.36)	−0.063 (−1.12)	−0.106 (−1.00)	−0.005 (−0.57)
Hardware dummy	−0.127 (−1.51)	−0.116** (−2.59)	−0.156 (−1.41)	−0.197* (−2.03)
Misc. service dummy	−0.016 (−0.24)	−0.0001 (−0.00)	0.007 (0.07)	−0.005 (−0.05)
The first period dummy	0.032 (0.96)	0.028 (0.85)	0.104* (1.98)	0.044 (0.75)
Intercept	0.071 (0.82)	0.068 (0.88)	−0.124 (−0.93)	−0.141 (−1.14)
Number of enterprises	128	128	207	207
R^2	0.21		0.15	
First-stage F		27.56**		12.95**
Over-identification test χ^2		1.59		0.92

[a]The dependent variable is the annual growth rate, approximated by the difference between the log of the number of employees and its lagged value, divided by the number of years between the two observations. Numbers in parentheses are t-statistics based on the robust standard errors. **Significant at the 1% level, *at the 5% level.
[b]The lagged employment variable is instrumented in 2SLS regressions in columns (ii) and (iv).

no significant effect on enterprise growth. In the later two periods, however, the 2SLS estimate of the effect of the initial employment size is much larger in absolute terms than the OLS estimate, and the effect of the years of schooling is positive and highly significant in both specifications. The result, that the effect of schooling was strengthened in the later periods, supports Hypothesis 5-1. To the extent that initial employment size is endogenous, the OLS estimates are inconsistent. That the consistent 2SLS estimate of the effect of initial size becomes greater in absolute terms lends strong support to Hypothesis 5-3.

Although not reported in the table, here, too, the effects of the explanatory variables on growth remain qualitatively unchanged if the leavers are included in the sample. The magnitudes of the effects are changed as follows. Firstly, the inclusion of the leavers weakens the negative effect of the initial employment size compared with the result in column (iv) of Table 5.8. Put differently, the growth constraint is estimated to be less severe if the leavers are included in the sample. This suggests that relocation from Kariobangi to the formal industrial area relaxes the growth constraint. Secondly, the inclusion of the leavers strengthens the growth effect of schooling, especially in the later periods. This is probably because the leavers tend to be highly educated and their growth rates were much higher than average, especially after their relocation.

Table 5.9 shows the estimates of the functions explaining marketing to quality-conscious customers and the direct procurement of materials. The first two columns indicate clearly that the positive effect of schooling became stronger and that of vocational training became weaker in 2005 than in 1998/2000. Although not shown in the table, the estimates of these effects for 2002 are in between. These results support Hypothesis 5-2. If the leavers are included in the sample, the effect of schooling becomes stronger each year. It is difficult to explain why the effect of years of management was negative and significant in 1998/2000 and insignificant in 2005, and why the effect of years of prior experience was negative and significant in 2005 but insignificant in 1998/2000. But these results suggest that experience as a worker or an entrepreneur is not much help in increasing sales to quality-conscious customers.

According to columns (iii) and (iv), formal schooling became more important in 2005 than in 1998/2000 for entrepreneurs to increase the direct procurement of materials as well. Vocational training, prior experience, and management experience did not have any significant effects on direct procurement in either year. Nothing else in these columns is worth mentioning.

Table 5.9 Determinants of marketing to quality-conscious customers and direct procurement in the sample excluding the leavers, hardware shops, and miscellaneous service providers in a metalwork cluster in Kenya (Tobit regression)[a]

	Marketing		Procurement	
	1998/2000 (i)	2005 (ii)	1998/2000 (iii)	2005 (iv)
Years of schooling	0.041*	0.049*	0.050	0.101*
	(1.81)	(2.11)	(1.57)	(2.24)
Years of vocational	0.081*	0.038	0.058	0.107
training	(2.33)	(0.91)	(1.31)	(1.60)
Years of prior	0.002	−0.025*	−0.035	−0.040
experience	(0.10)	(−1.78)	(−1.24)	(−1.19)
Years of management	−0.029**	−0.004	0.038	−0.010
	(−2.63)	(−0.36)	(0.26)	(−0.52)
Soap dummy	0.721**	0.911**	−0.002	−0.008
	(2.79)	(3.17)	(−0.00)	(−0.02)
Car repair dummy	0.517**	0.462**	0.193	−0.360
	(3.39)	(2.78)	(0.85)	(−0.92)
Parts dummy	−0.060	−0.091	−0.067	−0.297
	(−0.47)	(−0.71)	(−0.34)	(−1.23)
Balance dummy	−0.229	−0.386*	0.515*	0.205
	(−1.16)	(−1.68)	(2.24)	(0.70)
Year 2000 dummy	0.116		−0.122	
	(1.12)		(−0.85)	
Intercept	−0.442	−0.406	−0.962*	−1.639**
	(−1.65)	(−1.49)	(−2.31)	(−2.59)
Number of enterprises	120	96	121	93
Number of left-censored obs.	54	45	94	78

[a]The dependent variable is the fraction of sales revenue from special orders and exports in columns (i) and (ii) and the fraction of material cost for procurement from special sources in columns (iii) and (iv). Numbers in parentheses are *t*-statistics based on the robust standard errors. **Significant at the 1% level, *at the 5% level.

Table 5.10 reports the panel fixed-effects estimates of the effects of being formal, marketing to quality-conscious customers, and procuring directly from factories on employment size. In these regressions, we included the leavers. As mentioned in the previous section, the data on employment in 1998, 2000, 2002, 2005, and 2006 are available, but the data on marketing and procurement are unavailable only in 2006. This is why the number of observations is larger in column (i), which does

Table 5.10　Panel fixed-effects estimates of the effect of moving to the formal sector on employment size, 1998, 2000, 2002, 2005, and 2006 in the sample excluding the leavers in a metalwork cluster in Kenya[a]

	(i)	(ii)	(iii)	(iv)	(v)
Being formal	0.742**	0.762**	0.453	0.313	7.452**
	(3.53)	(2.91)	(1.56)	(1.06)	(3.43)
Direct procurement		0.470*		0.447*	0.068**
		(2.46)		(2.38)	(2.79)
Marketing to			1.079**	1.041**	0.025*
quality-conscious			(3.26)	(3.16)	(1.79)
customers					
Year 2000 dummy	0.060	0.058	0.088	0.080	0.644
	(0.74)	(0.79)	(1.20)	(1.09)	(1.26)
Year 2002 dummy	0.054	0.095	0.144*	0.139*	1.176**
	(0.70)	(1.34)	(2.01)	(1.95)	(2.27)
Year 2005 dummy	0.344**	0.368**	0.426**	0.407**	2.794**
	(4.54)	(5.16)	(5.95)	(5.68)	(5.38)
Year 2006 dummy	0.326**				
	(4.25)				
Intercept	1.065**	0.944**	0.958**	0.848**	2.346**
	(17.47)	(12.61)	(14.41)	(10.46)	(3.99)
Number of observations	476	352	348	344	351
Number of enterprises	122	119	117	116	116
Average number of observations per enterprise	3.9	3.0	3.0	3.0	3.0
R-squared	0.15	0.22	0.23	0.25	0.28

[a]The dependent variable is the logarithm of the number of employees in columns (i) to (iv) and the number of employees in column (v). Numbers in parentheses are t-statistics. **Significant at the 1% level, *at the 5% level.

not include marketing and procurement on the right-hand side of the regression, than in the other columns.

In columns (i) and (ii), the effect of being formal on the logarithm of employment size is positive and highly significant. These results lend support to the argument that relocation to a formal industrial area enhances enterprise growth by removing the growth constraint faced by the enterprises in the *Jua Kali* cluster. The positive and significant effect of direct procurement, shown in columns (ii), (iv), and (v), indicates that increasing direct procurement is part of the multifaceted improvements, as discussed in the previous section.

In columns (iii) and (iv), the significance of the effect of being formal is lost because the marketing variable is included on the right-hand side of regression, which is correlated with being formal. Most likely this correlation arises from the fact that relocation to a formal industrial area relaxes the growth constraint largely by making it easier to increase quality-conscious customers, as the leavers explained to us. In column (v), however, the positive effect of being formal is highly significant despite the inclusion of the marketing variable. This is because the dependent variable in this column is not the logarithm but the number of workers. With this specification, the estimate of the effect is more influenced by the changes in employment at enterprises with high employment. The contrasting results between the estimates in columns (iv) and (v) indicate that the growth constraint in the Jua Kali cluster is not just the difficulty in increasing quality-conscious customers but also the difficulty in finding space for expansion.

The dummy for year 2005 has a positive and highly significant effect in all specifications, and that for year 2002 has a positive and significant effect in some columns. In other words, the employment size in 2005 was larger than that in 2002, which was larger than that in earlier years. The effect of the year 2006 dummy has about the same magnitude as that of the year 2005 dummy in column (i), which indicates that the large employment sizes in 2005 tended to be retained in 2006. These results remain the same if the leavers are excluded from the sample. Thus, it is reasonable to argue that the growth constraint is increasingly binding in the cluster, and begging to be relaxed by the transformation of the enterprises from informal to formal entities.

5.4   Concluding remarks

This chapter investigated the determinants of the size and growth of informal enterprises in SSA, taking a *Jua Kali* cluster in Nairobi as an example. Based on the experience of East Asia described by Sonobe and Otsuka (2006), we hypothesized that the entrepreneurs become increasingly motivated towards multifaceted improvements that improve profitability, and that entrepreneurs endowed with larger managerial human capital are more likely to succeed in achieving the improvements. We also hypothesized that the multifaceted improvements (and the resulting growth in enterprise size) are difficult to implement as long as the enterprises remain in the informal cluster. The testable implications derived from these basic hypotheses are strongly supported by the data.

The results of the regression analyses clearly indicate that, while the relative advantage of improving product quality is increasing in the *Jua Kali* cluster, it is difficult to find customers who appreciate the high quality of products and to find space for the expansion of operations. The growth constraints faced by the enterprises remaining in the cluster is becoming more severe. The question may arise as to why they hesitate to move to formal industrial areas, where they can progress multifaceted improvements and expand operations. For them to become formal, they will need to be able to generate high profits that exceed the moving cost and other costs associated with relocation and transformation from an informal to a formal enterprise. In addition to such costs, uncertainty seems to make them hesitant. To sum up, while the majority of enterprises in SSA do not grow partly because of the growth constraints of congested clusters and partly because of the lack of managerial ability of entrepreneurs, some enterprises, managed by educated entrepreneurs, grow successfully by taking the risk of introducing new management strategies, including relocation.

Ability and uncertainty are the functions of knowledge, however. If the entrepreneur is more knowledgeable, he is more likely to generate high profits by successfully achieving multifaceted improvements, and his assessment of profitability will be more accurate. Indeed, those entrepreneurs who have already moved their enterprises to formal industrial areas are more highly educated than the remaining entrepreneurs.

It seems clear from the analyses of Chapters 4 and 5, as well as Chapters 2 and 3, that managerial human capital, acquired particularly by formal schooling, is of the utmost importance in upgrading the products and their quality, marketing channels, and internal management, rendering strong support for Hypothesis 1. Qualitatively, we do not observe much difference in the importance of managerial human capital, either between Vietnam and Kenya or between these two countries and those northeastern countries studied by Sonobe and Otsuka (2006).

Part III
The China Shock and Quality Improvement

6
The Coping Strategy of the Electrical Fittings Industry in Pakistan

The China shock (massive, often sudden, and sharp increases in imports of cheap Chinese products) has affected many industries producing tradable products in a large number of low-income countries, including those in SSA (Zafar, 2007; Villoria, 2009). Part III of this book (Chapters 6 and 7) explores the issue of how such industries in low-income counties cope with the China shock, based on the case studies of a electric fittings cluster in Pakistan and a leather shoe cluster in Ethiopia. These two cases are intriguing examples of the China shock being successfully overcome by multifaceted innovations.

A major characteristic of the electrical fittings cluster in Sargodha, Pakistan, is that putting-out arrangements are common among outside traders, local traders, companies, subcontracting workshops, and household subcontractors, and in this way a fine division of labor is implemented. Many small entrepreneurs with poor endowments of managerial human capital have entered the industry as subcontractors. They are engaged in the production of a narrow range of products without undertaking any improvement of production methods and designs, whereas companies are engaged not only in production but also in the development of designs, setting new specifications for high-quality products, and seeking new marketing channels.

According to a UNIDO (2006) report, while the Sargodha cluster has experienced notable growth in terms of the number of enterprises, its activities have remained qualitatively the same over the last 30 years. The tools and machines used by enterprises in this cluster are outdated, the products are crude and of low quality and are sold solely in domestic markets, where low-quality products are still in demand. Thus, the development phase of this cluster is identified as the quantity expansion stage with low or declining profit. However, the increasing importation of electrical fittings from China is becoming a real threat to the producers in this cluster. The question is whether this cluster will shrink due to the China shock or will recover from this shock by entering the quality improvement phase.

In the same industry in China, the entry of a swarm of new enterprises producing poor-quality products was followed by the upgrading of product quality as well as the introduction of new marketing strategies, as reported by Sonobe et al., (2004). Facing fierce competition from Chinese products, do the enterprises in Sargodha attempt to upgrade their product quality and production processes? Will they succeed in leading the cluster towards the quality improvement phase? If the answer is affirmative, what are the major changes in the ways in which entrepreneurs operate their businesses, such as the development of new designs, procurement of high-quality raw material, and improvement in the channels for the marketing of finished products? What are the characteristics of the entrepreneurs who carry out multifaceted innovations? By using panel data on 126 companies, this chapter investigates whether the improvements that lead the cluster to enter the quality improvement phase have been taking place in the Sargodha cluster.[1]

The major finding of this chapter is that, to compete with the electrical fittings imported from China, entrepreneurs in Sargodha are attempting to improve the quality of their products, and that quality improvement is accompanied by the development of marketing channels appropriate for such improved products. Similarly to other currently developed industrial clusters in East Asia (Sonobe and Otsuka, 2006), such improvements are led by entrepreneurs who are relatively more educated and experienced in marketing and management. Aside from the managerial human capital, entrepreneurs' social capital, generated by their family ties with other entrepreneurs in the electrical fittings industry, also appears to be helpful in improving product quality and finding new marketing channels.

The rest of this chapter is organized as follows. Section 6.1 gives an overview of the Sargodha electrical fittings cluster. After briefly describing the strategies recently adopted by entrepreneurs to upgrade product quality, Section 6.2 advances testable hypotheses. Section 6.3 provides a descriptive analysis of sample enterprises, which is followed by a regression analysis in Section 6.4. Finally, the major findings are summarized and policy implications are discussed in Section 6.5.

6.1 An overview of the Sargodha electrical fittings cluster

The study site is called Sargodha. It is located in Punjab province, 172 km from Lahore, 261 km from Islamabad, the capital city of the country, and about 50 km from several interchanges of the 347 km-long Islamabad–Lahore motorway. Sargodha is not far from the well-known industrial districts, Sialkot, Gujarat, and Gujranwala in Punjab province, as the map of the northern part of the province in Figure 6.1 shows.[2] Sargodha is also well connected with many small cities and towns in Pakistan by a railway track built by British Royal before the partition in 1947.

Currently, Sargodha is a famous industrial cluster where a large number of small enterprises produce electrical fittings. Here "electrical fittings" refers to electric switches, sockets, plugs, bulb holders and main switches of not more than 30 amperes. According to UNIDO (2006), Sargodha has about 1,200 producers and accounts for about 70 percent of the domestic production of electrical fittings in Pakistan. Other major production sites are Lahore, the capital of Punjab province, and Karachi, the capital of Sindh province and the center of commerce and manufacturing of the country.

A survey of firms producing electrical fittings was conducted in Sargodha over a period of 3 months from August to October, 2008. In early August, a 2-week-long informal survey was conducted in which face-to-face interviews were held with officials of the Sargodha regional office of the Small and Medium-sized Enterprises Development Authority (SMEDA) and a selected group of entrepreneurs, in order to gather information on the historical development of the cluster and the major characteristics of entrepreneurs and their enterprises.

The major difficulty in conducting the formal random survey was that the list of enterprises, which is supposed to be collected by the Sargodha regional offices of the Federal Bureau of Statistics (FBS) and SMEDA, is neither reliable nor comprehensive.[3] The FBS regional office, however, could identify the parts of Sargodha where electrical fittings firms seemed to be most densely concentrated. With the assistance of local political agents (called union councilors) in the area, a list of 249 firms was collected and all of them were visited. Although seven entrepreneurs refused to provide us with any information, personal interviews were conducted with 242 entrepreneurs and reliable data were obtained from 232 entrepreneurs. Detailed information was collected on the history of the enterprise, the background of the enterprise

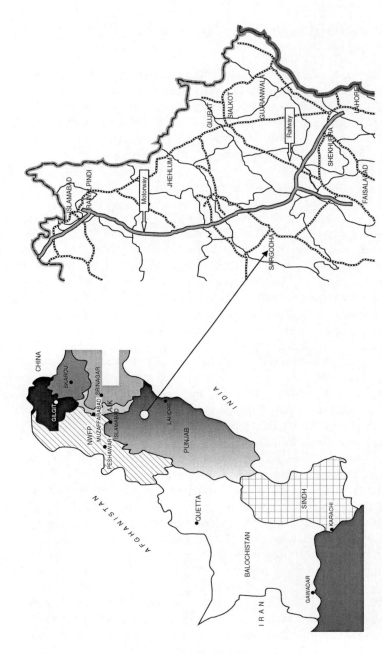

Figure 6.1 Location of the study site in Pakistan (the diagram on the left is the map of Pakistan and the diagram on the right shows the northern part of Punjab province)

owners, marketing, material procurement, and employment, among other things, in 2004, 2006, and 2008.

According to our respondents, the electrical fittings industry in Sargodha was initiated in the late 1960s when a local trader came back from Karachi, where he had acquired production skills and set up the first factory in Sargodha.[4] This pattern of development is similar to the cases of the garment clusters in Japan and China (Yamamura et al., 2003; Sonobe et al., 2002). A few years after the start of the electrical fittings industry in Sargodha, a relative of the pioneer, who is the owner of the currently leading enterprise, HERO electrical appliances company, entered the industry.[5] From these pioneering enterprises, a number of spin-off entrepreneurs emerged, who established their own factories or workshops while copying what they learned from the pioneers. The increasing number of enterprises attracted not only the traders of finished products but also die-makers, producers and suppliers of metal parts, and suppliers of Bakelite powder. This is reminiscent of the usual formation process of industrial clusters described in Chapter 1. According to a UNIDO (2006) report, in Sargodha there are about 600 suppliers of Bakelite powder, metal parts producers and suppliers, die-makers, and traders of finished products.

The main bodies of electrical fitting products are made of Bakelite, a synthetic material, which is electrically nonconductive and heat-resistant. Bakelite powder is heated and melted in a die and pressed into the shape of the die cavity by using a manual pressing machine. This is the most capital- and skill-intensive process. A small miscalculation in heating and pressing leads to disfigured products with substandard strength. Following this process is assembly, in which metal parts, such as tiny pins and springs, are fitted manually into a Bakelite part. The final stage includes the inspection of the assembled products and packing.

Figure 6.2 classifies the producers of electrical fitting products into three groups: (1) companies; (2) subcontracting workshops; and (3) household subcontractors. Since enterprises in the third group perform only assembling jobs, they are not included in our sample. Enterprises in the first two groups produce finished products. However, companies and subcontracting workshops are distinct from each other. Companies produce a variety of final products while engaging in the design and production of sample products, setting specifications, quality control, and conducting their own marketing. Moreover, all the companies use their own brand names to facilitate the marketing of their products. By contrast, subcontracting workshops specialize in the production of one or two particular

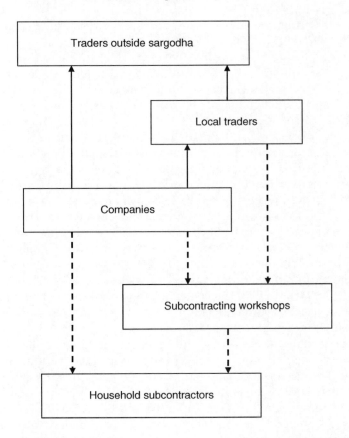

← – – Putting-out contracts (household subcontractors receive parts from and
deliver assembled products to subcontracting workshops and companies.
Subcontracting workshops receive raw material from and deliver finished
products to companies and local traders).

———→ Marketing Channels (companies sell products to local traders or sell
directly to outside buyers).

Figure 6.2 Subcontracting and marketing relationships among firms in an
electric fitting cluster in Pakistan

products, simply following the specifications set by their contractors,
and do not have their own brand names.

Table 6.1 gives the breakdown of the number of sample enterprises
by type and period of establishment. Among the 232 enterprises in

Table 6.1   The number of new entrants by enterprise type in an electric fitting cluster in Pakistan

	Enterprises established as	
	Companies	Subcontracting workshops
Up to 1980	6	3
1981–90	13	18
1991–2000	23	46
2001–8	34	89
Total	76	156

Source: The 2008 survey.

our sample, 76 started as companies and 156 started as subcontracting workshops. The number of new entrants per decade increased gradually, indicating that this industry is still in the quantity expansion phase. The initial investment required for a firm to be a company is several times larger than that required to be a subcontractor. At present, out of the 232 sample enterprises, 106 are subcontracting workshops and 126 are companies, 50 of which have been transformed from subcontracting workshops. Buyers of finished products are classified into local and outside traders. Local traders maintain retail or wholesale shops in the marketplace in Sargodha, while outside traders buy electric fittings from the local buyers or directly from the companies.

The putting-out contracts between subcontracting workshops and companies or local traders are not written contracts, but are usually long-term and based on their trust relationships. The proprietors of subcontracting workshops often visit their contractors to receive orders and discuss the specifications, designs, strength, and weight of the sample products. Companies and local traders often provide raw material and dies to the subcontracting workshops, but never provide the pressing machines. Payment to the subcontracting workshops by the companies or local traders is made on a piece-rate basis, usually at the end of every month. The subcontracting workshops put out the assembling job to household subcontractors. Subcontracting workshops receive the assembled products from the households, pack these products after inspecting each one, and finally deliver the finished products to their contractor. Putting-out contracts for assembling are also observed between household subcontractors and companies.

6.2   Quality improvement and testable hypotheses

This section explores the strategies recently adopted by the entrepreneurs in Sargodha to improve the product quality, in order to postulate testable hypotheses about the role of entrepreneurs' managerial human capital as well as social capital in upgrading the product quality and improving the overall performance of their enterprises.

6.2.1   Quality improvement

Companies in Sargodha use two types of Bakelite powder: domestic powder produced in Gujranwala, Sheikhupura, and Gadoon, and imported powder from China and Italy. Almost all the companies procure both types of Bakelite powder from local suppliers in Sargodha. Many producers produce metal parts in this cluster, and companies buy metal parts primarily from the marketplace through anonymous spot transactions, probably because it is time-consuming to procure different metal parts such as springs, screws, pipes, pins, and arms directly from different producers, or because these standard parts are qualitatively no different. The brass parts such as pipes, pins, and arms used in electrical fittings produced in Sargodha are of low quality and often cause sparking. Companies procure dies from local die-makers in Sargodha, who use conventional machine tools which cannot precisely control the sizes of the multi-cavity dies. Therefore, the dies made by these methods make it difficult to produce homogeneous standardized products. Multifaceted innovations in the sense of Sonobe and Otsuka (2006) used to be lacking in this cluster. Recently, however, some entrepreneurs have been attempting to improve the quality of their products, because the increasing imports of electrical fittings from China have intensified the quality competition and lowered the profitability of producing low-quality standard products.

As mentioned previously, the electrical fittings produced in Sargodha include electric switches, sockets, plugs, bulb holders, and main switches of not more than 30 amperes. These products fall under various subcategories of items specified as HS (Harmonized Commodity Description and Coding System) Code 8536. Even within the same subcategory, imported items are often not similar to those produced in Sargodha, such as switches and sockets of high voltage, and other types of lamp holders. Therefore, it is very difficult to obtain accurate data on the imports of electrical fittings that are very similar to those produced in Sargodha. Yet it is believed by entrepreneurs, as well as by the officials of Sargodha regional office of SMEDA, that the imported electrical fittings which are very similar to those produced in Sargodha all come from China. Thus, we show the imports of electrical fittings and related items from China from 1998/9 to 2008/9 in Figure 6.3. These imports from China increased by 10 times between 2003 and 2008 but decreased by 25 percent in 2009 as compared with 2008 imports.[6]

According to our respondents, the Chinese electrical fittings imported to Pakistan were made of plastic, which is less heat-resistant than Bakelite, but is easy to market because plastic allows the production of electrical fittings with better designs and finishing, at lower cost. We collected information on the prices of three major products (switches, sockets, and combined switch–sockets) from 63 companies, and data on the average price of their products relative to their Chinese counterparts from all the sample companies. The low quality of the Chinese electrical fittings is reflected in the high relative price of the Pakistani products, shown in Figure 6.3: throughout the period under study, the relative price exceeds 1, which indicates that the products made in

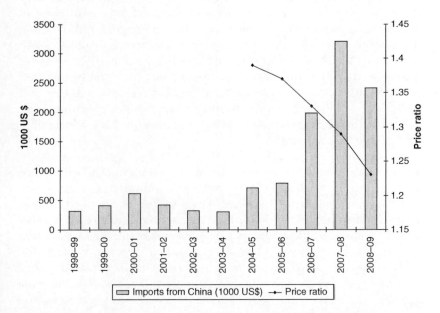

Figure 6.3 Imports of electrical fittings and related items (in 1,000 US$) from China, 1999/8 to 2008/9, and price ratio of Pakistani products to their Chinese counterparts

Sargodha are of higher quality than their Chinese equivalents. The gap between the prices of Pakistani products and Chinese products, however, has been decreasing over time. The first possible reason is that, due to fierce competition, the prices of Pakistani products have been falling in the order of 15 percent to 30 percent from 2004 to 2008 in nominal terms. The second reason is that Pakistani importers started importing relatively high-quality electrical fittings from China. The third reason is that the prices of Chinese products increased due to the depreciation of the Pakistani currency.

As the imports of low-priced but better designed electrical fittings from China intensified competition, leading entrepreneurs in Sargodha began attempting to improve the designs, finishing, and overall quality of their products and production processes. As mentioned before, die-makers in Sargodha use conventional machine tools. According to the entrepreneurs, the conventional machine tools used by local die-makers cannot control the sizes required for sophisticated and multi-cavity dies. Moreover, with conventional machine tools, it takes as long as 6 months to make a die, and by that time new designs have already entered the market. Thus, to produce new and differentiated designs and improve productivity, leading entrepreneurs began outsourcing their die requirements to China and big cities in Pakistan where the Computerized Numerical Control (CNC) technology for making sophisticated dies is available. Another trend clearly seen among the largest companies was the creation of their own CNC die-making sections within their factories. As of 2009, CNC die-making sections had been established in five sample companies. These companies hired staff holding diplomas in CNC die-making from recognized institutes.

As mentioned earlier, companies in Sargodha use both domestically produced and imported powders. The latter are roughly double the price of the former. According to the entrepreneurs, imported powder is easier to mold than domestically produced powder, and the use of the former improves the strength and finishing of the main body of the product. For these reasons, companies have increased the use of imported powder. To reduce the production cost and to increase productivity, a few companies have started using injection molding machines and polycarbonate instead of manual pressing machines and Bakelite powder. Our interviews with the entrepreneurs reveal three reasons for the use of polycarbonate instead of Bakelite powder. First, polycarbonate is cheaper than Bakelite. Second, unlike Bakelite, polycarbonate can be recycled. Third, as polycarbonate is easier to mold than Bakelite, it is suitable for the production of sophisticated products. According to a very knowledgeable entrepreneur, the time required to mold polycarbonate is five times shorter than that required to mold Bakelite. However, injection machines are required to use polycarbonate, which many small companies cannot afford. Thus, this change is limited to only six large companies.

Aside from the poor design and finish of the products, staff at the World Bank office in Islamabad and in the Sargodha regional office of SMEDA consistently pointed out the poor quality of the brass parts used in the electrical fittings produced in Sargodha. Brass is an alloy of copper and zinc and a conductor of electricity. The proportions of copper and zinc can be varied to create a range of brasses with varying properties. A greater quantity of copper improves the conductivity of the brass. As discussed earlier, so far companies have bought brass and other metal parts from the marketplace through anonymous spot transactions. Recently, however, a small number of companies have started procuring high-quality brass and other metal parts directly from producers. According to the entrepreneurs, the brass parts procured through anonymous spot transactions may be "lemons" containing metals other than copper and zinc. In contrast, the brass parts procured to order directly from producers are of higher quality.

Similarly to the East Asian experience reported by Sonobe and Otsuka (2006), along with the improvement in product quality, changes in marketing channels were observed in the Sargodha cluster. Local traders in Sargodha were interested in marketing the products of various producers. Moreover, they have strong unions, possess price-setting powers, and do not allow the producers to charge sufficiently high prices for improved high-quality products. Therefore, in order not to mingle their products with the standard products of others, to obtain higher prices for improved products, and to save brokerage fees, companies producing differentiated designs and better finished products have increased their direct sales to outside traders. While a few of the companies have appointed marketing staff or hired sales agents who deal only in that company's products, most of the entrepreneurs personally visit big cities with sample products and receive orders.

In the sense of Sonobe and Otsuka (2006), the strategies recently adopted by entrepreneurs in Sargodha can be called "multifaceted innovations," even though they have not developed truly new products using the most advanced scientific discoveries. According to the innovative entrepreneurs, they have succeeded in recovering their share in the domestic market by adopting these upgrading strategies.

6.2.2   Testable hypotheses

As can be seen, the imports of electrical fittings from China have intensified the competition, and thus entrepreneurs in Sargodha are attempting to improve the product quality and marketing channels by such means as the production of differentiated designs, increased use of imported Bakelite powder, direct procurement of improved quality metal parts, and increased direct sales to traders from outside Sargodha. As we argued in Chapter 1, generally highly educated entrepreneurs lead the industries to the quality improvement phase by taking the initiative in improving product quality, production organization, and marketing channels. In addition to formal education, the entrepreneurs' industry- and job-specific human capital, acquired through experience, is vital in improving the quality of products. It has also been empirically established that entrepreneurs who have previously been traders or engaged in marketing activities have superior abilities to sell higher-quality products directly to urban traders. According to our interviews with the entrepreneurs, specific human capital acquired by experience in marketing also helps in obtaining raw material at low cost and selling the finished products at high prices. Thus, we test the validity of Hypothesis 1 (i.e., the importance of managerial human capital in carrying out multifaceted innovations) by using the data of companies collected in Sargodha, with particular reference to the roles of formal schooling and experience of trading and management.

Several studies have attempted to analyze the roles of social capital in industrial development. For example, in a study of small-scale manufacturing entrepreneurs in Ghana, networks of business-related contacts improved the flow of technical information among enterprises (Barr, 2000). Furthermore, in a surgical cluster in Pakistan, where many of the enterprises belong to the same extended families, family ties provide the enterprises with a network of outside business contacts and valuable information on how to conform to new quality control pressures (Nadvi, 1999b). Personal networks have been shown to help entrepreneurs gain access to credit in a garment cluster in Kenya (Akoten et al., 2006) and in a farm equipment cluster in Pakistan (Caniëls and Romijn, 2003). The importance of family ties in the garment and steel bar industries in Vietnam has also been reported in Chapters 2 and 4. Our informal interviews with the entrepreneurs indicate that their social ties with people in the same industry help them gain access to trade credit from local traders, and that important business-related information is shared among groups of friends and relatives. Regarding the role of entrepreneurs' social capital, measured by their personal ties with people in the same industry, in improving product quality and marketing channels, we would like to postulate the following hypothesis:

Hypothesis 6-1: The entrepreneurs' social capital enhances the production of differentiated designs, use of imported powder, direct procurement of high-quality metal parts, and direct sales to outside traders.

Since improvements in product quality and marketing channels are expected to increase profits, entrepreneurs who are more successful at carrying out these improvements accumulate profits faster. It is also expected that these entrepreneurs reinvest the profits in fixed and working capital, thereby expanding their business size. Thus, in view of the increasing importance of multifaceted improvements, the following hypothesis is also advanced:

Hypothesis 6-2: Entrepreneurs' managerial human capital (both general and specific human capital) and social capital (measured by their ties with people in the same industry) have positive effects on the size and growth of enterprises.

6.3   Characteristics of sample enterprises

Table 6.2 presents the data on the characteristics of the sample companies and their entrepreneurs. In Tables 6.3 and 6.4, the sample companies are divided into three cohorts based on the years of operation as a company. Since many companies have upgraded from subcontracting workshops, the years of operation as companies have been separated from years of operation as subcontractors. Enterprises that have operated for longer years as companies, on average, have longer total years of operation. According to Table 6.2, the entrepreneurs in the three groups are not very different in their personal and family characteristics. However, the entrepreneurs operating companies from the beginning were more highly educated and had richer experience in marketing, and a greater network of connections with people in the same business, than those who entered the industry as subcontractors.

In our sample, the average years of schooling of the entrepreneurs is as low as 9.4, and only 31.2 percent of the entrepreneurs have completed high school, which is equivalent to 12 years of schooling. This is low compared with the East Asian cases (Sonobe and Otsuka, 2006). Only one-third of the sample entrepreneurs have prior experience in marketing as former merchants or in sales in other companies. The percentage of entrepreneurs having prior experience in marketing

Table 6.2   Characteristics of companies and entrepreneurs in an electric fitting cluster in Pakistan, 2009

| | Years of Operation as a Company | | | |
	Less than 5 years	5 to 9 years	More than 10 years	All
Number of observations	34	41	50	125
Number of subcontractors turned companies	18	20	13	51
Average total years of operation	5.4	10.7	18.9	12.6
Average years of schooling of entrepreneurs	9.9	8.8	9.4	9.4
% entrepreneurs with 12+ years of schooling	38.2	26.8	30.0	31.2
Average years of prior experience in marketing	2.3	2.5	2.7	2.5
% entrepreneurs with prior experience in marketing	23.5	31.7	46.0	35.2
Average years of prior experience in production of electrical fittings	4.3	4.4	3.5	4.0
% entrepreneurs with prior experience in production of electrical fittings	55.9	56.1	56.0	56.0
% entrepreneurs having father in same business	2.9	7.3	10.0	7.2
Average no. of friends and relatives in same industry	3.2	2.6	4.1	3.3

Source: The 2008 and 2009 surveys.

is highest among those operating companies for 10 or more years and lowest among those operating companies for less than 5 years. Table 6.2 also shows that 56 percent of the entrepreneurs had worked at electrical fittings enterprises before becoming entrepreneurs, which indicates the importance of spinoffs in the formation of the Sargodha industrial cluster. Moreover, this table indicates that in total nine entrepreneurs (or about 7 percent) had fathers in the same industry. Of these nine entrepreneurs, only two inherited their businesses from their fathers.

Table 6.3 presents the data on the number of workers, production of differentiated designs, use of imported powder, direct procurement of metal parts, and direct sales in 2009, where the sample entrepreneurs are grouped into those with 12 or more years of schooling and those with

Table 6.3 Number of workers, production of differentiated designs, use of imported powder, direct procurement of metal parts, and direct sales by entrepreneur's years of schooling in an electric fitting cluster in Pakistan, 2009

	Years of Operation as a Company			
	Less than 5 years	5 to 9 years	More than 10 years	All
Entrepreneurs with 12 years or more of schooling				
Number of observations	13	11	15	39
Number of workers	10.0	18.2	35.5	22.1
% companies producing differentiated designs	7.7	36.4	40.0	28.2
Imported powder (%)	76.2	91.8	97.7	84.6
Direct procurement of metal parts (%)	7.8	20.0	31.6	20.4
Direct sales (%)	68.7	85.5	91.0	82.0
Entrepreneurs with less than 12 years of schooling				
Number of observations	21	30	35	86
Number of workers	7.2	10.6	14.4	11.3
% companies producing differentiated designs	14.3	10.0	22.8	16.3
Imported powder (%)	55.2	76.4	84.5	74.6
Direct procurement of metal parts (%)	1.3	6.5	7.5	5.7
Direct sales (%)	63.1	71.1	71.5	69.3

Source: The 2008 and 2009 surveys.

less than 12 years of schooling. The companies operated by the relatively highly educated entrepreneurs are about double the size, measured by the number of workers, than those operated by their less educated counterparts. Similarly, the percentage of companies producing differentiated designs is high among the relatively highly educated entrepreneurs, except for those operating for less than 5 years as a company. Companies operated by relatively highly educated entrepreneurs make greater use of imported powder in the total consumption of Bakelite powder. The percentage of high-quality metal parts directly procured from producers is roughly four times greater among the relatively highly educated entrepreneurs than among their less educated counterparts. Moreover, the percentage of revenue from direct sales with outside traders is higher among the relatively highly educated entrepreneurs. All these observations are consistent with Hypothesis 6-1.

Table 6.4 Number of workers, production of differentiated designs, use of imported powder, procurement of metal parts, and direct sales by entrepreneur's prior experience in marketing in an electric fitting cluster in Pakistan, 2009

	Years of Operation as Company			
	Less than 5 years	5 to 9 years	More than 10 years	All
Entrepreneurs with prior experience in marketing				
Number of observations	8	13	23	44
Number of workers	5.6	15.1	24.5	18.3
% companies producing differentiated designs	12.5	17.4	20.6	18.2
Imported powder (%)	85.0	93.5	95.1	92.8
Direct procurement of metal parts (%)	5.0	16.5	20.5	16.5
Direct sales (%)	81.4	93.5	94.6	91.9
Entrepreneurs without prior experience in marketing				
Number of observations	26	28	27	81
Number of workers	8.6	10.7	18.7	12.7
% companies producing differentiated designs	11.5	14.3	37.0	21.0
Imported powder (%)	61.2	71.9	75.0	69.5
Direct procurement of metal parts (%)	3.4	3.9	13.3	6.9
Direct sales (%)	52.7	63.3	73.2	63.2

Source: The 2008 and 2009 surveys.

Table 6.4 examines the effects of the entrepreneur's prior experience in marketing on various aspects of quality improvement. Out of 125 sample companies in 2009, 44 were run by entrepreneurs having experience in marketing before establishing their own businesses. The percentage of companies producing differentiated designs is high among entrepreneurs having prior experience in marketing except for those companies operating for less than 10 years. Similarly to the case of educated entrepreneurs, the percentages of using imported powder, of high-quality metal parts directly procured from producers, and of revenue generated from direct sales with outside traders are higher among entrepreneurs having prior experience in marketing. These observations are consistent with Hypothesis 6-2.

In Tables 6.3 and 6.4, regardless of the entrepreneurs' years of schooling and prior experience in marketing, the percentage of companies producing differentiated designs, using imported powder, procuring high-quality metal parts directly from producers, and selling direct to outside traders is higher among companies operating for more years. Moreover, the size of enterprises, measured by the number of workers, tends to increase with the years of operation as a company, for which the respondents provided two explanations. Firstly, the size of the company is constrained by both the fixed and working capital. As entrepreneurs operate their businesses for longer periods and accumulate capital, they can increase the size of their enterprises. Secondly, enterprise size also depends on the competence of the entrepreneurs in terms of managing workers, designing new products, and marketing, which can be gained through learning by doing.

6.4   Estimation methods and results

In this section regression analyses are employed to determine the quantitative impacts of human and social capital on various aspects of quality improvement and enterprise performance, while accounting for the effects of other factors to verify the validity of the hypotheses advanced in Section 6.2. Subsection 6.4.1 specifies the estimation model to be used, and Subsection 6.4.2 examines the empirical results.

6.4.1   Model specification

To test the hypotheses advanced in Section 6.2, let us examine the determinants of the following five dependent variables: (i) whether a company produces differentiated designs; (ii) the fraction of imported powder in the total consumption of Bakelite powder by a company; (iii) the fraction of the value of metal parts directly procured from producers; (iv) the fraction of revenue from direct sales to outside traders, and (v) enterprise size measured by the number of workers and its growth. According to our hypotheses, the companies operated by entrepreneurs with relatively high general human capital measured by schooling, specific human capital measured by experience in marketing and management, and social capital measured by whether an entrepreneur's father used to work in the same industry and the number of friends and relatives in the same industry tend to be associated with more differentiated designs, the use of a greater fraction of imported powder, and the greater importance of the direct procurement of metal parts and direct sales. Also, we postulate that these companies tend to be larger and grow faster.

To test Hypotheses 6-1 and 6-2, we regress the above-mentioned dependent variables (i) to (iv) on the entrepreneur's years of schooling, prior experience in marketing, years of operation as a company and as a subcontracting workshop, father's involvement in the same business, and the number of friends and relatives in the same business as well as other exogenous variables. The data on dependent variables are available for 2004, 2006, 2008, and 2009. Since the coefficients of the independent variables are expected to change in a dynamic setting, we estimate the regression functions separately for each year. Hence, the dependent variable may be denoted Y_{it} with subscript i and t indicating enterprise and year, respectively. The explanatory variables are all time invariant, and a vector of these variables is denoted by X_i without subscript t. Thus, the estimated regression equations are of the following form:

$$Y_{it} = X_i \beta_t + u_{it}, \tag{6.1}$$

where β_t is a vector of the parameters to be estimated and u_{it} is an error term with white noise properties. Since the production of differentiated designs is represented by a dummy variable that assumes the value of 1 if a company uses the CNC dies and zero otherwise, the model for this analysis is estimated using the Probit estimator. The functions explaining the fraction of imported powder, fraction of the value of metal parts directly procured from producers, and fraction of revenue from direct sales are estimated with the two-limit Tobit estimator, because the data on these variables are censored at 0 and 100.

To test Hypothesis 6-2, the size of the company in terms of the logarithm of employment size (E) is regressed on X_i:

$$LnE_{it} = X_i \gamma_t + v_{it}, \tag{6.2}$$

where γ_t are the coefficients which are allowed to vary over time, and v_{it} is an error term with white noise properties. I also ran a growth regression using a specification extensively used in the empirical literature on economic and enterprise growth. It can be derived from equation (6.2) as follows. Let δ be a convergence parameter to be estimated and let E_{it-1} denote the lagged employment size. By adding δLnE_{it-1} to the right-hand side of equation (6.2) and then subtracting its equivalent, $\delta(X_i \gamma_{t-1} + v_{it-1})$, one can obtain

$$LnE_{it} = \delta LnE_{it} + X_i (\gamma_t - \delta\gamma_{t-1}) + (v_{it} - \delta v_{it-1}). \tag{6.3}$$

Subtracting LnE_{it-1} from both sides of equation (6.3) and rearranging gives the well-known growth equation,

$$LnE_{it} - LnE_{it-1} = \lambda_1 \, LnE_{it-1} + X_i \, \lambda_2 + w_{it}, \tag{6.4}$$

where $\lambda_1 = \delta - 1$, $\lambda_2 = \gamma_t - \delta\gamma_{t-1}$, and $w_{it} = v_{it} - \delta v_{it-1}$.

6.4.2 Estimation results

Table 6.5 presents the estimated functions explaining whether the company produces differentiated designs. Companies operated by relatively highly educated entrepreneurs are more likely to produce differentiated designs than others, as the effects of the entrepreneur's formal schooling were always positive and significant. Moreover, the coefficients are larger in the later period, which provides support for Hypothesis 1. Similarly, the coefficients of the years of operating as a company were also positive and significant in all the years. The coefficients of the years of operation as a subcontractor, however, were insignificant in all regressions. These findings indicate the clear influence of experience of running a company on the entrepreneur's ability to produce differentiated designs. The production of differentiated designs requires not only technical abilities to produce sophisticated designs but also a sizeable amount of fixed capital to purchase CNC dies. Thus, it is likely that enterprises that have operated for a longer period as companies have stronger capability to meet the financial requirements for using CNC dies.

Table 6.5 also shows that the coefficient of the dummy variable representing the entrepreneur's prior experience in marketing is weakly significant in 2008 and 2009, which weakly supports Hypothesis 6-2. The coefficients of the dummy variable representing the entrepreneur's father's involvement in the same industry, and the number of friends and relatives who were in the electrical fittings industry when the entrepreneur established his firm, were insignificant.

Table 6.6 reports the estimated function explaining the determinants of the fraction of imported powder. Consistently with Hypothesis 6-1, the effects of the entrepreneur's schooling, marketing experience, and years of operation as a company on the fraction of imported Bakelite powder are all positive and significant. As may be expected, the coefficients of the years of operation as a subcontractor are insignificant. The coefficients of the number of friends and relatives in the same industry when the entrepreneur started his firm are positive in all periods but significant only in 2008 and 2009. Similarly, the coefficients of the

Table 6.5 Determinants of the production of differentiated designs by companies in an electric fitting cluster in Pakistan (Probit model)[a]

	Production of differentiated designs			
	2004	2006	2008	2009
	(1)	(2)	(3)	(4)
Entrepreneur's years of	0.012*	0.019*	0.024*	0.030**
schooling	(1.88)	(1.82)	(1.97)	(2.52)
Years of operation as a	0.015*	0.017*	0.021*	0.025*
company	(1.93)	(2.07)	(2.39)	(2.41)
Years of operation as a	−0.013	−0.001	0.006	0.001
subcontractor	(−0.49)	(−0.12)	(0.64)	(0.12)
Prior marketing	−0.063	−0.044	0.014	0.017*
experience	(−1.18)	(−1.27)	(1.69)	(1.73)
Prior experience of	0.001	−0.061	−0.035	−0.097
electrical	(0.39)	(−0.79)	(−0.42)	(−0.98)
fittings production				
Number of friends and	0.000	0.003	0.001	0.013
relatives	(0.11)	(0.51)	(0.10)	(1.39)
in the same industry				
Father in the same	0.074	0.244	0.264	0.111
industry	(0.59)	(1.28)	(1.46)	(1.63)
Father in high-income	−0.050	−0.035	−0.071	−0.100
occupation	(−0.78)	(−0.42)	(−0.77)	(−1.11)
Entrepreneur's and	0.045	0.025	0.035	0.020
father's	(1.02)	(1.08)	(1.18)	(1.13)
share in initial				
investment				
Entrepreneur's age	0.002	0.005	−0.001	−0.001
	(0.85)	(1.09)	(−0.18)	(−0.28)
Intercept	−2.623*	−2.860*	−1.941*	−2.789*
	(−1.96)	(−2.24)	(−1.94)	(−2.26)
Pseudo R-square	0.3223	0.2602	0.2955	0.3127
Number of observations	91	111	126	125

[a]The estimates reported are the marginal effects. Numbers in parentheses are z-statistics.
**Significant at the 1% level, *at the 5% level.

dummy variables representing the proprietor's father's involvement in the same industry and father's high-income occupations were positive and significant in all periods except for 2004. These findings indicate that entrepreneurs with greater social capital tended to make greater use of imported powder, which is consistent with Hypothesis 6-1. It appears that entrepreneurs having fathers or friends and relatives in the same industry tend to have improved access to trade credit and information

Table 6.6 Determinants of the use of imported Bakelite powder by companies in an electric fitting cluster in Pakistan (Tobit model)[a]

| | Use of imported powder | | | |
| | 2004 | 2006 | 2008 | 2009 |
	(1)	(2)	(3)	(4)
Entrepreneur's years of	0.689*	0.776*	0.986*	1.042*
schooling	(2.18)	(2.28)	(2.24)	(2.05)
Years of operation as a	0.967**	1.058**	1.236**	1.288**
company	(3.02)	(4.16)	(4.53)	(3.95)
Years of operation as a	−0.411	−0.579	−0.494	−0.444
subcontractor	(−1.56)	(−1.35)	(−1.66)	(−1.71)
Prior marketing	27.266**	26.869**	24.453**	22.352**
experience	(8.87)	(6.17)	(7.88)	(6.69)
Prior experience of	1.503	1.411	2.164	3.119
electrical	(0.37)	(0.40)	(0.65)	(0.71)
fittings production				
Number of friends and	0.634	0.445	0.538*	0.556**
relatives	(1.38)	(1.08)	(1.84)	(2.01)
in the same industry				
Father in the same	7.971	11.221*	14.755**	16.182*
industry	(1.13)	(1.82)	(2.70)	(2.20)
Father in high-income	1.632	3.540*	5.409**	7.577**
occupation	(0.94)	(2.07)	(2.76)	(4.62)
Entrepreneur's and	0.016	−0.006	−0.025	−0.079
father's	(0.30)	(−0.12)	(−0.58)	(−1.30)
share in initial				
investment				
Entrepreneur's age	0.105	−0.013	−0.171	−0.197
	(0.55)	(−0.08)	(−1.10)	(−0.92)
Intercept	24.486	31.073**	36.578**	40.965**
	(1.79)	(2.70)	(3.99)	(4.03)
Pseudo R-square	0.2067	0.2076	0.1889	0.1928
Number of observations	91	111	126	125
Number of censored obs.				
Left	15	18	15	14
Right	28	35	48	50

[a]The estimates reported are the marginal effects. Numbers in parentheses are z-statistics.
**Significant at the 1% level, *at the 5% level.

on new sophisticated designs, new products, and new marketing channels through informal communications among groups of friends and relatives. However, as we noticed in Table 6.5, none of the variables representing the entrepreneur's social capital significantly affects the

Table 6.7   Determinants of the procurement of metal parts directly from producers in an electric fitting cluster in Pakistan (Tobit model)[a]

	Direct procurement of metal parts			
	2004	2006	2008	2009
	(1)	(2)	(3)	(4)
Entrepreneur's years of schooling	0.743 (1.14)	0.879 (1.59)	1.117* (1.70)	1.361* (1.87)
Years of operation as a company	0.301* (1.79)	0.348* (1.82)	0.593* (2.30)	0.616** (2.71)
Years of operation as a subcontractor	−0.066 (−0.28)	−0.013 (−0.22)	−0.034 (−0.11)	−0.114 (−0.56)
Prior marketing experience	0.331 (0.40)	0.233 (1.37)	0.138 (1.66)	0.140* (1.74)
Prior experience of electrical fittings production	−0.001 (−0.81)	−0.087 (−0.24)	0.004 (0.58)	0.028 (0.03)
Number of friends and relatives in the same industry	−0.010 (−1.14)	0.127 (0.72)	0.256 (1.42)	0.166 (1.45)
Father in the same industry	−0.116 (−0.09)	−0.016 (−0.38)	−0.166 (−0.07)	−0.040 (−0.02)
Father in high-income occupation	0.043 (0.64)	0.208 (0.67)	0.931 (1.16)	1.686 (1.33)
Entrepreneur's and father's share in initial investment	0.088 (1.42)	0.108 (1.39)	0.132 (1.02)	0.127 (1.03)
Entrepreneur's age	−0.031 (−0.70)	−0.027 (−0.81)	−0.291 (−1.35)	−0.205 (−1.57)
Intercept	−2.300 (−1.53)	−1.662 (−1.41)	−4.765 (−1.35)	−4.311* (−1.78)
Pseudo R-square	0.1898	0.1928	0.2201	0.1998
Number of observations	91	111	126	125
Number of censored obs.				
Left	82	98	109	106
Right	2	3	6	8

[a]The estimates reported are the marginal effects. Numbers in parentheses are z-statistics.
**Significant at the 1% level, *at the 5% level.

production of differentiated designs. This may indicate that kinship and connections with people in the same cluster matter in gaining access to credit from local traders located within the cluster but do not help in procuring CNC dies from die-makers located outside Sargodha.

Table 6.7 reports the results of the estimated function explaining the fraction of high-quality metal parts directly procured from producers. The years of operation as a company had positive and significant effects in all periods. Moreover, the coefficients in 2008 and 2009 were substantially larger than those in 2004 and 2006. The effects of the entrepreneur's schooling and marketing experience on the direct procurement of metal parts, however, were marginally significant only in 2008 and 2009. In 2009, only 19 companies were procuring metal parts directly from producers. Of these 19 companies, 16 were owned by entrepreneurs with at least 12 years of schooling and 13 with prior experience in marketing, while seven entrepreneurs had both. These results indicate that the entrepreneurs who are more educated and experienced and are former traders pay closer attention to those aspects of quality that are not easily visible, such as designs and the finishing of the products.

Table 6.8 reports the determinants of the percentage of revenue from direct sales. The effects of the entrepreneurs' schooling, marketing experience, and years of operation as a company are all positive and significant in all the periods. These results, together with the positive effects of the entrepreneurs' schooling, experience in marketing, and years of operation as a company on the production of differentiated designs and the use of imported powder, suggest the importance of entrepreneurs' general and specific human capital in carrying out multifaceted improvements, which is consistent with our hypotheses as well as the findings of Sonobe and Otsuka (2006) from East Asian countries. The coefficients of the number of friends and relatives are positive and significant only in 2008 and 2009. Furthermore, the coefficients of the dummy variable representing father's involvement in the same industry and father's high-income occupation were significant in all periods except in 2004. These findings suggest that the social ties of entrepreneurs with people in the same industry influence their ability to find new marketing channels suitable for the sale of improved high-quality products. Probably, the father's high-income occupation does not affect the sales to outside traders directly, but indirectly through its impact on the use of high-quality raw material. Also, it must be pointed out that, although implicit, outside traders seem to contribute to quality improvement, which supports Hypothesis 2 formulated in Chapter 1.

Finally, Table 6.9 presents the results of the estimated function explaining the determinants of the enterprise size in terms of the number of workers and its growth.[7] Columns (1) to (4) of Table 6.9 show that an entrepreneur's schooling and management experience learned by running a company have positive and significant effects on the

Table 6.8 Determinants of the direct sales of finished products with outside traders in an electric fitting cluster in Pakistan (Tobit model)[a]

	Direct sales			
	2004	2006	2008	2009
	(1)	(2)	(3)	(4)
Entrepreneur's years of	0.478*	0.507*	0.595**	0.642**
schooling	(1.86)	(2.27)	(2.59)	(2.60)
Years of operation as a	0.589**	0.666**	0.685**	0.693**
company	(2.93)	(3.99)	(3.33)	(3.87)
Years of operation as a	−0.301	−0.144	−0.245	−0.441
subcontractor	(−1.34)	(−0.86)	(−1.36)	(−1.07)
Prior marketing	10.017**	9.842**	8.621**	8.607**
experience	(3.39)	(3.79)	(3.33)	(3.21)
Prior experience of	−0.986	−0.092	0.688	0.758
electrical	(−0.47)	(−0.05)	(0.38)	(0.39)
fittings production				
Number of friends and	0.204	0.286	0.388*	0.398*
relatives	(1.41)	(1.61)	(1.88)	(1.99)
in the same industry				
Father in the same	3.997	4.112*	4.803*	4.902*
industry	(1.31)	(1.68)	(2.08)	(2.29)
Father in high-income	0.815	1.263*	1.603**	1.714**
occupation	(0.84)	(1.96)	(2.81)	(2.91)
Entrepreneur's and	0.051	0.008	−0.011	−0.035
father's share in	(1.30)	(0.29)	(−0.43)	(−0.22)
initial investment				
Entrepreneur's age	−0.153	0.054	−0.010	0.006
	(−0.35)	(0.64)	(−0.12)	(0.06)
Intercept	−115.961	−108.444	−90.168	−84.886
	(−0.75)	(−1.59)	(−1.60)	(−1.17)
Pseudo R-square	0.1805	0.1877	0.1927	0.2002
Number of observations	91	111	126	125
Number of censored				
obs.				
Left	17	11	14	14
Right	44	53	59	60

[a]The estimates reported are the marginal effects. Numbers in parentheses are z-statistics.
**Significant at the 1% level, *at the 5% level.

employment size in all periods. The effects of experience in marketing, production of electrical fittings, and management experience while running a subcontracting workshop were insignificant. Moreover, the number of friends and relatives and having a father in the same

Table 6.9 Determinants of enterprise size and growth in an electric fitting cluster in Pakistan (OLS estimation)[a]

	Log(employment size)				Growth rate	
					2004 to 2006	2006 to 2009
	2004	2006	2008	2009		
	(1)	(2)	(3)	(4)	(5)	(6)
Log of initial employment size					−0.060* (−2.42)	0.003* (1.91)
Entrepreneur's years of schooling	0.028* (1.69)	0.030* (1.83)	0.032* (1.93)	0.033* (2.06)	−0.002 (−0.05)	0.001* (1.82)
Years of operation as a company	0.074** (5.40)	0.079** (5.77)	0.089** (5.36)	0.088** (6.96)	−0.002 (−0.53)	0.002* (1.72)
Years of operation as a subcontractor	0.011 (1.05)	0.023 (1.29)	0.016 (1.25)	0.018 (1.27)	−0.028* (−2.18)	−0.003* (−2.09)
Prior marketing experience	−0.246 (−1.58)	−0.343 (−1.56)	−0.351 (−1.26)	−0.361 (−1.37)	0.007 (0.16)	−0.015 (−1.40)
Prior experience of electrical fittings production	0.031 (0.28)	0.021 (0.19)	−0.091 (−0.68)	0.002 (0.01)	0.053 (1.43)	0.008 (0.86)
Number of friends and relatives in the same industry	0.016 (1.63)	0.017* (1.74)	0.019* (1.93)	0.023** (2.08)	0.001 (0.34)	0.001 (0.84)
Father in the same industry	0.247 (0.68)	0.123* (1.83)	0.143* (1.81)	0.160* (1.79)	−0.076 (−1.12)	−0.011 (−0.45)
Father in high-income occupation	0.081 (0.74)	0.058 (0.51)	0.011 (0.18)	0.020 (0.37)	−0.018 (−1.06)	−0.001 (−0.20)
Entrepreneur's and father's share in initial investment	0.001 (0.73)	0.001 (0.63)	−0.001 (−0.47)	0.000 (0.32)	0.014 (1.16)	0.003 (1.02)
Entrepreneur's age	0.003 (0.58)	0.004 (0.61)	0.004 (0.62)	0.001 (0.14)	−0.001 (−0.30)	0.000 (1.00)
Intercept	1.525** (4.65)	1.377** (5.13)	1.278** (4.77)	1.267** (4.20)	0.125 (1.33)	−0.023 (−0.90)
Adjusted R-square	0.2469	0.2558	0.2610	0.2518	0.0897	0.0824
Number of observations	91	111	126	125	90	107

[a]Numbers in parentheses are *t*-statistics. **Significant at the 1% level, *at the 5% level.

industry had positive effects on enterprise size in all periods except in 2004.

Columns (5) and (6) in Table 6.9 exhibit the determinants of enterprise growth covering the periods from 2004 to 2006 and from 2006 to 2009, respectively. The coefficient of the initial employment size of the enterprise is negative and significant in the first period. However, it becomes positive and significant during the second period, implying that larger enterprises have tended to grow faster in more recent years, which is consistent with the prediction of the endogenous model of cluster development regarding enterprise size in the quality improvement phase. In other words, once the industry enters the quality improvement phase, even large and long-established enterprises can grow faster in size. Similarly, the coefficients of the entrepreneur's schooling and years of operation as a company are insignificant during the first period, but become positive and significant during the second period. Recall that the China shock took place in the second period. Thus, the estimation results strongly indicate that the entrepreneur's managerial human capital plays a critical role in upgrading product quality and improving marketing and internal management. The coefficient of the years of operation as a subcontracting workshop was negative and significant in both periods.

6.5   Concluding remarks

The role of industrial clusters in industrial development has attracted much attention in the last two decades from development economists and policymakers, partly because of their capacity to generate employment opportunities, reduce poverty, and enlarge the growth opportunities of the industry by creating economies of agglomeration, and partly because they are ubiquitous even in developing economies. Sargodha's electrical fittings cluster is long established and the largest in the country, with a 70 percent share of the total domestic production of electrical fittings. However, the electrical fittings produced in Sargodha are crude and of low quality. Moreover, the increasing import of low-priced electrical fittings from China has become a serious threat to the producers operating in this cluster. This chapter has attempted to inquire whether and how the enterprises in Sargodha are able to compete with the Chinese products.

The empirical analyses revealed that entrepreneurs with relatively high education, marketing experience, and skills acquired through learning by doing began showing signs of carrying out multifaceted innovations by introducing new designs and adopting new methods of material procurement and marketing. These findings clearly support Hypothesis 1. Some of these multifaceted innovations are beginning to impact enterprise performance. These findings are consistent with the recent literature on industrial clusters in East Asia, which indicates that more educated and experienced producers are the carriers of multifaceted innovations. Moreover, the entrepreneur's social capital, based on social ties with people in the same industry, contributed to the multifaceted improvements in Sargodha.

It seems that the China shock has actually provided incentives to introduce multifaceted innovations for those entrepreneurs who are endowed with sufficient managerial human capital, acquired by schooling, trading experience, and the experience of managing companies. As will be demonstrated in the next chapter, similar changes have been observed in the leather shoe industry in Ethiopia, responding to another China shock. In contrast, we observed the lack of such changes in the garment cluster in Nairobi reported in Chapter 3. It may well be that the endowment of managerial human capital determines whether the China shock brings about the substantial reduction or expansion of the industrial clusters outside China in the longer run. It is also clear that intensified competition may facilitate the transition from the quantity expansion phase to the quality improvement phase, regardless of whether it is endogenously created or exogenously provided, as in the case of the China shock.

7
The V-Shaped Growth in the Leather Shoe Industry in Ethiopia

Manufacturing industries in sub-Saharan Africa (SSA) have generally been stagnant or shrinking for the last three decades (Bigsten and Söderbom, 2006). As Collier and Gunning (1999) and Fafchamps (2004) and many others argue, industrial development in Africa has been hindered by a myriad of problems ranging from high transportation costs, high transaction costs due to imperfect information, and imperfect contract enforcement to highly risky business and political environments. Moreover, both the provision of public services and the development of grass-roots institutions and social capital are considered to be insufficient in Africa to cope with such problems. Added to these problems is the "China shock," a massive and sudden increase in the imports of cheap Chinese products that impacts upon stagnant domestic industries in SSA.

The World Bank and other organizations have collected large sets of enterprise data from many industries in various African countries in the 1990s. Using these data, a number of empirical analyses have been carried out to provide insights into the major constraints on industrial development.[1] Few attempts, however, have been made to learn from prosperous industries, presumably because of the lack of successful cases of industrial development in sub-Saharan Africa (McCormick, 1999). According to Bigsten and Söderbom (2006, p. 242) and Gunning and Mengistae (2001, p. 50), however, some African firms "have performed extremely well" and "African manufacturing firms are highly profitable."

This chapter presents the results of our case study of successful industrial development based on field surveys conducted in one of the most labor-intensive industries in one of the poorest countries, namely the leather-shoe industry in Addis Ababa, Ethiopia.[2] We collected primary data on the performance and characteristics of 90 private enterprises and two state-owned enterprises (SOEs) in this industry. It is widely believed by those who are engaged in this industry that well over 1,000, probably nearer 2,000, factories are producing leather shoes in Addis Ababa. Most of them employ only 10 workers or fewer, but several factories have hundreds of workers. In the early 2000s, China-made leather shoes flooded into the Ethiopian market, plunging the local industry into a slump. Remarkably, however, the industry soon resumed vigorous growth, not only taking back the domestic market but even finding its way into the international market. How the China shock has been overcome is a major issue, as it has caused many industries in SSA simply to shrink, as in the case of the garment industry in Nairobi reported in Chapter 3. In contrast, the electric fittings industry in Pakistan, reported in Chapter 6, seems to have been successful in regaining the market share of domestic production at the expense of Chinese imports.

While the majority of Ethiopian factories sell their products to domestic markets, some export shoes in bulk to Italy and other developed countries as well as neighboring African countries. These high-performing enterprises are not SOEs but private enterprises. They are building or planning to build new large factories to start mass production of high-quality leather shoes for foreign markets. Thus, the leather shoe industry in Addis Ababa is exceptionally successful in Africa. We believe that this is a case worth investigating, since it is expected to provide insight into the key to successful industrial development in this region. A major finding is that the growth of this industry was driven initially by the massive entry of new enterprises established by former employees of the existing shoe factories, but more recently by the growth in enterprise sizes due to improvements in the quality of products, marketing, and management. Such improvements were first made by highly educated entrepreneurs and subsequently followed by other enterprises. While the followers have grown in size, the leading enterprises have grown faster. Such a development pattern appears similar to the experience of successful cluster-based industrial development in China, Taiwan, and Japan, as is reported by Sonobe and Otsuka (2006).

The rest of the chapter is organized as follows. Section 7.1 reviews the empirical literature on cluster-based industrial development in East Asia in comparison with the Ethiopian case and postulates several testable hypotheses. Section 7.2 describes our data collection method and the basic statistics concerning enterprise size, the educational and occupational backgrounds of owners, marketing and procurement, and enterprise growth. The results of the regression analyses are presented in Section 7.3, followed by a summary of the findings and policy implications in Section 7.4.

7.1   A comparative perspective and hypotheses

The production of leather shoes in Ethiopia dates from the late 1930s, when Armenian merchants founded two shoe factories in Addis Ababa.[3] These factories nurtured a number of shoemakers, who opened their own factories in Addis Ababa and trained their workers. Today, the neighborhood of Merkato, a huge marketplace in the city, swarms with shoemakers, wholesale shops dealing in leather, soles, and shoe accessories, and shoe retail stores.

Industrial clusters like this are ubiquitous in developing as well as developed countries because of the benefits of agglomeration economies originally pointed out by Marshall (1920). If transacting parties are located near each other, transport costs are saved, transaction costs due to imperfect information and imperfect contract enforcement are lowered, and good products and superior production practices diffuse quickly. Thus, industrial clusters enhance the division and specialization of labor among enterprises, the development of the market for skilled workers, and the dissemination of technical and managerial knowledge. Such agglomeration economies attract new enterprises to a cluster, making the cluster larger and reinforcing the agglomeration economies.

This leather shoe cluster in Addis Ababa is as large as successful shoe clusters in other countries, such as Agra in India (Knorringa, 1999), the Sinos Valley in Brazil (Schmitz, 1995; Bazan and Navas-Aleman, 2004), and Leon and Guadalajara in Mexico (Rabelloti, 1995). Yet, as in East Asia and elsewhere (Sonobe and Otsuka, 2006), the number of enterprises in the Ethiopian shoe industry grew rapidly in the early stage of industrial development due to spin-offs, that is, the establishment of new enterprises by workers who had formerly worked for pioneering enterprises and who copied their production methods. Many industries in developing countries, however, ceased to grow after they had expanded in terms of the number of enterprises, for example the garment cluster in Nairobi (Chapter 2; Akoten et al., 2006). An industry ceases to grow when the profitability of producing low-quality products falls as their market supply increases relative to market demand. This is typically the case if the increase in market supply is not accompanied by improvements in product quality. By contrast, those clusters where product quality was successfully improved have continued to grow, as clearly indicated by the case studies conducted by Sonobe and Otsuka (2006) in East Asia and Schmitz and Nadvi's (1999) compilation of case studies conducted in Latin America and South Asia.

According to the emerging literature on cluster-based industrial development in East Asia, quality improvement is accompanied by the introduction of new marketing methods and new production organizations (e.g., Sonobe et al., 2002, 2004, 2006). For example, the improvement of product quality is followed by branding and advertisement, since profits increase only after the improved quality is correctly perceived by potential buyers. The operation of own retail shops and the employment of sales agencies are useful in protecting brand names of differentiated products. The production of high-quality and differentiated products requires the use of high-quality and specially designed parts. The establishment of a brand name and dedicated marketing and procurement systems generates positive size effects, making a larger-scale operation advantageous, so that large enterprises emerge in the quality improvement phase.[4] Thus, the case studies of cluster-based industrial development commonly indicate that the further development of an industry after cluster formation is made possible by *multifaceted* innovations (or improvements) in technology, marketing, and organization, as was discussed in Chapter 1.

In view of the vital role played by multifaceted innovations in industrial development, questions arise as to what types of entrepreneurs carry them out and what characterizes early and late imitators. In all the eight case studies conducted by Sonobe and Otsuka (2006) in East Asia, the general human capital or formal education of entrepreneurs assumed greater importance in carrying out multifaceted innovations, even though there is no denying that the industry- and job-specific human capital acquired through experience is also important.

To investigate how similar the development pattern of the leather shoe industry in Ethiopia is to the East Asian experience, we advance the following testable hypotheses based on the above review of the literature on cluster-based industrial development in East Asia:

Hypothesis 7-1: Leading enterprises operated by highly educated and experienced entrepreneurs produce high-quality products and market them through their own distribution systems designed to reach customers directly.

Hypothesis 7-2: To produce high-quality differentiated products, such leading enterprises purchase high-quality inputs directly from producers.

Hypothesis 7-3: To take advantage of improved product quality, established brand names, and direct marketing and procurement systems, the leading enterprises operate on a larger scale than others.

Note that these three hypotheses are variants of Hypothesis 1 postulated in Chapter 1, that "the managerial human capital of enterprise managers is the major determinant of successful multifaceted innovations."

7.2 Characteristics of sample enterprises

7.2.1 Sampling

In early January 2005, we began conducting informal interviews with the shoemakers who were members of the Ethiopian Tanners, Footwear, and Leather Garments Manufacturing Association. After several interviews, we decided to conduct a formal survey of enterprises and began considering the sampling method. We visited the Central Statistics Authority and found that they did not have much information on leather shoe producers. They recommended that we visit the association for information, but the association had only the 14 largest shoemakers as members and knew little about non-members, who make up the vast majority of the shoe enterprises. Thus, we began visiting micro and small factories in back alleys behind the large marketplace named Merkato. Since these factories were trying to escape detection by the government authorities, including the statistical office, it was impossible for us to find them without being guided by a knowledgeable person. We were able to become acquainted with two such persons and to hire them as guides. Since each guide knew the whereabouts of only a limited number of shoemakers, making a comprehensive list of shoemakers even within a small part of the cluster would have required an unrealistically large number of guides. Instead, we requested several shoe store owners and our guides to write down the names of all the shoemakers that they knew, whether large or small, and then selected 100 enterprises randomly. Very new enterprises, founded in 2003 or later, are not included in the sample, partly because our guides were not familiar with such new enterprises, and partly because we were interested in the analysis of enterprise growth during the China shock, in which the data on very new enterprises could not be used. We conducted a survey in February and early March 2005 and obtained reliable data from 90 private enterprises.

In addition, we interviewed the managers of two SOEs, Tikure Abbay and Anbessa, the oldest shoe factories, founded by Armenians in the late 1930s. They were nationalized by the military government in 1974 and remained the largest and second largest shoemakers in the country. In recent years, private enterprises had caught up with these SOEs, and, thus, the latter were in process of privatization.[5] Although we obtained reliable data from these two SOEs, our analysis below focuses on the private enterprises because they were so different in behaviors.

7.2.2 Entrepreneur cohorts and enterprise sizes

Some entrepreneurs in the sample are second-generation shoe entrepreneurs in the sense that their parents were shoe factory owners, shoe workers, or shoe traders. In Table 7.1 as well as the other descriptive tables, the 90 private enterprises in the sample are classified into six types according to whether the owner was first-generation or second-generation and the years of operation by the current head of the enterprise. As column 4 of Table 7.1 shows, 18 sample enterprises were run by second-generation entrepreneurs. The oldest private enterprise in the sample is OK Jamaica, which was founded in 1969 by a former shoe factory worker, succeeded by his son in 1985. Another two private enterprises in the sample were founded by the current owners' parents. The rest, comprising 15 second-generation entrepreneurs, had not inherited their businesses from their parents, but their parents had engaged in shoe manufacturing or trading.

As shown in column 1 of Table 7.1, 47 sample enterprises were founded in 2001 or 2002. According to our respondents, the worst year for the industry was 2001, when the market was flooded with Chinese shoes, and the industry was still in poor shape in 2002. Figure 7.1 shows the changes in imports and exports of leather shoes and their average prices (c.i.f. (cost, insurance and freight) price in the case of imports and f.o.b. (free on board) price in the case of exports) from 1997 to 2006.[6] Since it is known that most, if not all, imported leather shoes came from China, it is clear that the China shock took place primarily in 2001. Imports, however, sharply declined thereafter. According to our interviews, this can be explained partly by the fact that, although the Chinese shoes that came to Ethiopia had better finishing and were more fashionable, consumers quickly learned that they were much less durable and, hence, began to prefer locally produced shoes. The low quality of imported products would be reflected in their average price, which was much lower than the average price of the shoes exported from Ethiopia. Moreover, the quality of domestically produced shoes had improved, which would have culminated in the recent surge of exports of Ethiopian shoes. It must also be pointed

Table 7.1   Number of sample enterprises, their average sizes, and owners' observable human capital in 2004 by owner type in a leather shoe cluster in Ethiopia

	Years of operation			
	2 to 4 years	5 to 9 years	10 years +	All
	(1)	(2)	(3)	(4)
Owner without a parent in the shoe business				
Number of observations	43	23	6	72
Average number of workers	5.0	6.3	7.9	5.7
Value added (US$1,000)	7.1	9.6	17.0	8.7
(Annual growth rate, 2002–4, %)	(27.6)	(13.3)	(24.0)	(23.1)
% entered university	2.3	0	0	1.4
Years of prior experience	10.2	10.7	10.8	10.4
Owner with a parent in the shoe business				
Number of observations	4	9	5	18
Average number of workers	5.8	20.6	58.8	27.9
Value added (US$1,000)	5.9	84.8	107.7	73.6
(Annual growth rate, 2002–4, %)	(44.0)	(44.6)	(9.8)	(34.3)
% entered university	25.0	44.4	60.0	44.4
Years of prior experience	7.1	4.4	4.5	5.0

out that the remaining imports from China are primarily women's footwear, of which durability is not the most important trait. The focus of this study, as well as almost all sample enterprises, is on the production of men's leather shoes.

Since shoe manufacturing is highly labor-intensive, the international competitiveness of this industry is determined largely by wage rate. Table 7.2 compares the average annual nominal wage earnings of workers in the urban leather industry in China with those of the leather shoe industry in Ethiopia based on our own survey data, both expressed in US dollars using the respective official exchange rates.[7] It is clear that the wage rate in Ethiopia is very low, less than one-half of that in China, which suggests that potentially Ethiopia has a comparative advantage in the shoe industry vis-à-vis China, to the extent that its production technology and management efficiency are not significantly inferior. This low wage rate in Ethiopia would also explain, at least partly, the decline in imports of leather shoes from China.

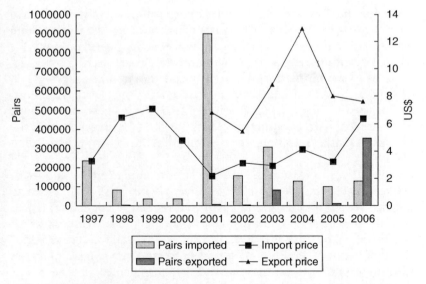

Figure 7.1 Number of pairs of imported and exported leather shoes and their average prices in Ethiopia, 1997–2006

Data source: Ethiopian Foreign Trade Statistics (various years).

Table 7.2 Comparison of nominal annual wage earnings in the urban leather industry in China and in the leather shoe industry in Ethiopia (US$ per year)[a]

	China (1)	Ethiopia (2)	Ratio (2) / (1)
2000	967	406	0.42
2001	992	–	–
2002	1,100	412	0.37
2003	1,164	–	–
2004	1,296	517	0.4
2005	1,526	–	–

[a]The urban leather industry in China refers to the manufacturing industries of leather, fur, feather, and their products in urban areas. The wage data of the leather shoe industry in Ethiopia are based on our own data. Wage earnings in local currencies are converted to US dollars using the official exchange rates.

Sources: *China Labor Statistical Yearbook* (various issues) for wage data and *China Statistical Yearbook* (2005) for the exchange rate between US dollars and Chinese Yuan, and IMF (2007) for the exchange rate between US dollars and Ethiopian birr.

Despite the China shock, the entry of new enterprises was very active in 2001 and 2002. The fact that the majority of the enterprises were new also indicates that only a small number of enterprises could survive in the face of intense market competition. Our guides were good examples: their own businesses had recently ended in failure, and they had become shoe workers employed on a piece-rate wage basis. Thus, both new entry and factory closure occurred frequently. These observations are consistent with Gunning and Mengistae's (2001) argument that the process of market selection was as strong in Africa as anywhere else in the 1990s.

Table 7.1 also presents the average size in terms of the number of workers and value added in 2004.[8] Clearly, enterprise size tended to increase with years of operation by the current entrepreneur, for which respondents provided two explanations. Firstly, the size of production is constrained by the size of working capital, especially cash for the purchase of leather and other materials. As an entrepreneur accumulates working capital, he can increase the size of his enterprise. Secondly, enterprise size also depends on the competence of the entrepreneur at managing personnel, designing shoes, costing, marketing, and so on, which is gained through learning by doing, including both his own development of useful ideas and imitation.

As shown in Table 7.1, the enterprises of the second-generation entrepreneurs tended to be larger, given the years of their operation. Their advantage over the first-generation entrepreneurs would arise from diverse sources, such as inherited talents, the home environment in which they were raised, and advice and financial support provided by parents. As mentioned earlier, only three second-generation entrepreneurs in the sample inherited enterprises from their parents. Moreover, one of these enterprises was smaller than the average of all the sample enterprises in 2004. Thus, most of the advantage of the second-generation shoe entrepreneurs is likely to come from channels other than the inheritance of the parent's business itself.

7.2.3   Characteristics of entrepreneurs

Almost all the parents of those entrepreneurs born outside Addis Ababa were farmers, whereas the parents of those entrepreneurs born in Addis Ababa were shoemakers, traders dealing in shoes, grains, and textiles, tailors, carpenters, mechanics, and a soldier.[9] In the parents' era, new shoemakers were young dwellers in Addis Ababa. Later on, young men and women also came from the provinces to become shoemakers. The parents of the second-generation entrepreneurs tended to have some education because most of them were raised in Addis Ababa. By contrast, a majority of the parents of the first-generation entrepreneurs had no education.

Of the 52 entrepreneurs born outside Addis Ababa, 45 were born in Butajira, which is located about 170 km south of Addis Ababa and is the heartland of Gurage, one of more than 80 ethnic groups in Ethiopia. Gurage people account for about 2 percent of the total population, but are said to play a disproportionately active part in the business world. In Mengistae's (2001) sample, which covers registered businesses in various industries in Addis Ababa, a third of the manufacturing enterprises are owned by Gurage entrepreneurs. In Lika's (1997) sample of shoemakers, two-thirds are Gurage.[10] In our sample, the presence of Gurage entrepreneurs is even stronger: they account for 86 percent in the full sample and 82 percent in the subsample of entrepreneurs born in Addis Ababa. The first- and second-generation entrepreneurs were similar in terms of ethnicity and the number of family members and relatives working in the leather shoe industry.

On average, the first-generation entrepreneurs had only 8.5 years of schooling, whereas the second-generation entrepreneurs had 11.8 years. The difference is statistically significant at the 1 percent level. During the survey, we obtained the impression that entrepreneurs tended to consider themselves highly educated if they had entered a university. If we apply this criterion, the first- and second-generation entrepreneurs appear even more different, as shown in the fifth and 11th rows in Table 7.1. Interestingly, the percentage of the second-generation entrepreneurs who entered a university increased with the years of operation. This observation suggests that high education increased the likelihood of enterprise survival, even though it seems difficult to establish the causality. The fact that highly educated sons chose to work in the shoe industry instead of going to the public and other sectors suggests that the shoe business had been expected to be profitable.[11] The majority of them majored in accounting.

The occupational backgrounds of the entrepreneurs were homogeneous. All but six of them were spin-offs, who had worked at shoe factories before becoming entrepreneurs. Of the six exceptions, two were former shoe traders, who were second-generation, and four came from other industries. The first- and second-generation entrepreneurs differ, however, in the years of prior experience in this industry. While the first-generation entrepreneurs had spent 10 years on average on acquiring skills and accumulating funds before starting up their own businesses, the second-generation entrepreneurs had spent only 5 years in preparation (see the sixth and 12th rows in Table 7.1).

7.2.4   Quality improvement

Because shoes were mainly handcrafted at micro and small factories, new entry required the purchase of only a small amount of leather and other materials for use in the first few weeks, and thus there was little sunk cost. As a result, a massive entry of new enterprises occurred every year. As mentioned earlier, however, many entrants exited the industry soon after, even though accurate statistical data on exit are unavailable. According to a knowledgeable respondent, the key to the survival and growth of a new entrant is to establish a good reputation for producing durable and attractive shoes with good leather, and in this way the currently large enterprises have grown large. This view seems to be shared widely in the shoe industry in Addis Ababa, as all the respondents agreed on the importance of product quality and reputation.

Table 7.3 shows the average factory price of men's leather shoes as a proxy for product quality.[12] Consistent with Hypothesis 7-1, the average price tended to be higher for those enterprises operated by experienced, second-generation entrepreneurs. The highest average price in 2004 was $17.34, recorded by OK Jamaica, the oldest and the fifth largest enterprise in our sample. Relatively new enterprises did not produce expensive shoes, partly because they could not afford to procure expensive leather, and partly because they had neither good marketing channels suitable for high-quality shoes nor the ability to develop attractive designs as yet. Thus, there was a wide spectrum of shoe prices, even though the importance of product quality was recognized by every shoemaker.[13]

Table 7.3 presents the data on marketing channels in 2004 as well. New enterprises were totally dependent on retail shops in Addis Ababa, wholesalers who hawk shoes in the provinces, and their agents for marketing. They did not have any other marketing channels such as their own retail shops, exports, or special orders of working shoes from the government and large companies. Consistent with Hypothesis 7-1, long-established enterprises, especially those operated by second-generation entrepreneurs, tended to develop some such channels to directly reach the ultimate customers. The table also indicates that the fraction of sales revenues from such direct marketing was positively correlated with the average price, and that the experienced, second-generation entrepreneurs increased this fraction.

Export was negligible in 2004 in the sample as a whole, but it accounted for 25 percent of the sales at Ramsey and 5 percent at three enterprises, including OK Jamaica. Ramsey was the fourth largest private enterprise in the sample in 2004, and exported military shoes

Table 7.3 Price of men's shoes and marketing channels of products and materials in 2004 by owner type in a leather shoe cluster in Ethiopia

	Years of operation			
	2 to 4 years	5 to 9 years	10 years +	All
	(1)	(2)	(3)	(4)
Owner without a parent in the shoe business				
Men's shoe price (USD)	6.14	6.90	8.03	6.54
Direct marketing (%)	0	0.7	15.8	2.8
Leather directly from tanneries[a]	0	3.0	13.3	2.1
Soles imported (%)[b]	0	0	10.0	0.8
Soles directly from factories (%)[c]	0	0	23.3	1.9
Owner with a parent in the shoe business				
Men's shoe price (USD)	6.66	9.28	12.52	9.60
Direct marketing (%)	0	4.4	76.0	23.3
Leather directly from tanneries[a]	0	11.1	100	22.2
Soles imported (%)[b]	0	0	38.0	10.6
Soles directly from factories (%)[c]	0	44.4	22.0	28.3

[a]This row shows the percentage of the value of leather bought directly from leather tanneries. The other source of leather is the wholesalers of shoe materials, whose shops are located in Merkato.
[b]This is the percentage of the value of shoe soles imported.
[c]This is the percentage of the value of shoe soles bought directly from sole factories, including enterprises' own sole factories. Other soles are procured from shoe material wholesalers, whose shops are located in Merkato.

to neighboring countries. OK Jamaica was exporting high-quality men's shoes mainly to South Africa, Botswana, and Israel. To increase exports, both enterprises were building large factories in an industrial park newly developed by the government. In this industrial park, about eight other large shoemakers were building or planning new factories. As in the case of the metalwork cluster in Kenya reported in Chapter 5, here too successful enterprises move from the congested cluster to industrial parks or zones. Among them was Peacock, the third largest private enterprise in 2000 and the largest in 2004 in our sample. Its new factory had commenced operation just before we visited it in January 2005, and it had just shipped the first batch of OEM (own equipment manufacturing) exports to an Italian company, under the guidance of a few Italian technicians dispatched by that company. After our survey, we revisited this factory twice. In June 2005, the entrepreneur said that its production had doubled in a half-year with the same workforce and machines. In February 2006, he said that its export business had been growing fast. Such development is consistent with the export data shown in Figure 7.1.

Table 7.3 also presents the data on material procurement, which are available only for 2004. Whether large or small, most shoemakers in Addis Ababa purchase leather, soles, and accessories. Large and small enterprises, however, differed in procurement sources. Consistent with Hypothesis 7-2, large enterprises purchased leather and soles in bulk directly from tanneries and factories or from abroad, whereas small enterprises procured materials completely from material wholesalers in the marketplace. Bulk purchases were associated with volume discounts and were hence cost-effective.

In Table 7.3, imported Chinese soles used by the producers of low-price shoes are not treated as imports, because they were bought in the marketplace. What the table treats as imported soles are high-quality soles imported from Italy, Spain, and some other European countries. Beginning by importing soles, these shoemakers gradually developed connections with European enterprises and obtained information from them on advanced technology and the latest fashions. Another trend clearly seen among the largest enterprises was to establish their own factories to produce rubber soles using molds imported from Taiwan or China. As of 2004, three sample enterprises and some other large shoemakers owned sole factories.

Thus, old enterprises run by second-generation entrepreneurs improved product quality by using expensive leather and soles, increased direct transactions with customers, and reduced procurement costs by purchasing materials directly from factories. In addition, they went to the United States and Europe as well as neighboring countries to visit factories, shoe stores, and trade fairs. The leaders of the industry made a variety of observations abroad, which led them to adopt different business models. In fact, the second-generation entrepreneurs with more than 10 years of operation had visited European countries twice a year in the last 5 years, while others never did. Although it is difficult to prove statistically the importance of learning from abroad in the development of enterprises in developing countries, it seems clear that successful international technology transfer is the key to success in this industry in Ethiopia.[14] Such an observation is consistent with Hypothesis 3 specified in Chapter 1. While some found it profitable to specialize in unfashionable products, such as military boots, others attached importance to learning from Europe through OEM export. While some were eager to mechanize production processes, one entrepreneur was determined to develop the flexible division of labor among a large number of shoemakers by taking full advantage of the fact that they are clustered, which is reminiscent of the flexible specialization developed in central and northwestern Italy, as described by Piore and Sabel (1984).

With these active leaders, the private sector of the industry achieved strong recovery from the China shock. The numbers in parentheses in Table 7.1 show the average annual growth rates of the US dollar equivalent of value added by the type of entrepreneur. The China shock hit the enterprises operated by the experienced, second-generation entrepreneurs most seriously, but even they were able to record positive growth in value added in the latter 2 years under study. Many other enterprises that survived the market competition maintained positive growth even in the middle of the China shock and achieved fast growth in more recent years. The average annual growth rate of the sample enterprises was 10 percent from 2000 to 2002 and 25 percent from 2002 to 2004.[15]

7.3   Estimation methods and results

7.3.1   Specification

To test Hypotheses 7-1 to 7-3 advanced in Section 7.1, we examine the determinants of five dependent variables: (i) the price of men's shoes, (ii) the fraction of sales revenue from direct marketing, (iii) the fraction of the amount of leather that was directly procured from tanneries, (iv) the fraction of soles directly procured from sole factories, and (v) enterprise size in terms of value added. We also estimate a function that explains the determinants of enterprise growth, following the lead of the existing studies of enterprise growth in Africa. According to Hypotheses 7-1 and 7-2, the enterprises with highly educated and experienced entrepreneurs tend to produce more expensive shoes, and have greater proportions of direct marketing and direct procurement of materials. Hypothesis 7-3 predicts that these enterprises tend to be larger in production size. To capture the effects of high education, we use a dummy variable, called university dummy, which is equal to 1 if the entrepreneur was admitted to a university and 0 otherwise. To capture the effects of management experience, we use the years of operation by the current entrepreneur.

To test Hypotheses 7-1 and 7-2, we regress the dependent variables (i) to (iv) on the university dummy and the years of operation as well as other exogenous variables. Of the four dependent variables, shoe prices and marketing are available for 2000, 2002, and 2004. Hence, these dependent variables may be denoted Y_{it} with subscripts i and t indicating enterprises and years, respectively. The data on the direct procurement of materials are available only for 2004. The explanatory variables, which characterize enterprises, are all time-invariant, and the vector of these variables is denoted by X_i without subscript t. The coefficients of X_i may change over time. Thus, the regression equations we estimate are of the following form:

$$Y_{it} = X_i \alpha_t + e_{it}, \tag{7.1}$$

where α_t is a vector of parameters to be estimated and e_{it} is an error term. Since all the explanatory variables are time-invariant, panel data models (i.e., fixed- and random-effects models) are not worth considering here. The shoe price equation is estimated with OLS, but the functions explaining the direct marketing proportion and the proportion of the direct procurement of leather are estimated with the two-limit Tobit estimator because the data on these variables are censored at 0 and 1. The model for the direct procurement of soles degenerates into a Probit model because this proportion happens to be either 0 or 1 at all the sample enterprises.

To test Hypothesis 7-3, enterprise size in terms of the logarithm of value added (V) is regressed on X_i:

$$\ln V_{it} = X_i \beta_t + u_{it}, \tag{7.2}$$

where β_t are coefficients which are allowed to vary over time, and u_{it} is an error term. We also ran growth regressions using the specification extensively used in the empirical literature on economic growth (e.g., Barro and Sala-i-Martin, 1992) and enterprise growth (e.g., Evans, 1987). This can be derived from equation (7.2) as follows. Let γ be a convergence parameter to be estimated, and let V_{it-1} denote the lagged value added. By adding $\gamma \ln V_{it-1}$ to the right-hand side of equation (7.2) and then subtracting its equivalent, $\gamma(X_i \beta_{t-1} + u_{it-1})$, we obtain

$$\begin{aligned}\ln V_{it} &= X_i \beta_t + u_{it} + \gamma \ln V_{it-1} - \gamma(X_i \beta_{t-1} + u_{it-1}) \\ &= \gamma \ln V_{it-1} + X_i(\beta_t - \gamma_{t-1}) + (u_{it} - \gamma u_{it-1}).\end{aligned} \tag{7.3}$$

Subtracting $\ln V_{it-1}$ from both sides of equation (7.3) and rearranging yields the familiar growth regression equation,

$$\ln V_{it} - \ln V_{it-1} = \delta_1 \ln V_{it-1} + X_i \delta_2 + w_{it},\qquad(7.4)$$

where $\delta_1 = \gamma - 1$, $\delta_2 = \beta_t - \gamma\beta_{t-1}$, and $w_{it} = u_{it} - \gamma u_{it-1}$. In the literature on enterprise growth in Africa, McPherson (1996), Ramachandran and Shah (1999), Gunning and Mengistae (2001), and Mengistae (2001) commonly find that initial enterprise size, $\ln V_{it-1}$, and the years of operation have negative effects on enterprise growth, $\ln V_{it} - \ln V_{it-1}$.[16] McPherson (1996), Ramachandran and Shah (1999), and Mengistae (2001, 2006) find positive effects of entrepreneur's schooling on enterprise growth.

7.3.2 Estimation results

Table 7.4 presents the estimated functions that explain the determinants of shoe prices (see columns 1 to 3), the direct marketing proportion (column 4), and the direct procurement proportion (columns 5 and 6). The dummy for the second-generation entrepreneurs does not have a significant effect in any column. These results clearly indicate that the differences in product quality, marketing, and procurement behaviors between the first- and second-generation entrepreneurs, as indicated in Tables 7.4 and 7.5, came from the differences in their education levels or some other attributes.

In column 1, the data in the 3 years under study are pooled, and the coefficients are assumed to be constant over time. This assumption is valid except for the coefficient of the university dummy, which became much smaller in 2004 than in 2000 and 2002, as shown in columns 2 and 3. The years of operation or the management experience always had a positive and highly significant effect on shoe prices. The effect of high education was weakened in 2004 by the fact that some of the highly educated entrepreneurs, including the owners of Ramsey and Peacock, increased production of less expensive military boots and casual shoes. These entrepreneurs had just begun focusing on the mechanized mass production of standardized shoes for export markets. The coefficients of the year dummies in column 1 indicate that the average shoe price in 2000 and 2002 was a little less than 90 percent of that in 2004.

Consistently with Hypothesis 7-1, column 4 of Table 7.4 shows that the university dummy and the years of operation of the current entrepreneur had positive and significant effects on the proportion of direct marketing. Although not reported in the table, we ran regressions separately for the 3 years and found that the coefficient of the university

Table 7.4   Determinants of product pricing, marketing, and input procurement in a leather shoe cluster in Ethiopia[a]

Dependent variable	ln(price)			Direct marketing	Direct procurement	
					Leather	Soles
Sample year	00, 02, 04	00, 02	04	00, 02, 04	04	04
Estimator	OLS			Tobit		Probit
	(1)	(2)	(3)	(4)	(5)	(6)
Second-	0.085	−0.010	0.166	0.108	0.864	0.918
generation	(1.18)	(−0.10)	(1.65)	(0.49)	(0.52)	(1.52)
University	0.211*	0.348**	0.103	0.652**	2.327	0.467
	(2.25)	(2.58)	(0.80)	(2.54)	(1.14)	(0.60)
Years of	0.029**	0.029**	0.028**	0.083**	0.367*	0.079*
operation	(6.05)	(4.49)	(4.00)	(5.78)	(1.79)	(2.10)
Years of prior	−0.004	−0.001	−0.006	0.023*	0.043	−0.103
experience	(−1.12)	(−0.31)	(−1.18)	(2.27)	(0.67)	(−1.52)
Gurage	−0.052	−0.027	−0.048	−0.082	−1.232	−0.145
	(−0.76)	(−0.26)	(−0.52)	(−0.42)	(−0.77)	(−0.18)
Year 2000	−0.119*	0.003		0.017		
	(−1.92)	(0.05)		(0.11)		
Year 2002	−0.135**			−0.086		
	(−2.85)			(−0.57)		
Intercept	1.782**	1.611**	1.799**	−1.518**	5.415	−1.575
	(23.10)	(14.65)	(17.77)	(−4.20)	(1.62)	(−1.79)
Sample size	204	109	89	216	90	90
R-squared	0.34	0.34	0.34			
No. of left- and right-censored obs.				Left: 188 Right: 4	Left: 81 Right: 6	

[a]Numbers in parentheses are *t*-statistics. **Significant at the 1% level, *at the 5% level (one-sided tests except for the intercept).

dummy increased from 0.54 in 2000 to 0.65 in 2002 and to 0.77 in 2004. While these increases are not drastic, they lend further support to Hypothesis 7-1. An additional finding is that years of prior experience in the shoe industry had a positive and significant effect on direct marketing. This result, together with the positive effect of years of operation, suggests that the importance of direct marketing was strongly recognized by those who had long experience in shoemaking.

In columns 5 and 6, the effects of the university dummy and management experience on direct procurement proportions are all positive, consistent with Hypothesis 7-2. Those of the university dummy, however, are insignificant, and the effect of management experience on the direct procurement of leather is only marginally significant. Although not reported in the table, the OLS estimates of these effects are positive and significant. In the Tobit and Probit estimations, the statistical significance of these effects is low because only a very small number of the sample enterprises procured materials directly from producers. Indeed, only nine enterprises procured leather directly from tanneries, and nine enterprises procured soles directly from factories, of which six did both. Five of these six enterprises were owned by entrepreneurs with more than 10 years of management experience, and four were owned by highly educated entrepreneurs. These enterprises were all eager to export their products to large foreign markets.

Table 7.5 presents the estimated functions that explain the determinants of enterprise size and enterprise growth. While the coefficients in the size function are related to those in the growth function, as shown in equations (7.3) and (7.4), the relationships among the estimated coefficients in Table 7.5 are not exact because the samples used in estimating the size function for $t-1$ and t and the growth function for the period from $t-1$ to t were a little different due to new entry and missing data. As in Table 7.4, the dummy for the second-generation entrepreneurs does not have a significant effect in any column in Table 7.5.

Consistent with Hypothesis 7-3, both the university dummy and the years of management experience had positive and highly significant effects on enterprise size, as shown in columns 1 to 4. The negative and significant coefficients of year dummies in column 1 indicate that the average enterprise size in 2000 and 2002 was as small as Exp(−0.53), or about 60 percent of that in 2004, because of the China shock. Columns 2 to 4 show that the magnitude of the effect of high education on enterprise size declined in 2002 and increased in 2004. The effect was weaker in 2002 because the large enterprises operated by highly educated entrepreneurs were most seriously hit by the China shock. For example, the sales revenue of Kangaroo, the largest private shoemaker in 2000, was reduced by half in 2 years. In accordance with the drastically weakened effect of the university dummy on enterprise size, its effect on growth was negative and significant in the period from 2000 to 2002, as shown in column 5. Such an impasse might drive the highly educated entrepreneurs to seriously consider the mass production of standardized but high-quality shoes for export.

In the recovery phase from 2002 to 2004, the university dummy had an increased effect on enterprise size and a positive and significant effect on growth, as shown in columns 4 and 6, respectively. Its

Table 7.5   Determinants of enterprise size and growth in a leather shoe cluster in Ethiopia[a]

Dependent variable	lnV$_t$				lnV$_t$– lnV$_{t-1}$	
Sample year and period	00, 02, 04	00	02	04	00–2	02–4
Independent variables	(1)	(2)	(3)	(4)	(5)	(6)
lnV$_{t-1}$					0.041	−0.143**
					(0.34)	(−2.48)
Second- generation	−0.011	−0.191	−0.081	0.135	0.266	0.301
	(−0.04)	(−0.32)	(−0.18)	(0.31)	(0.76)	(1.33)
University	1.618**	2.415**	1.157*	1.547**	−1.525*	0.529*
	(4.71)	(3.25)	(2.07)	(2.73)	(−2.42)	(2.03)
Years of operation	0.115**	0.130**	0.123**	0.101**	−0.042	−0.011
	(6.16)	(3.22)	(4.09)	(3.27)	(−1.66)	(−0.79)
Years of prior experience	−0.018	−0.014	−0.030	−0.009	−0.042**	0.017
	(−1.25)	(−0.40)	(−1.31)	(−0.37)	(−3.19)	(1.21)
Gurage	−0.024	−0.033	−0.167	0.111	−0.846**	0.271
	(−0.09)	(−0.05)	(−0.41)	(0.27)	(−3.34)	(1.54)
Year 2000	−0.543*					
	(−2.27)					
Year 2002	−0.526**					
	(−2.86)					
Intercept	8.055**	7.266**	7.778**	7.911**	1.556*	1.227*
	(26.79)	(8.80)	(17.54)	(17.85)	(2.32)	(2.52)
Sample size	214	39	86	89	36	85
R-squared	0.37	0.53	0.33	0.30	0.41	0.12

[a]Numbers in parentheses are *t*-statistics. For columns 5 and 6, *t*-statistics are calculated based on the White standard errors robust to heteroskedasticity. **Significant at the 1% level, *at the 5% level (one-sided tests except for the intercept).

effect on enterprise size, however, did not regain the magnitude that it had had just before the China shock. There are two possible explanations for this. One is that Chinese shoes still occupy the women's shoe segment of the leather shoe market, which used to be monopolized by some domestic enterprises with highly educated entrepreneurs. Another explanation is that multifaceted improvements led by highly educated entrepreneurs were just at the incipient stage. The size expansion of the innovative enterprises observed in the shoe industry in Addis Ababa was not yet as spectacular as Sonobe et al., (2004, 2006) have observed in several industries in East Asia, such as the electric appliance industry in Wenzhou and the motorcycle industry in Chongqing, where innovative enterprises achieved tremendous expansion in size. Qualitatively, however, the way in which the development process unfolds itself in Addis Ababa is similar to that in East Asia; that is, quality improvement is accompanied by the adoption of new marketing and procurement strategies, improvements in production organization, and the emergence of large enterprises, and these multifaceted improvements are led by highly educated and experienced entrepreneurs.

While Mengistae (2001) found that enterprises owned by Gurage entrepreneurs were larger and grew faster than other enterprises, our estimates of the Gurage effect on enterprise size are insignificant, as shown in columns 1 to 4. Our result differs from Mengistae's probably because the overwhelming majority of our sample entrepreneurs are Gurage. The Gurage effect on enterprise growth is negative and highly significant in column 5 but it is positive and insignificant in column 6. We are unable to explain these results. In column 5, years of prior experience as shoe workers have a negative and significant effect, which suggests that those entrepreneurs experienced in trading performed better than former shoe workers when the industry suffered from the China shock. This finding reinforces the importance of trading experience in managing manufacturing enterprises, as argued in Hypothesis 1 in Chapter 1.

The existing analyses of enterprise growth in SSA use enterprise data gathered from various industries, and find that old incumbents hardly grow, even though they are more likely to survive than new entrants. This is because industries in SSA as a whole are so static, without technological and managerial progress, that only newly established enterprises have the opportunity to grow by learning what incumbents already know. Unlike these results, our estimates of the growth effect of the years of operation are insignificant, as shown in columns 5 and 6, which suggests that old enterprises grow as rapidly as new ones. By contrast, this variable has positive and persistent effects on the enterprise size (see columns 1 to 4). Probably these estimation results reflect the fact that the industry under study is dynamically growing based on learning from abroad.

7.4 Concluding remarks

The leather shoe industry in Ethiopia is producing shoes exportable to the markets in the developed countries. The industry took back the domestic market from Chinese shoes, which had flooded the market around 2001. Since then, the industry has been growing vigorously. These developments are good news to those who are interested in poverty reduction in SSA, because Ethiopia is one of the poorest countries and the leather shoe industry is one of the most labor-intensive industries, which provide ample employment opportunities for the poor.

This chapter has found that the industry's growth has been driven not only by the entry of new enterprises but, more importantly, by the growth of leading enterprises and followers, as in East Asia. Moreover, it has presented supportive evidence for the hypothesis that highly educated entrepreneurs endowed with ample managerial human capital introduce new ideas on product design, production methods, labor management, marketing, and procurement because they face fierce competition from China as well as from a swarm of micro-entrepreneurs, who enter the market with little investment. These findings strongly support Hypothesis 1. Note that, although we emphasize the effect of declining output prices due to active entry of new enterprises on the effort to undertake innovations in our endogenous model of cluster-based industrial development discussed in Chapter 1, declining output prices due to imports of cheap commodities may also induce quality improvement.

In order to compete with cheap imported products or to promote exports, there is no choice but to carry out multifaceted innovations. Fortunately for Ethiopia, some entrepreneurs who are endowed with large managerial human capital actively learned production methods, product designs, and marketing methods from Italy and other advanced countries. Entrepreneurs in East Asia also learn regularly from more advanced countries. It is, therefore, no wonder that, qualitatively, the development process of the leather shoe industry in Ethiopia bears close similarities to the process of the cluster-based industrial development observed in East Asia. The lessons we should learn from the recent experience of the leather shoe industry in Ethiopia are that international technology transfer and the role of managerial human capital, which are complementary, are of the utmost importance. This conclusion also applies to the case of the electric fittings industry in Pakistan discussed in Chapter 6, where managers endowed with managerial human capital introduced new ideas through learning from India and China. These Ethiopian and Pakistani experiences are in contrast to the experience of the garment industry in Kenya analyzed in Chapter 2, where entrepreneurship is scarce and learning from abroad is totally lacking.

Part IV

The Success and Failure of Industrial Development Strategies

8
International Knowledge Transfer in a Garment Cluster in Bangladesh

Having demonstrated the importance of traders and managerial human capital in carrying out multifaceted innovations in previous chapters, Part IV (Chapters 8 and 9) explores how the success or failure of industrial development is governed by the development strategies of the private sector and the government, based on the case studies of the garment clusters in Bangladesh and Ethiopia. It will be shown that successful cluster-based development requires not only active roles of traders and competent managers but also international technology transfer.

Whether knowledge spills over from foreign ventures to local enterprises in developing countries depends on the absorptive capacity of the latter, according to the excellent survey of the literature by Crespo and Fontoura (2007). Similarly, producers of garments, shoes, and toys in developing countries may or may not have the capacity to learn how to undertake high value-added activities, such as designing, marketing, and branding, from their transactions with large companies in developed countries, according to the interesting case studies of global value chains compiled by Schmitz (2004). These findings are reminiscent of Arrow's (1985, p. 201) explanation for the vast differences in income levels among countries: "Information exchange is costly not so much because it is hard to transmit but because it is difficult to receive. A teacher realizes all too painfully the difficulty of getting information into a student's head. Perhaps we should not be totally surprised that the acquisition of information is not the same as its transmission."

We have only meager empirical knowledge about what helps entrepreneurs in developing countries acquire knowledge conducive to industrial development. How difficult is it for them to receive knowledge from developed countries? How easily does new knowledge that they acquire spill over to other entrepreneurs or workers? What types of institutions may be developed to internalize spillover externalities? Appropriate development policies depend on the answers to these questions.

This chapter attempts to answer some of these questions by examining primary enterprise data collected from the export-oriented garment industry in Bangladesh. The industry has received foreign direct investments and sold products to large foreign buyers in developed countries. These contacts with large companies in developed countries are said to have provided garment producers in Bangladesh with ample opportunity to absorb advanced technological and managerial knowledge (e.g., Rhee, 1990; Quddus and Rashid, 2000; Siddiqi, 2005). Indeed, the industry in this least developed country has achieved spectacular growth for the last 25 years, as Easterly's (2002) popular book has attested to. However, the success in learning is not the same as having the opportunity to learn. This study explores how the industry has absorbed knowledge from developed countries and how such knowledge contributed to the growth of the industry as a whole.

Knowledge transmission and absorption are difficult to measure, however. Proxies that have been used in the existing studies tend to be rough. For example, a number of studies of spillovers from foreign direct investment use the presence of foreign ventures in the vicinity of a domestic enterprise as a proxy for the enterprise's access to new knowledge (Crespo and Fontoura, 2007). To construct a better proxy, we interviewed 132 entrepreneurs, that is, businessmen called managing directors, general managers, or proprietors, running garment trading houses and knitwear factories, including the largest factories in the country. We asked, among other things, how they acquire and update their knowledge of technology, management, and marketing.

We find that more highly educated entrepreneurs have better business results, and that the average education level of the entrepreneurs in this industry is very high. This is probably a reason why they have succeeded in continuously updating their knowledge of mass production, marketing, management, and fashion. We also find that the good performers in the industry tend to be those enterprises that are operated by entrepreneurs who have received intensive training in developed countries. In addition to the training of entrepreneurs, the employment of foreign experts is also found to be effective in improving the performance of enterprises. Another important finding of this study is that the advanced knowledge acquired through training abroad became of benefit to a large number of enterprises through the division of labor between producers and traders as well as through knowledge spillovers.

If some ex-trainees did not have enough financial or physical capital to start manufacturing, they became traders and made use of their advanced knowledge for the benefit of producers who did not possess such knowledge. While some existing case studies of industrial development in developing countries discuss the role of traders in knowledge absorption, they do not provide any statistical evidence of the manner in which traders contribute to the industrial development because of the lack of data on traders (e.g., Schmitz and Nadvi, 1999; Sonobe and Otsuka, 2006).

The rest of this chapter is organized as follows. The next section briefly reviews the development of the garment industry in Bangladesh. Section 8.2 advances three hypotheses to be tested with the enterprise data. Section 8.3 explains our method of data collection and presents a descriptive analysis to characterize the sample enterprises. Hypothesis testing is carried out in Section 8.4, followed by the summary of the findings and the policy implications contained in Section 8.5.

8.1 Historical background and hypotheses

In the late 1970s, Bangladesh had negligible exports of garments and was not subject to export restriction under the Multi-Fiber Arrangement (MFA). To take advantage of the lack of export restriction and the abundance of low-wage labor, the Daewoo Corporation of South Korea planned to develop a production base in Bangladesh, and teamed up with Desh Garment Ltd. Daewoo sent 130 workers from Desh to South Korea to train them for 8 months. Within 2 years after the training, however, almost all the trainees had left Desh to start their own garment businesses (Rhee, 1990). Easterly (2002, pp.147–8) comments: "This explosion of garment companies started by ex-Desh workers brought Bangladesh its $2 billion in garment sales today."

In 1982, the government launched a new industrial policy to promote the garment industry with such instruments as the duty-free import of garment machinery and bonded warehouse facilities (e.g., Quddus and Rashid, 2000; Siddiqi, 2005). Textile and garment companies in South Korea and other newly industrialized countries (NIEs) in East Asia continued to invest in their factories in export processing zones in Dhaka, the capital city, and Chittagong, the largest port city, in Bangladesh. As in the case of the Desh–Daewoo training, they sent Bangladeshi workers to their home countries for intensive training, and many of the trainees, some time after returning to Bangladesh, moved to other factories or started their own factories or trading houses.

As a result of the rapid growth, the garment industry was brought under the quota system in 1986. The system is said to have favored Bangladesh producers because it protected them from foreign competitors and because the quota given to Bangladesh was generous relative to those given to India and Sri Lanka (e.g., Mlachila and Yang, 2004; Siddiqi, 2005; Saxena and Wiebe, 2005). Another important event in 1986 was that the Export Promotion Bureau of Bangladesh and the United Nations Development Programme (UNDP) sent several knitwear producers to Italy, Germany and Poland, which helped the industry understand the latest production techniques and export market conditions, according to Hoq (2004). It is curious that, unlike the case in other countries, both the government and donor agencies support learning from abroad.

From the late 1980s through the 1990s, the center of gravity of the industry shifted from foreign ventures to local producers and traders. The local producers and traders increased exports to large retailers and branded marketers in Europe and North America. These customers developed new designs at their headquarters and sold the new products under their own brands through their own distribution channels. However, the production was subcontracted to producers in developing countries. The case studies of such global value chains connecting suppliers in Asia and Latin America to developed countries find that working to the specifications set by global buyers helped the suppliers improve production efficiency and adopt sophisticated product lines, even though global buyers discouraged suppliers from developing their own designs, brands, and marketing channels (e.g., Gereffi, 1999; Tewari, 1999; Schmitz and Knorringa, 2000; Bazan and Navas-Aleman, 2004; Giuliani et al., 2005). The same seems to hold true in the case of the suppliers in Bangladesh.

Table 8.1 shows how the number of garment producers, their employment, export value, and the share of garment export in the country's total export earnings increased from 1983 to 2005. In 2005, the industry earned more than 5 billion US dollars from exports, comprised 4,100 manufacturing enterprises, employed 2 million workers, and accounted for 75 percent of the country's total export earnings (Bangladesh Export Promotion Bureau, 2005). Although not shown in the table, the number of garment traders, intermediating local producers, and global buyers has also increased. Today, about 600 traders are registered (BGMEA, 2005/6), but they represent the tip of the iceberg because traders have no legal obligation to register, unlike producers. The location of garment producers and traders is concentrated in the greater Dhaka and

Table 8.1   Growth of the garment industry in Bangladesh

	Number of producers	Employment (million workers)	Export value (billion USD)	% of garments in the country's export earnings
1983/4	134	0.04	0.03	3.9
1987/8	685	0.28	0.43	35.2
1991/2	1,163	0.58	1.18	59.3
1995/6	2,353	1.29	2.55	65.6
1999/00	3,200	1.60	4.35	75.6
2004/5	4,107	2.00	5.17	74.3

Source: Bangladesh Export Promotion Bureau (2005).

Chittagong areas. The Dhaka area has approximately 3,500 producers and is sprawling out to the north, whereas the Chittagong area has 600. Most traders are located in Dhaka.

When the garment industry in Bangladesh was small, global buyers used their offices in other Asian cities to deal with their suppliers in Bangladesh. As the industry grew, it became profitable for some global buyers to set up buying offices in Dhaka. With buying offices in Dhaka, it became easy for them to procure garments directly from local producers. By bypassing local traders, the buyers and producers save brokerage fees and may improve quality control. Moreover, some global buyers use the internet to seek competing bids for export orders. These developments have considerably reduced the importance of local traders in intermediation (Rahman, 2005). In response, some local traders have launched their own production of garments, particularly knitwear.

In 1994, the international community decided to abolish the MFA. The quota system was gradually phased out, starting in 1995, and abolished in 2005. Quota elimination allows global buyers to import as many garments as they like from their favorite suppliers, thereby putting competitive pressure on suppliers (e.g., Khan, 2004; Rahman, 2004). Their competition centers around higher quality, lower prices, and quicker delivery. In Bangladesh, the emphasis on quick delivery due to intensified competition has put the producers of woven garments, such as shirts and skirts, at a disadvantage relative to knitwear producers. This is because the woven garment producers depend heavily on imported woven textile, which is prone to delays in delivery, whereas the knitwear producers have an abundant and quick supply of domestically produced yarn (Siddiqi, 2005). Moreover, knitwear producers in Bangladesh were able to find new markets for sweaters and cardigans.

As a result, the knitwear sector has grown much faster than the woven garment sector since 1995 in terms of both the number of producers and export earnings, as shown in Table 8.2.

Intensified competition has triggered various reactions from garment producers and traders, according to our interviews with the leaders of the Garment Manufacturers and Exporters Association (BGMEA) and the Knitwear Manufacturers and Exporters Association (BKMEA). For example, producers hire an increasing number of foreign experts, mostly from India and Sri Lanka, in order to improve product quality and production efficiency. In China, the state owned enterprises (SOEs) absorbed technologies from Japan and other developed countries, and private enterprises poached engineers from SOEs (Sonobe et al., 2006). For Bangladesh, important sources of foreign experts are India and Sri Lanka. Another example is the large investment in equipment and the improvement of working conditions undertaken by the garment producers to comply with the standards and regulations of developed countries regarding labor, safety, environment, and human rights protection (e.g., Rahman, 2005). Global buyers prefer factories that comply with these codes of conduct, because they are under pressure from consumer groups and labor unions in their home countries (Schmitz, 2005).

During the phasing-out period of the quota system, the garment industry in Bangladesh continued to increase its world market share from 1.2 percent in 1995 to 2.0 percent in 2000, and further to 2.3 percent in 2005 (WTO, 2007). In the year after the quota abolition,

Table 8.2 Number of enterprises and export value by sector in Bangladesh, 1995–2005[a]

Year	Woven garment sector			Knitwear sector		
	No. of enterprises	Export value (million USD)		No. of enterprises	Export value (million USD)	
		Total	Per enterprise		Total	Per enterprise
1995/96	1,646	1,835	1.11	350	393	1.12
2000/01	2,318	3,364	1.45	1,044	1,496	1.43
2002/03	1,997	3,258	1.63	1,229	1,654	1.35
2004/05	1,928	3,220	1.67	1,523	2,536	1.66

[a] A fiscal year starts in July and ends in June.

Sources: BGMEA (various years), BKMEA (2005), and Bangladesh Export Promotion Bureau (2005).

the industry increased its export earnings by 23 percent, according to BGMEA.

Among various issues related to the development process of the garment industry in Bangladesh, we are particularly interested in the impact of the training that the entrepreneurs received in developed countries, including South Korea. The high growth of the industry began with the training of 130 workers from Desh at Daewoo. We are also interested in the determinants of entrepreneurial ability or managerial human capital to adjust to the intensified competition, because the sustainability of the growth of the industry will depend on this human capital. To address these issues, this section develops three testable hypotheses.

To our surprise, Hypothesis 3 of this study, that the transfer of knowledge from developed to developing countries is the key to successful industrial development in developing countries, has not been widely accepted. For example, the literature on foreign direct investment spillovers has yielded mixed results (Crespo and Fontoura, 2007), and the studies of global value chains seldom carry out statistical analyses. Thus, we would like to advance the following testable hypothesis:

Hypothesis 8-1: The producers and traders who received intensive training in developed countries tend to hire foreign experts to improve production efficiency, thereby expanding the size of their operation.

Here, conceptually we assume that the training and employment of foreign experts shift the marginal profit curve upward and that the enterprise operates at the size where the marginal profit equals zero. In this sense, operation size serves as an indicator of enterprise performance. The effect of training on performance will be difficult to capture accurately because knowledge leaks or spills over to untrained entrepreneurs, but it is hard to imagine that knowledge spillovers equalize enterprise performances completely.

Easterly (2002, pp.146–8) emphasizes that the knowledge transferred from developed countries contributed to the development of the industry as a whole because the "knowledge leaks." Although there is no doubt that the knowledge leaked, it does not follow that all the knowledge possessed by the ex-trainees spills over. Because the ex-trainees have an advantage in knowledge-intensive activities, they would benefit from transactions with those who have a disadvantage in such activities. According to the case studies in Asia and Latin America, traders often play an important role in bringing technological knowledge and market information to producers (Schmitz and Nadvi, 1999; Sonobe and Otsuka, 2006). It is likely that those ex-trainees who are endowed with such knowledge, but not financial and physical capital, would act as traders.

Such division of labor between traders and producers would be fostered by the cluster of numerous garment enterprises. Becker and Murphy (1992) and Sonobe and Otsuka (2006) argue that transaction costs tend to be low in industrial clusters, where opportunistic behaviors are quickly spotted by a large number of enterprises engaged in the same and related transactions. Since Marshall (1920), economists have identified both knowledge spillovers and the development of the division of labor as major benefits of industrial clusters (e.g., Krugman, 1991). Through both channels, the use of advanced knowledge would be shared by a large number of entrepreneurs and workers in the garment industry in Bangladesh. Thus, it seems reasonable to hypothesize as follows:

Hypothesis 8-2: Trained traders provide producers with more knowledge-intensive services than untrained traders, whereas untrained producers rely on intermediation by traders more than trained producers.

We will measure the dependence of a producer on traders by the fraction of the producer's exports through traders. According to the endogenous growth theory, knowledge accumulation is the vehicle of growth because it can be used repeatedly and simultaneously without causing rivalry, regardless of whether it is excludable and transacted or whether it is non-excludable and leaks (e.g., Romer, 1990a, b). Contrary to Easterly (2002), who emphasizes the importance of non-excludable knowledge only, we have advanced Hypothesis 8-2 to shed light on the importance of excludable knowledge and the role of traders.

As mentioned earlier, increased competition has pressured garment suppliers in developing countries to improve product quality, reduce product prices, and deliver products quickly, as in the case of the China shock analyzed in Chapters 6 and 7. As a result, their profit maximizing point may shift toward the greater employment of foreign experts and higher propensity to export directly. Such changes will shift the marginal profit curve upward, even though they will increase fixed costs. As a result, the new profit maximizing size of an enterprise will be larger than the original size. Responding to increasing direct exportation by producers, some traders have counteracted by entering manufacturing. An interesting question is who will take the initiative in adjustment to the shifting equilibrium. The accepted view of human capital, as articulated by Schultz (1975), attributes the value of human capital to the ability to deal with dynamic disequilibria. The case studies of industrial development in East Asia lend strong support to this view

(Sonobe et al., 2003; Sonobe and Otsuka, 2006). Thus, we advance the following hypothesis:

Hypothesis 8-3: Highly educated traders tend to enter into manufacturing, whereas highly educated producers tend to export directly, hire a larger number of foreign experts, and have large enterprise sizes.

8.2 Characteristics of sample enterprises

In August and December 2005, we conducted preliminary surveys of producers, traders, and consultants for nearly 4 weeks in total. We visited both woven garment and knitwear factories of various sizes, ranging from fewer than 10 workers to a few thousand workers. We found it interesting to study the development of the knitwear sector and the trading sector, because the knitwear sector has led the growth of the industry recently and because the roles of traders in economic development remain an enigma. Our sample was selected randomly from the member lists of the three associations: BGMEA, BKMEA, and Bangladesh Garments Buyers and Association (BGBA). After establishing a rapport with some leaders of these associations, we were able to request that they introduce us to the entrepreneurs, whom we selected randomly. For 3 months, from late December 2005 to early March 2006, we visited 40 traders and 100 knitwear producers in the greater Dhaka area,[1] and we were able to interview the entrepreneur at each enterprise except for eight factories.

Our sample consists of 40 traders, 55 T-shirt producers, and 37 sweater producers.[2] They provided us with recall information on the number of workers, production and costs, and export revenues in 1998, 2000, 2002, 2004, and 2005, as well as information on their educational and occupational backgrounds.[3] Because a number of new enterprises have entered the knitwear sector every year, as is shown in Table 8.2, only 33 of the 92 knitwear producers in our sample were operating in 1998, and 74 in 2002. Because new entry continued in the trading sector as well, only 27 of the 40 sample traders were operating in 1998, and 36 in 2002. The data were collected directly from the entrepreneurs and the managers, who were instructed by the entrepreneurs to cooperate with us.

Table 8.3 presents the data on the average employment size of the sample enterprises by sector in selected years. A typical trader employs about 20 regular workers and no part-time workers. He pays his workers on a time-rate basis but not on a piece-rate or commission basis, probably because the qualitative performance of individual workers is difficult to measure. Unlike traders, producers pay the majority of their employees on a piece-rate basis.[4] The average number of employees of

Table 8.3 Number of employees per enterprise by sector in selected years in a garment cluster in Bangladesh

		Knitwear production sector	
Year	Trading sector	T-shirts	Sweaters
1998	16.1	508.1	894.4
2002	18.2	587.0	1,302.3
2005	23.2	828.1	1,831.6

the sweater producers is much larger than that of the T-shirt producers, even though the two sectors share similar sizes of average value added per enterprise. This is because the sweater sector is more labor-intensive than the T-shirt sector, which is clear to visitors to the two types of factories.

As shown in Table 8.3, the growth of the average employment size has been faster in the sweater sector. Although not shown in the table, the growth of the number of producers has also been faster in the sweater sector. The faster growth of the sweater sector can be attributed to the labor-intensive nature of its production, because a labor-abundant country like Bangladesh has a comparative advantage in such a sector.

The garment enterprises are operated by highly educated entrepreneurs, in their forties on average, as shown in Table 8.4. Five trading houses in the sample are subsidiaries of foreign trading houses.[5] All the other enterprises in the sample are owned and operated by Bangladeshis. In Bangladesh, it takes 16 years to receive a specialized degree, and the majority of our sample entrepreneurs have such degrees. In the subsamples of traders and sweater producers, 50 entrepreneurs went to school for 16 years and the remaining 27 entrepreneurs for 14 years. Only these two levels of education are found among these entrepreneurs, whereas there is a greater variation in the subsample of T-shirt producers. The important point, however, is that the entrepreneurs in this industry are highly educated by any standard.[6] In view of the abundance of low-wage labor in the country, it is little wonder that they have achieved the high growth of their industry. Yet, the extent to which the high education of entrepreneurs helps industrial development is worth examining statistically.

Table 8.4 also presents the data on the experience of the entrepreneurs in the garment business. The number of years of garment trading measures the prior experience of an entrepreneur as a proprietor or employee of a garment trading house, a yarn or fabric trader, or the marketing

Table 8.4 Education and work experiences of entrepreneurs by sector in a garment cluster in Bangladesh

	Trading sector	Knitwear production sector	
		T-shirts	Sweaters
Age (in 2005)	43.0	44.0	45.7
Education			
Years of schooling	15.2	14.7	15.4
% of entrepreneurs with more than 16 years schooling	60.0	52.7	67.6
Years of prior experience			
garment trading	8.0	9.4	4.6
garment production	4.2	8.4	5.4
Years of operation of the current business	9.8	7.9	5.3

division of a garment factory, before he established his current enterprise. As was postulated in Hypothesis 1 in Chapter 1, the prior experience of garment trading seems critically important for the managerial human capital of entrepreneurs. The number of years of garment production measures the prior experience as a proprietor or employee of a garment factory before the establishment of the current enterprise. The number of years of operation is equal to the age of the enterprise, as the current entrepreneurs are founders. Compared with the traders and T-shirt producers, the sweater producers are less experienced in garment trading and production, because many of them entered the garment industry after they had succeeded in other businesses or after they returned from foreign countries. Although not shown in the table, about 30 percent of the traders in the sample have experienced working at trading houses owned and operated by traders from India, Sri Lanka, and other foreign countries, and about 10 percent have experienced working at foreign venture garment factories.

According to Table 8.5, seven traders and six knitwear producers in the sample had received intensive training at foreign training institutions. Their training was financed by three sources: donor agencies, their employers, and themselves. A trader received intensive training in Japan with financial support provided by the Association for Overseas Technical Scholarship (AOTS) of Japan. UNDP provided support for the training of three knitwear producers in Europe. Three traders and two knitwear producers in the sample received intensive training in South

Table 8.5   Number of entrepreneurs trained abroad and their operation sizes in 2005 in a garment cluster in Bangladesh

	Trading sector		Knitwear production sector	
	No. of traders	Average export value (million USD)	No. of producers	Average value added (million USD)
Trained	7	8.8	6	8.4
financed by				
donor agency	1		3	
employer	3		2	
self or partner	3		1	
Untrained	33	4.0	86	5.1
Total	40	4.8	92	5.3

Korea and Singapore when they were employed by foreign ventures. Among them is one of the 130 ex-Desh workers who received training at Daewoo. According to him, when Desh recruited 130 workers, it announced its plan to dispatch workers to South Korea for training. This attracted university graduates, including himself, to Desh, even though intellectual young men in those days were in general uninterested in jobs in the manufacturing sector. He now owns and operates woven garment factories besides a trading house. The rest of the ex-trainees in the sample received intensive training in China, Taiwan, and Sri Lanka at their own expense. In each case, the entrepreneur received the training before he established his enterprise.

Table 8.5 also shows the average export value for traders and value added for knitwear producers in 2005. Usually, the operation size of an enterprise is measured by value added. Calculating value added, however, requires either the data on sales revenue, production costs, and inventories, or the data on profits, wage payments, and land rents. Both sets of data are difficult to obtain from traders. We thus use export values of traders and value added of knitwear producers to capture their operation sizes. Table 8.5 demonstrates that the trained entrepreneurs operate businesses of much larger scale than the untrained entrepreneurs. However, the training took place many years ago. Why, then, are the operation sizes in 2005 so different between the trained and the untrained? We will attempt to answer this question in the next section.

Table 8.6 Percentage of traders providing extra services and percentage of value of export through traders in selected years in a garment cluster in Bangladesh

	(i)	(ii)	(iii)	(iv)
	Trading sector		Knitwear production sector	
	% of traders making samples	% of designs re-engineered	% of revenues through traders	% of producers without marketing staff
1998	67.7	22.6	43.8	39.4
2002	64.9	20.0	50.3	13.5
2005	75.0	28.8	41.4	6.5

Table 8.6 presents the data relevant to Hypothesis 8-2. When the transaction begins, there are exchanges of samples between producers and buyers. Producers make counter samples in order to assure foreign buyers that they are able to make exactly the same products as the samples made by the buyers. When producers are busy, they may ask traders to make counter samples in their place. Producers also ask traders to make sellers' samples. Column (i) of Table 8.6 shows that about two-thirds of the traders have equipment and staff for sample-making, which is a relatively knowledge-intensive activity.

Column (ii) pertains to design re-engineering. In this buyer-driven garment industry, the designs of all the products come from foreign buyers. After production begins, however, it may turn out that modifying the original design makes the product more attractive or easier to produce in a larger quantity in a shorter time period. Sometimes foreign buyers allow producers to modify designs. Few producers, however, have the capacity for design re-engineering in Bangladesh. Instead, some traders can re-engineer designs. According to Table 8.6, the traders modified the designs of more than 20 percent of the products that they dealt with. This is a clear example of knowledge-intensive services.

A reasonable measure of the dependence of producers on intermediation by traders is the percentage of their values of export through traders. This percentage is higher among sweater producers than among T-shirt producers, but it did not increase or decrease clearly in either sector. However, the disintermediation in the industry has been clearly progressing; the percentage of producers who did not employ any marketing staff but depended completely on traders decreased from 39.4 percent to 6.5 percent, as shown in column (iv) of Table 8.6.

Table 8.7   New strategies of traders and knitwear producers and the size of their operation in a garment cluster in Bangladesh

	(i)	(ii)	(iii)	(iv)	(v)
	Traders		Knitwear producers		
	Operating factories (%)	Average export value (million USD)	With int'l certificates (%)	Hiring foreign experts (%)	Average value added (million USD)
1998	29.6	3.6	9.1	6.1	3.0
2002	39.8	3.5	45.9	12.2	3.3
2005	57.5	4.8	54.3	20.6	5.3

The response of traders to the disintermediation is to enter directly into garment manufacturing. According to column (i) of Table 8.7, more than half of the traders had entered garment manufacturing by 2005. According to our interviews with these traders, they export their products through their own trading houses, and almost all of them continue to provide trading services to producers. The average operation size of the traders increased to 4.8 million USD in 2005. In the next section, we will characterize the traders who entered manufacturing and examine whether their entry contributed to the increase in operation size.

The compliance with the code of conduct is difficult to measure. Instead, column (iii) of Table 8.7 shows that an increasing number of producers have obtained certification from international auditing bodies, such as International Organization for Standardization (ISO), in order to win popularity among global buyers. According to column (iv), an increasing number of producers hire foreign experts, which is consistent with the results of our interviews with entrepreneurs. Column (v) shows that the enterprise size increased considerably during the quota phase-out era, despite the fact that the new entrants tended to have smaller sizes than the average incumbents and hence reduced the average size.

8.3   Estimation methods and results

8.3.1   Specification

In order to test Hypothesis 8-1, we begin by estimating a reduced-form regression equation in which the operation size of a trader or producer is on the left-hand side and his training, schooling, and other characteristics are on the right-hand side. To estimate the effect of the employment of foreign experts on the value added of a producer, we use the instrumental variable method or the two-stage least squares (2SLS) because the decision on employment is highly likely to be endogenous. Because of knowledge spillovers, the effect of the training is likely to be attenuated over time. Thus, we include an interaction term, that is, the training dummy times the number of years that have passed since the training was conducted. The effect of the training may also be affected by the level of education of the trainee. To see this, we include another interaction term, which is the product of the training dummy and the education variable.

To test Hypothesis 8-2, we run the three reduced-form regressions that explain (1) sample-making, (2) design re-engineering by traders, and (3) the propensities of producers to export indirectly through traders. The sample-making function is specified as a probit model because the data on sample-making are binary. The design re-engineering function and the indirect exportation function are specified as two-limit tobit models because the data on these variables are censored at 0 and 1.

Hypothesis 8-3 is partially tested by the estimation of the reduced-form function that explains the operation sizes, which is also used to test Hypothesis 8-1. Similarly, the effect of education on the propensity of a producer to export directly is assessed when we test Hypothesis 8-2, because this propensity is 1 minus the propensity to export indirectly through traders. As noted in the previous section, the sample traders were educated for either 14 years or 16 years, without exception. Although the education levels of the sample producers have a little more variation, the vast majority of the producers went to school for 14 years or 16 years. Thus, to represent the education levels, we use the higher education dummy, which is equal to 1 for those who went to school for 16 years or longer and 0 for others.

The effect of the education levels of the producers on their employment of foreign experts is estimated by running a probit regression, because the data on the employment of foreign experts are binary. This regression serves as the first stage for the 2SLS regression of the operation sizes of the producers. In this 2SLS regression, we will also include the propensity to export directly as another endogenous right-hand side variable. For the traders, too, we will run a 2SLS regression to estimate the effects of their entry into manufacturing and design re-engineering on their export revenues.[7]

We have observations from five different years, but the exogenous variables are all time-invariant. Hence the panel-data specification of the regression models is not worth considering here. Although not shown in this paper, we ran regressions for the different years separately. For the early years in the sample, the estimates of the effects in which we are interested tend to be unstable and statistically insignificant due to the small sample size. However the qualitative results are unchanged regardless of the years. The estimates obtained from the subsamples for 2002, 2004, and 2005 are stable. Thus, we pool the data from the different years and use year dummies to control for time effects. For the sample of producers, the data on the T-shirt producers and sweater producers are pooled because we obtained similar results from the regressions treating them separately. The results of these separate regressions are reported by Mottaleb (2007).

8.3.2   Estimation results

Table 8.8 presents the estimates of the reduced-form functions explaining the export values of traders and the value added of producers. Consistently with Hypothesis 8-1, the training dummy has a positive and highly significant effect on the export value of traders. The interaction of the training dummy and the years since the training has no effect, which suggests that part of the training does not easily spill over to other traders or that the trained traders were able to grow as fast as imitators. Our attempt to include another interaction term in the regression, the product of the training dummy and the high education dummy, failed because of multicollinearity. According to our interviews, the trained traders are also highly educated simply because the training was implemented in English.

In columns (iii) to (v), the effect of high education is positive and highly significant, which is consistent with Hypothesis 8-3. However, the training dummy has no significant effect on the operation sizes of the producers. The reason is found in the multicollinearity between the training and the years of prior experience in garment production. If the latter variable is excluded from the regression, the effect of training becomes positive and significant, as shown in column (v). If the years of prior experience in garment marketing are also excluded, the effect of training becomes even stronger. These results were obtained because the trained entrepreneurs had worked longer as employees of garment factories or trading houses than the untrained entrepreneurs. Overall, the estimates of the effects of training lend strong support to Hypothesis 8-1.

For both traders and producers, one of the most important determinants of their operation sizes is the years of operation. This is partly

Table 8.8 Determinants of the operation sizes of traders and knitwear producers in a garment cluster in Bangladesh[a]

	(i)	(ii)	(iii)	(iv)	(v)
	Traders		Knitwear producers		
	ln(export value)		ln(value added)		
Higher education	0.09	0.08	0.53**	0.53**	0.47**
dummy	(0.47)	(0.41)	(3.51)	(3.49)	(3.07)
Training dummy	0.77**	0.73**	0.14	0.26	0.42*
	(4.42)	(3.20)	(0.61)	(0.80)	(1.99)
Training dummy*		0.00		−0.01	
Years since the		(0.20)		(−0.52)	
training					
Age	−0.05*	−0.05*	0.003	0.003	0.003
	(−2.37)	(−2.34)	(0.33)	(0.37)	(0.32)
Years of prior	0.03	0.03	0.05**	0.05**	
experience in	(1.49)	(1.19)	(4.91)	(4.97)	
garment production					
Years of prior	0.03	0.03	0.02**	0.02**	0.01
experience in	(1.07)	(1.05)	(3.23)	(3.24)	(1.40)
garment marketing					
Years of operation	0.13**	0.13**	0.10**	0.10**	0.10**
	(5.58)	(5.42)	(8.22)	(8.28)	(8.57)
Foreign venture	0.15	0.14			
experience dummy	(0.81)	(0.80)			
Foreign ownership	0.80**	0.79**			
dummy	(3.84)	(3.79)			
Sweater producer			0.82**	0.83**	0.74***
dummy			(6.60)	(6.54)	(5.79)
Dhaka dummy			−0.21	−0.20	−0.22
			(−1.59)	(−1.51)	(1.56)
Central district	0.36*	0.35*			
dummy	(1.86)	(1.85)			
Year 2000 dummy	0.09	0.08	−0.23	−0.22	−0.22
	(0.31)	(0.30)	(−0.87)	(−0.85)	(−0.86)
Year 2002 dummy	0.07	0.06	−0.23	−0.22	−0.21
	(0.21)	(0.19)	(−0.92)	(−0.89)	(−0.83)
Year 2004 dummy	0.20	0.19	−0.10	−0.10	−0.12
	(0.64)	(0.60)	(−0.49)	(−0.44)	(−0.51)
Year 2005 dummy	0.28	0.27	0.16	0.17	0.15
	(0.87)	(0.82)	(0.77)	(0.81)	(0.66)
Constant	14.7**	14.7**	13.00**	12.97**	13.28**
	(21.3)	(20.0)	(34.0)	(32.8)	(33.3)
R squared	0.40	0.40	0.30	0.31	0.26

[a]The sample size is 176 in columns (i) to (iii) and 341 in columns (iv) and (v). Numbers in parentheses are *t*-statistics. **Significant at the 1% level, *at the 5% level.

because operation sizes expand as the entrepreneurs reinvest profits in their businesses and partly because they accumulate expertise over time through learning by doing. Given the enterprise age, younger traders tend to have greater operation sizes than older traders, but there is no such tendency among producers. The foreign ownership dummy indicates whether the trader is based in a foreign country. The positive and highly significant effect of this variable on operation sizes supports the view that there is still room for Bangladeshi traders to learn from traders in developed countries.

The positive effect of the sweater producer dummy indicates that the sweater producers tend to have much larger operation sizes than the T-shirt producers, with their education, training, and experiences being equal. The marginally significant effect of the central district dummy may suggest either that being located in the center of Dhaka is advantageous for traders or that only high-performing traders can afford to stay in the center. Even if this dummy variable is excluded from the regression, the estimates of the operation size function remain almost unchanged.

Table 8.9 shows the results of the reduced-form regressions of sample-making, design re-engineering, and indirect export depending on the intermediation of traders. The training dummy has positive and highly significant effects on sample-making and design re-engineering in columns (i) and (iii), and it has a negative and significant effect on indirect export in column (v). These results strongly support Hypothesis 8-2. Like the training dummy, years of operation have positive and highly significant effects on sample-making and design re-engineering by traders and a negative and significant effect on indirect export through traders. Moreover, in columns (v) and (vi), years of prior experience in garment marketing have a negative and significant effect. Thus, trained producers and producers experienced in trading can dispense with transactions with traders.

In column (ii) of Table 8.9, the effect of the training dummy is absorbed by the interaction term, and the negative effect of the prior experience in garment production increases if the interaction term is included. These results are difficult to interpret, but they are likely to result from the correlation between years of prior experience and years since the training. In column (iv), the interaction term between training dummy and years since the training has a negative and significant effect on design re-engineering, implying the declining effect of training on trainees relative to non-trainees over time, and its insertion increased the positive estimate of the effect of training. However, note that the overall effect of training on the provision of design re-engineering

Table 8.9 Determinants of sample-making and design re-engineering by traders and the dependence of knitwear producers on intermediation in a garment cluster in Bangladesh[a]

	Probit		Two limit tobit			
	(i)	(ii)	(iii)	(iv)	(v)	(vi)
	Trading sector				Knitwear sector	
Estimation method	Sample-making		Proportion of designs re-engineered		Export through traders	
Higher education	0.19	−0.05	−0.14	−0.02	−0.53**	−0.53**
dummy	(0.82)	(−0.19)	(−1.58)	(−0.23)	(−5.98)	(5.98)
Training dummy	1.53**	0.41	0.63**	0.85**	−0.39*	−0.04
	(3.72)	(1.04)	(4.93)	(5.97)	(−2.35)	(−0.12)
Training dummy*		0.14**		−0.04**		−0.04
Years since the		(3.55)		(−3.19)		(−1.13)
training						
Age	−0.05*	−0.06*	−0.01	−0.01	−0.001	−0.00
	(−1.93)	(−2.31)	(−1.30)	(−0.65)	(−0.28)	(0.46)
Years of prior	−0.06	−0.11**	−0.01	0.01	−0.003	0.00
experience	(−1.68)	(−2.56)	(−0.92)	(0.53)	(−0.34)	(−0.11)
in garment						
production						
Years of prior	0.02	0.02	0.02	0.02	−0.02**	−0.02**
experience in	(0.63)	(0.49)	(0.85)	(0.97)	(−3.18)	(−2.56)
garment marketing						
Years of operation	0.12**	0.14**	0.04**	0.03**	−0.06**	−0.06**
	(4.27)	(4.71)	(3.21)	(2.63)	(−6.84)	(−6.75)
Foreign venture	−0.66**	−0.72**	0.42**	0.43**		
experience dummy	(−2.49)	(−2.69)	(3.84)	(4.26)		
Foreign ownership	0.46	0.46	1.74**	1.70**		
dummy	(1.17)	(1.17)	(8.02)	(8.38)		
Left censored			107	107	83	83
observations						
Uncensored			50	50	144	144
Right censored			19	19	114	114

[a]Each regression includes an intercept, four year dummies, and either the central district dummy or the Dhaka dummy. Columns (vii) and (viii) also include a product dummy to distinguish T-shirt producers and sweater producers. The sample size is 176 in columns (i) to (vi) and 341 in columns (vii) and (viii). Numbers in parentheses are z-statistics. **Significant at the 1% level, *at the 5% level.

service is positive, as shown in column (iii). These results suggest that there were spillovers, but that the difference in service provision due to training remains for many years.

The coefficients of the foreign venture experience dummy indicate that those traders who used to work at foreign trading houses or foreign venture factories do not make samples but re-engineer designs. The very strong effect of the foreign ownership dummy on design re-engineering, as shown in columns (iii) and (iv), reflects the fact that traders from South Korea, Sri Lanka, India, and Italy have superior ability to provide knowledge-intensive service. Overall, the results shown in Table 8.9 support our argument that the advanced knowledge acquired by traders from developed countries is of benefit to producers who did not have training, not only through spillovers but also through transactions of knowledge-intensive services.

Table 8.10 reports the results of the regressions that examine the determinants of their own garment production by traders and the operation sizes of their trading businesses. Supporting a part of Hypothesis 8-3, the higher education dummy has a positive and significant effect on their own production. Not only the highly educated traders but also the trained and experienced traders are more likely to enter into manufacturing. As in Table 8.9, the insertion of the interaction term between the training dummy and years since training reduces the effect of the training dummy and the effects of prior experience in production and in marketing. Both the foreign venture experience dummy and the foreign ownership dummy have negative and highly significant effects on traders' own production. Although we are not sure why this is true, the greater expertise of those traders with international experience may encourage them to focus on trading.

Columns (iv) and (v) of Table 8.10 report the 2SLS and GMM estimates of the export value function, respectively.[8] Own production and design re-engineering have positive and highly significant effects on export value, as we expected. However, the effect of sample-making turned out to be insignificant, probably because sample-making services are abundantly provided by the majority of the traders. The export value increases with the years of operation, suggesting the importance of experience in the trading business. According to the results of over-identification tests, education and training as well as other exogenous variables do not have significant effects on export value once the effects of own production and design re-engineering are controlled for. These results indicate that their positive and significant effects on export value, as shown in Table 8.8, come indirectly through own production and design re-engineering.

Table 8.10   Determinants of own production and export by traders in a garment cluster in Bangladesh[a]

	(i)	(ii)	(iii)	(iv)
	Own production		ln(export)	
Estimation method	Probit	Probit	2SLS	GMM
Higher education dummy	0.49*	0.34		
	(1.94)	(1.32)		
Training dummy	0.79**	−0.10		
	(2.47)	(−0.22)		
Training dummy* Years since the training		0.12** (3.22)		
Age	−0.02	−0.03		
	(−1.04)	(−1.44)		
Years of prior experience in garment production	0.12** (3.31)	0.08* (1.87)		
Years of prior experience in garment marketing	0.08* (2.22)	0.07* (1.92)		
Years of operation	0.05	0.06*	0.07**	0.07**
	(1.57)	(1.89)	(2.85)	(3.06)
Foreign venture experience dummy	−0.86** (−2.96)	−0.92** (−3.05)		
Foreign ownership dummy	−1.40** (−3.50)	−1.50** (−3.63)		
Central district dummy	0.82**	0.79**		
	(2.72)	(2.54)		
Own production (instrumented)			1.42** (2.84)	1.43** (3.15)
Sample making (instrumented)			−0.03 (−0.06)	−0.20 (−0.47)
Design re-engineering (instrumented)			0.07** (2.85)	0.07** (3.06)
Year 2000 (yes=1)	0.09	0.01	0.03	0.07
	(0.27)	(0.04)	(0.09)	(0.24)
Year 2002 (yes=1)	0.31	0.20	−0.10	−0.05
	(0.88)	(0.54)	(−0.29)	(−0.18)
Year 2004 (yes=1)	0.48	0.34	−0.10	−0.04
	(1.27)	(0.88)	(−0.29)	(−0.13)
Year 2005 (yes=1)	0.92*	0.78*	−0.31	−0.22
	(2.31)	(1.94)	(−0.86)	(−0.68)
Constant	−0.78	−0.13	13.1**	13.2**
	(−0.90)	(−0.15)	(40.7)	(45.6)
R squared	0.19	0.22		

[a]The instrumental variables are the right-hand side variables other than years of operation and year dummies. The *F* statistic for the joint significance of their effects on own production is 4.94, that on sample-making is 4.57, and that on design re-engineering is 20.81. The chi-squared for the over-identification test is 2.9 for 2SLS and 2.2 for GMM. The number of observations is 176. Numbers in parentheses are *z*-statistics or *t*-statistics.
**Significant at the 1% level, *at the 5% level.

Table 8.11 Determinants of the employment of foreign experts by knitwear producers and the value added function in a garment cluster in Bangladesh[a]

	Employment of foreign experts		ln(value added)	
	Probit	Probit	2SLS	GMM
Higher education dummy	0.84** (3.36)	0.85** (3.23)		
Training dummy	0.92** (3.04)	2.69** (5.78)		
Training dummy * Years since the training		−0.17** (−4.96)		
Age	0.01 (0.48)	0.01 (1.06)		
Years of prior experience in garment production	0.03* (1.90)	0.05** (3.03)	0.04** (3.51)	0.04** (4.06)
Years of prior experience in garment marketing	0.03* (2.13)	0.04** (2.50)	0.01 (1.40)	0.02** (2.47)
Years of operation	0.05* (2.39)	0.05* (2.26)	0.07** (4.84)	0.08** (5.28)
Dhaka dummy	−0.25 (−1.06)	−0.12 (−0.52)		
Sweater producer dummy	1.05** (4.00)	1.27** (4.32)	0.36* (2.08)	0.42** (2.55)
Employment of foreign experts (instrumented)			1.02* (1.98)	1.12* (2.18)
Proportion of revenues from direct export (instrumented)			0.72* (1.87)	0.68* (1.82)
Year 2000 dummy	0.09 (0.20)	0.23 (0.45)	−0.19 (−0.73)	−0.25 (−0.97)
Year 2002 dummy	0.34 (0.83)	0.65 (1.31)	−0.21 (−0.86)	−0.25 (−1.05)
Year 2004 dummy	0.38 (0.95)	0.71 (1.47)	−0.11 (−0.53)	−0.11 (−0.52)
Year 2005 dummy	0.68* (1.74)	1.03* (2.16)	0.09 (0.44)	0.12 (0.58)
Constant	−3.45** (−5.47)	−4.37** (−5.91)	13.28** (54.4)	13.14** (34.8)

[a]The instrumental variables are the high education dummy, training dummy, training dummy *years since the training, age, and Dhaka dummy. The F statistic for the joint significance of their effects on foreign expert employment is 50.42 and that on direct export proportion is 13.74. The chi-squared for the over-identification test is 5.6 for 2SLS and 5.2 for GMM. The number of observations is 341. Numbers in parentheses are t-statistics. **Significant at the 1% level, *at the 5% level.

Table 8.11 presents the results of the regressions that examine the determinants of the employment of foreign experts by the producers and their value added. Several important observations can be made. First, both higher education and training experience lead to more frequent employment of foreign experts, even though the training effect seems to erode over time. These findings are consistent with Hypotheses 8-1 and 8-3. Second, experience in garment production, garment marketing, and the operation of producers' own firms all affect the employment of foreign experts, suggesting that the knowledge acquired through such experience is a complement to the knowledge provided by the foreign experts. Third, these three experience variables also have positive and significant effects on the value added, according to the last two columns. Fourth, sweater producers employ more foreign experts, presumably because this sector is newer and faster-growing than the T-shirt sector. Fifth, the predicted foreign expert dummy variable and the proportion of revenues from direct exports have positive and significant effects on value added, signifying the importance of employing foreign experts and direct exports in improving management efficiency. These findings are once again consistent with Hypotheses 8-1 and 8-3.

8.4   Concluding remarks

This chapter has explored the successful process of industrial development in developing countries, taking the rapidly growing garment industry in Bangladesh as an example. This case may appear quite different from the successful process of industrial development in East Asia. According to previous studies of East Asian cases, industries begin by producing low-quality imitated imported products, and their products remain low-quality until highly educated producers take the initiative in introducing new knowledge of production, marketing, and management in response to the declining profitability of producing low-quality products (Sonobe and Otsuka, 2006). While many industries in East Asia have succeeded in such a transformation, many in Africa have failed. In contrast to both cases, the Bangladeshi garment industry produced garments for developed country markets even before the producers proliferated, and it has continuously improved product quality and production efficiency.

The East Asian cases and the Bangladeshi case share the same vehicle of successful development, however. Consistent with Hypotheses 1 to 3 formulated in Chapter 1, the key is the absorption of advanced knowledge from developed countries by highly educated entrepreneurs who often have trading experience. The previous studies of industrial development in East Asia and Africa, including those reported in Chapters 2 to 7, have provided evidence that the managerial human capital of entrepreneurs assumes importance when the transformation begins. However, they failed to provide direct evidence for the importance of advanced knowledge transferred from developed countries. The analysis of this chapter clearly indicates that both elements are important. Moreover, it finds that advanced knowledge was made available to a large number of enterprises through both knowledge spillovers and the division of labor between producers and traders in a long-term process. These findings of this study strongly support the proposition that providing entrepreneurs with training programs that teach technology, marketing, and management in a continuous fashion is critically important for the promotion of industrial development in developing countries.

9
Misfired Promotion of the Export-Oriented Garment Industry in Ethiopia

The US preferential trade policy AGOA (the African Growth and Opportunity Act) was signed into law in 2000. It has provided garment industries in sub-Saharan Africa with duty-free and quota-free access to the US market while allowing the use of third-country fabric as an input. This opportunity is similar to the one given to the Bangladeshi garment industry around 1980 through the export restriction on Korean and other East Asian garment producers under the Multi-Fiber Arrangement (MFA). Following the lead of Daewoo, a number of East Asian garment producers undertook technology transfers to and direct investments in Bangladesh in response to the MFA export restriction. Bangladeshi businessmen and the government of Bangladesh took full advantage of this new opportunity to develop their garment industry into one of the leading garment exporters in the world and the single most important industry in the country, as we saw in the previous chapter. Is this success of Bangladesh being replicated in sub-Saharan Africa (SSA)?

According to USITC (2007), substantial growth in the value of exports from sub-Saharan Africa was found during 2001–5 in the sectors producing energy-related products, minerals and metals, and agricultural products. During the same period, however, Africa's garment export value grew by 13 percent (for the 4 years), whereas the world's garment export value grew by 31 percent. Factors that could positively affect Africa's garment export include the tariff preferences and trade agreements, such as the Cotonou Agreement and AGOA, the quota on US imports of garment products from China, and government policies to promote the garment industry, such as the development of industrial zones and export processing zones. Why was the growth rate of Africa's garment export so low despite these favorable factors?

In an attempt to answer this question, the present chapter investigates the recent development of the garment industry in Addis Ababa, Ethiopia. This country deserves special attention for several reasons. It has the second largest population and is among the lowest income countries in SSA. In 2001, the country had the smallest value of garment export among the six selected countries in SSA considered by USITC (2007). The Ethiopian government has provided various support measures for export-oriented garment enterprises in order to take full advantage of the opportunity offered by AGOA.[1] Ethiopia's garment export increased from 0.66 million US dollars in 2001 to 4.74 million dollars in 2005, an increase of 624 percent. The question arises as to whether this high growth indicates that the country's untapped comparative advantage in garment production was at last unleashed by the government's promotion policy, or whether the high growth took place simply because the initial level was negligible.

This chapter uses enterprise data collected in 2007 from the garment industry in Addis Ababa. The data set covers all the export-oriented garment producers and other ready-made garment producers catering to the local market as well as randomly selected tailors located in the city. A major finding is that the export-oriented garment enterprises have much lower labor productivity than other ready-to-wear (RTW) garment enterprises and slightly lower labor productivity than tailors, whose production is much less capital-intensive. The export-oriented garment enterprises do not seem to be actively gaining expertise in production, marketing, procurement, and management from abroad. The export-oriented enterprises have not only lower productivity but also poorer growth performance than other types of garment producers. These observations indicate that the government support measures have not helped the export-oriented enterprises to sprint from the start as their Bangladeshi counterparts were able to in the 1980s.

The rest of this chapter is organized as follows. After describing the support provided by the government for the garment industry, Section 9.1 advances testable hypotheses. Section 9.2 examines the characteristics of the sample enterprises by enterprise type, which is followed by the presentation of the regression results in Section 9.3. Section 9.4 compares the Ethiopian and Bangladeshi cases to see what made the growth paths of the export-oriented garment industries in their early stages of development so different.

9.1 Promotion policy and testable hypotheses

As discussed in the previous chapter, the export garment market is dominated by global buyers, who are large retail, wholesale, or manufacturing companies based in North America or Western Europe. The global buyers place orders for the production of garment items to vendors or suppliers in developing countries, where labor costs are low. The parameters of the outsourcing contract between the two parties are specified by the global buyers. In the 1960s and 1970s, a limited number of developing countries in Asia and Latin America were able to satisfy the global buyers' demand for garment production at low cost (Gereffi, 1999). In the 1980s and 1990s, the global buyers diversified the sources of supply to other developing countries, such as the Philippines, Bangladesh, and Vietnam, and a number of countries emerged as new entrants in global value (or commodity) chains after transforming themselves from planned economies to market economies, liberalizing foreign trade and capital flows, and improving governance. As a result, competition among producers in different developing countries heated up, and the global buyers became increasingly choosy about prices, delivery times, and product quality.

In the world of global value chains, there is a ladder of functions that producers in developing countries are required to perform by global buyers. The level of function rises as the supplier upgrades from just sewing imported fabric following given designs and other specifications, to taking care of the sourcing of fabric and modifying designs, to designing products, and to selling products under their own brand names (Schmitz and Knorringa, 2000). There is also a ladder of the quality level of products that the developing country producers produce for global buyers. A producer climbs these ladders by accumulating the managerial human capital of the manager and the technical skills of workers. In the early era of global value chains, global buyers provided substantial support to developing country producers so that the latter could climb the ladder (Gereffi, 1999). In recent years, however, global buyers have not worked with producers whom they had to help. Needless to say, operating at the bottom of the ladders is a cut-throat business, with thousands of potential competitors all over the world. To be profitable, a developing country producer has to have improved managerial human capital and technical skills so as to earn quasi-rents.

The government of Ethiopia is eager to achieve export-led industrialization.[2] Since garment production is labor-intensive and Ethiopia is labor-abundant, it seems reasonable that the government regarded the export-oriented garment industry as one of the key industries that deserved government support. When AGOA was enacted, the Ethiopian government decided to take full advantage of AGOA by providing various incentive schemes to the export-oriented garment enterprises, such as (i) preferential financing with a long grace period (3 years), a long repayment term (15 years), and an interest rate lower than the market interest rate, (ii) export credit guarantee loans up to the equivalent of export earnings in the previous year without collateral, (iii) the preferential supply of land, (iv) duty-free imports of machinery (including second-hand machines), (v) a 100 percent duty drawback given to the purchase of intermediate inputs for commodities to be exported, and (vi) subsidies to employ foreign experts to train workers. Two points are noteworthy. First, the government tried to be highly conducive to the development of the export-oriented garment industry. Second, the gist of the policy was to provide financial incentives but not to infuse managerial human capital and industry-specific skills.

It was intended that the recipients of these support measures would be garment producers with the ability to export garment products to developed country markets. Such enterprises, however, were nonexistent when the policy was established. While Ethiopian garment producers had exported their products to neighboring countries on a small scale, none had been admitted into a global value chain covering European and North American markets, even though garment exports to developed country markets might have taken place through some other channels. Moreover, the manufacturing sector of Ethiopia as a whole exported few items to foreign markets, and mass production in the factory system was not common. Probably, workers in the manufacturing sector would have had highly limited technical skills and awareness of the importance of product quality, efficiency, and punctuality, and managers would not have developed much expertise in managing such workers. In short, technical skills specific to the export-oriented garment industry, skilled workers in manufacturing, international marketing expertise, and managerial human capital were very scarce in this country. In such a case, there is no guarantee that the government will select promising enterprises for export promotion.

According to the Ricardian model of international trade, a tradable good industry is not viable without government support if labor productivity, given product quality, is too low relative to the wage rate and the international price of its product. Probably, the export-oriented garment enterprises needed government support in order to enter and grow in the international market. When the support to the export enterprises began, their labor productivity may have been lower than that of the garment enterprises catering to the domestic market under the pressure of import competition. A major question arises as to whether government support helps the enterprises become viable exporters.

Our answer to this question is negative. The reason can be decomposed into three parts. First, returns to productivity improvement are not wholly appropriated by the investor. Managers or engineers may be sent to foreign countries to acquire advanced management practices and technologies, but they may quit the job before contributing to the enterprise's profits. The fruit of inviting foreign experts to train Ethiopian managers and workers may dissipate because of job-hopping or poaching of trained managers and workers. Probably this is why the government provides a subsidy to export-oriented enterprises employing foreign experts and training workers. Yet, in our observation, only a small number of foreigners are employed by the garment enterprises. Second, the short-run return to such investments is low even without the dissipation or erosion of investment returns. At the low end of the quality ladder and the functional ladder in the international garment trade, the competition among producers is fierce, and the low wages of Ethiopia are not really helpful because there are other low-wage countries. To earn high returns or quasi-rents, the investor will have to undertake either long-term or sizable investment in managerial and technological human capital. Third, if the garment business turns out to be less profitable than expected, the investor may instead find it more profitable to take advantage of the fact that the government is willing to help the development of the export-oriented industry. In other words, seeking further support can be more profitable (Bhagwati, 1982). Based on these considerations, it seems reasonable to postulate the following hypothesis:

Hypothesis 9-1: Enterprises that have insufficient expertise in exporting receive subsidy for survival and, consequently, have lower labor productivity than enterprises receiving no subsidy.

If the subsidy for survival distorts the incentive of the export-oriented enterprises for growth, the effect of the managerial human capital of their managers on enterprise performance may not be significant. If specific expertise in a particular type of business is in short supply, the shortage should be made up by investments in the human capital of the enterprise manager or the core staff. To the extent that this is the case, the manager's human capital should be an important determinant of management efficiency and the pace at which his or her enterprise acquires the specific expertise in question. In the case of the export-oriented garment industry in Ethiopia, however, this argument may fail to hold true because the incentives of the enterprise manager or owner for learning and growth may be distorted such that rent-seeking is more important than maximizing profit from the enterprise operation without relying on government support. Thus, we advance the following hypothesis:

Hypothesis 9-2: Enterprises with more educated managers tend to be more productive and greater in employment size in the non-subsidized sector, whereas productivity and managers' education levels may not be closely related in the subsidized export-oriented sector.

While the garment industry in Ethiopia has not had expertise in the mass production of products with exportable quality and international marketing, it has had expertise in the international procurement of materials, because fabric and other materials have long been imported. The experience of a garment enterprise manager as an importer of materials will help his or her enterprise procure materials at lower costs, even though the favorable effect of such experience may be reduced by the distorted incentive in the subsidized sector. Thus, a testable hypothesis may be postulated as follows:

Hypothesis 9-3: An enterprise operated by a manager with experience of import trading tends to have higher labor productivity and larger employment sizes in the non-subsidized sector, but not necessarily so in the subsidized sector.

9.2   Characteristics of sample enterprises

Roughly speaking, the garment industry in Ethiopia has a dual structure in which modern large factories and conventional, micro- and small-scale enterprises (MSEs) coexist, just like many industries in developing countries. Large enterprises produce RTW Western-style garments in the factory system. Export-oriented garment enterprises are included in this category. As in other manufacturing sectors in Ethiopia, large garment factories were nationalized during the socialist regime in the 1970s and 1980s, and then they were privatized or are still being privatized. They are still among the largest garment enterprises in terms of employment and production volumes. The staple of their product lines is uniforms for military forces, police, schools, and factories. Schools seldom have their own unique uniforms, but share the same uniforms with other schools. Factory uniforms are even more standardized across factories and industries. The producers of uniforms in such a society thus do not have to be aware of updated fashions. In addition, because of the legacy of the socialist economy, large factories often lack cost-consciousness and the concept that consumer satisfaction is vital in selling products. It is easy to imagine that considerable efforts to reform management and workers' attitudes would be required for them to gain competitiveness in international markets.

Typical MSEs in the garment industry in Ethiopia are tailors, who stock rolls of cloth in their shops and make custom suits and dresses to order for customers at the shops. Their customers are relatively wealthy city dwellers. Hence, tailors are traditionally concentrated in a few commercial areas in Addis Ababa. The vast majority of tailors are former employees of tailors. After acquiring skills, they started their own tailor shops. Because of the high rents in commercial areas, the locations of new tailor shops have gradually spread over six out of the ten sub-cities in Addis Ababa, according to information obtained from the Business Registration Bureau. Besides tailors, producers of Ethiopian traditional clothes and subcontractors may be regarded as garment MSEs. They do not fall within the scope of our study, however, as Ethiopian traditional clothes are so distinct from the products of the export-oriented garment enterprises. Furthermore, the producers are the subcontractors, who often operate in premises provided by traders, so that they can hardly be regarded as independent enterprises.

In June 2007, we conducted in collaboration with the Ethiopian Development Research Institute a census survey of RTW factories and tailors operating in Addis Ababa, where the majority of garment enterprises in the country were said to be located.[3] After an exhaustive search, we found 35 RTW enterprises and 677 tailors and obtained reliable data from 32 RTW enterprises and 130 randomly selected tailors. As shown in Table 9.1, we classify the RTW enterprises into three groups. The first group consists of 14 export-oriented enterprises, which were 8.4 years old on average as of 2007. The three former state-owned enterprises are included in this group, and the majority of the other enterprises were just 3 years old or younger. After Ethiopia became eligible for apparel benefits provided by AGOA in August 2001, the number of export-oriented garment enterprises began increasing in 2002, and increased sharply in 2004 because of the government support measures (see Table 9.5 below).

The tailor-turned enterprises constituting the second group are the enterprises that had started as tailors but later adopted the factory production system to produce ready-made suits and other RTW garment items. They had not exported their products at the time of our survey. The third group of enterprises is referred to as the "others" or "other

Table 9.1   Sample size by enterprise type in the garment industry in Ethiopia

| | RTW enterprises | | | |
	Export-oriented	Tailor-turned	Others	Tailors
Number of sample enterprises	14	7	11	130
Years of operation as of July 2007				
Mean	8.4	10.3	7. 5	11.9
Median	3	10	4	8
Max	41	18	23	42
Number of owners with overseas experience	5	0	4	1

RTW enterprises." They had produced RTW clothes from the beginning, like the export-oriented enterprises, but were selling their products only within Ethiopia. The tailors are more homogeneous than the RTW enterprises. No enterprises in the sample are foreign-owned or foreign joint ventures, even though some owners are Ethiopian expatriates in the US, Canada, and Italy.

In indigenous industries in developing countries, the initial investments of business owners are self-financed or financed by their families. The first column of Table 9.2 indicates clearly that the export-oriented garment enterprises are exceptional in this respect, as seven of them financed their initial investment with bank loans. Note that, in this table, the total number of the export-oriented enterprises is 11 because the data on initial investment of the three former state-owned enterprises are not available. We asked the tailor-turned enterprises about how they financed their investments in the factory production system. Three of them were able to borrow from banks, as they had established good reputations by the time they wanted to extend their businesses.

The newly established export-oriented garment enterprises are owned by wealthy business persons, including diasporas, and cooperatives. Diasporas refer to Ethiopian migrants who emigrated to Europe and North America, especially during the period of the national crisis in the 1970s and 1980s. Many of them became successful in business in the places where they had settled and waited for a suitable opportunity to come back to or invest in their home country. Five export-oriented garment enterprises and four other RTW enterprises in Addis Ababa received investments from diasporas, as shown at the bottom

Table 9.2 Source of initial investment finance and investments by diaspora in the garment industry in Ethiopia[a]

	RTW enterprises			
	Export-oriented[b]	Tailor-turned	Others	Tailors
Self-financed completely	4	3	7	106
Loan financed partially or completely	7	4	4	24
Bank loan	7	3	2	4
Invested by owners with overseas experience	5	0	4	1

[a]The table shows the number of enterprises applicable to each case.
[b]Of the 14 export-oriented RTW enterprises, the three former state-owned enterprises are not included here since their data on initial investment finance are missing.

of Table 9.2. Some of the owners of the garment enterprises operate the businesses by themselves as general managers, and others leave the management to hired general managers.

Table 9.3 presents the data on the background attributes of the general managers. Perhaps the most important finding from this table is that the average education level of the export-oriented enterprise managers is very high; indeed, slightly higher than that in the export-oriented garment industry in Bangladesh (see Table 8.4). The average education level of the tailor-turned and other RTW enterprise managers, that is, 13 years of education, is a mediocre level in many industries in developing countries (see Table 10.2). The average education level of the tailors is much lower than that of the RTW enterprise managers.

Almost all the tailors in the sample are owners of businesses. Likewise, all the tailor-turned RTW enterprise managers are business owners. As we will see shortly, these two types share similar attributes, except for their education level. It seems reasonable to conjecture that their relatively high education levels helped them extend their tailor businesses to RTW production. Interestingly, however, the most innovative and successful entrepreneur in the garment industry is a tailor-turned RTW producer who went to school only for 9 years, just like the typical tailor. His innovation was imitated by relatively highly educated tailors, who turned into RTW producers following his lead. Anecdotes like this, with a less educated innovator and highly educated imitators, abound in the East Asian experience of industrial development (Sonobe and Otsuka, 2006, Chapters 2 and 5).

Table 9.3   Background attributes of general managers by enterprise type in the garment industry in Ethiopia[a]

| | RTW enterprises | | | |
	Export-oriented	Tailor-turned	Others	Tailors
Years of schooling	16.1	13.0	13.1	9.1
% of females	14.3	0	27.2	16.1
Age as of 2007	47.4	39.4	47.2	41.0
Parents in trading or white-collar occupations (%)	17.9	0	29.7	7.8
Work experience in garment sector (%)	35.7	100.0	54.5	84.6
Work experience in import trading (%)	7.2	0	18.2	3.1
Training (%)				
Garment production				
Vocational school	0.0	14.3	0.0	2.3
Formal training	42.9	14.3	18.2	10.8
Management				
Vocational school	0.0	0.0	0.0	0.0
Formal training	78.6	42.9	36.4	6.2

[a]Work experience in garment sector refers to work experience as an entrepreneur, worker, or hired manager at a tailor shop or garment factory before he or she became a garment entrepreneur.

Turning to other attributes, both tailors and tailor-turned RTW enterprise managers are about 40 years old on average, likely to be sons of farmers or tailors, and used to work as sewers at tailor shops. Hence, they did not need to receive short-term formal training in sewing skills. However, three out of the seven tailor-turned RTW enterprise managers participated in formal training in management, presumably because they needed to learn how to manage larger organizations than tailor shops, whereas few tailors had a need to learn management. The export-oriented enterprise managers and other RTW enterprise managers are about 47 years old, a little more likely to have parents in trading or white-collar occupations, and less likely to have had work experience in the garment sector before assuming their managerial positions. It may be noteworthy that three-quarters of the export-oriented enterprise managers participated in management training programs.

Table 9.4, which is based on the pooled data in the 4 years from 2004 to 2007, reports the most important results of our descriptive analysis. The export-oriented enterprises are smaller than the tailor-turned RTW

Table 9.4 Size and labor productivity by enterprise type in the garment industry in Ethiopia, 2004–7[a]

	RTW enterprises			
	Export-oriented	Tailor-turned	Others	Tailors
Real sales revenue (1,000 birr)				
Mean	2,751	8,342	812	31
Median	828	1,154	335	14
Real value added (1,000 birr)				
Mean	1,376	3,870	275	19
Median	404	480	144	10
Number of production workers				
Mean	192.5	121.7	35.1	2.3
Median	176.5	56.5	24.0	2.0
Total number of sewing machines				
Mean	248.4	92.1	50.7	2.7
Median	214.0	58.0	31.0	2.0
% of high-speed sewing machines	74.3	72.1	72.3	3.5
Real value added per worker (1,000 birr)				
Mean	5.6	22.2	8.2	7.2
Median	4.1	21.5	5.0	4.8

[a]Mean and median are taken from the pooled data covering four years from 2004 to 2007. Value added here is defined as sales revenue minus expenses on material, utility, and transportation. To obtain real values, nominal values were deflated by using the GDP implicit deflator taken from the World Bank Development Indicators database.

enterprises in terms of real sales revenue and value added, whether compared by mean or median. In terms of employment and equipment, however, the export-oriented enterprises are larger than the tailor-turned RTW enterprises. Therefore, the export-oriented enterprises have much lower value added per worker than the tailor-turned RTW enterprises. Moreover, they have lower value added per worker than the other RTW enterprises and even the tailors. The tailors are not just small in size in terms of value added and employment, but also poor in equipment. Their sewing equipment consisted of antiquated foot-treadle machines. By contrast, the export-oriented enterprises used electrically powered high-speed machines. Nonetheless, their value added per worker was lower than that of the tailors.

Value added per worker is not exactly the same as labor productivity, because it does not take labor hours into account. In 2007, workers worked only 44.7 hours per week at the export-oriented enterprises, whereas they worked 59.1 hours at the tailor-turned enterprises, 49.6 hours at the other RTW enterprises, and 52.8 hours at the tailors. Therefore, even if the differences in labor hours are taken into account, the productivity of the export-oriented enterprises is significantly lower than that of the tailor-turned enterprises. These observations support Hypothesis 9-1.

Real sales revenue and real value added have large discrepancies between their means and medians. The discrepancies are particularly large for the tailor-turned RTW enterprises. This is because there are two distinct large types of enterprise in this group. One is the above-mentioned innovator with relatively low education. The other has 12 years of education. Note, however, that, even if these particularly successful enterprises are excluded from the sample as outliers, the tailor-turned RTW enterprises still have higher labor productivity than the other enterprise types.

If the government support were helpful in improving productivity, real labor productivity would tend to rise over time and to be higher for the early entrants than for the new entrants. To see whether this conjecture holds true, Table 9.5 highlights the latest year in the study period and focuses on the export-oriented enterprises. The enterprises established between 2005 and 2007 (Group A) began exporting garment products in the second half of 2007 (or 2006.7), whereas those established between 1999 and 2004 (Group B) began exporting garment products around the middle of 2004 (or 2003.5). The three export-oriented enterprises established before 1998 (Group C) used to be state-owned and began exporting garment products around the end of 2005. The median of labor productivity is particularly low in Group B, which is the most experienced in exporting. Thus, labor productivity of export-oriented enterprises does not seem to increase over time. While Group C has slightly higher labor productivity than the tailors and the other RTW enterprises (see Table 9.4), it is not impressive compared with the very high labor productivity of the tailor-turned RTW enterprises.

The data on value added, employment, and sales revenues indicate that Group C is largest and that the size of Group B is almost the same as the size of Group A in terms of the median. The data on export as a percentage of sales revenue indicate that Group B is most strongly export-oriented. This group's small share of material cost in the current cost bears out its strong orientation toward exporting, because global buyers often put out materials to producers. By contrast, Group C has a relatively low export ratio and a high material cost ratio, which indicate

Table 9.5 Performance of export-oriented enterprises in the garment industry in Ethiopia, 2007[a]

	Established in		
	2005 to 2007	1999 to 2004	1998 or earlier
	Group A	Group B	Group C
Number of enterprises	7	4	3
Number of former state-owned enterprises	0	1	3
Year started exporting	2006.7	2003.5	2005.0
Real value added per worker (1,000 birr)			
Mean	3.5	4.7	5.4
Median	4.1	2.0	6.8
Real value added (1,000 birr)			
Mean	359	1,473	1,354
Median	275	256.1	1,820
Number of production workers			
Mean	144.1	170.75	266.3
Median	124	123.5	278
Real sales revenue (1,000 birr)			
Mean	740	1,662	5,358
Median	467	357	4,755
Export as % of sales revenue			
Mean	56.4	62.5	40.5
Median	64.3	70.0	46.0
Material cost as % of current cost			
Mean	29.1	6.8	71.0
Median	29.8	4.7	71.4

[a]Current cost refers to the sum of the expenses on materials, labor, rent, electricity and transportation.

that this group is less export-oriented. In sum, the more strongly export-oriented, the less productive and the slower in growth is the enterprise. These observations lend further support to Hypothesis 9.1.

The data indicating the effort to upgrade enterprise capacity are presented in Table 9.6. Among the 14 export-oriented enterprises, only six employed a foreign expert during the period under study, that is, between 2004 and 2007. Only one export-oriented enterprise and the innovative tailor-turned RTW enterprise employed foreign experts for 2 or 3 years. Most foreign experts came from India and Mauritius. The fact that only a small number of foreign experts are employed by the export-oriented enterprises is consistent with their low labor productivity.

Table 9.6 Upgrading of enterprise capacity in the garment industry in Ethiopia

	RTW enterprises		
	Export-oriented	Tailor-turned	Others
Number of enterprises hiring foreign staff[a]	6	1	0
In-house training program			
% of enterprises running training	92.9	71.4	64.0
% of workers receiving training	73.2	52.9	44.7
Average length of training (weeks)	5.6	5.5	7.8
Training programs at formal institutions			
% of enterprises sending workers to training	42.9	57.1	18.2
% of workers receiving training	25.9	2.6	21.9
Average duration of training (weeks)	2.1	5.4	3.4

[a]The first column indicates the number of enterprises which had hired foreign staff as managers, supervisors or technicians from 2004 to 2007.

Table 9.6 also shows the data on worker training. Apart from on-the-job training, the vast majority of the enterprises provide in-house training programs, which are provided to 40 to 70 percent of the workers and last more than 5 weeks on average. Some enterprises sent workers to short-term training programs held at formal institutions. The short-term programs, however, cannot be compared with the intensive training that Desh's workers received at Daewoo's factory in Korea when the export-oriented garment industry in Bangladesh emerged (see Section 8.1 in the previous chapter).

As shown in the upper panel of Table 9.7, the export-oriented enterprises had a low percentage of operating expenses on raw materials. As mentioned earlier, global buyers tend to put out materials to developing country producers. At the bottom of the product quality ladder of the global value chain, developing country producers are expected to provide simple processing services like sewing. This is why the export-oriented enterprises have a relatively low proportion of raw material cost and a relatively high proportion of labor cost. Probably, if they were fully admitted by the major global value chains, these tendencies would be much stronger. As we indicated in Table 9.5, however, completely export-oriented enterprises were in a minority in Addis Ababa, at least

Table 9.7 Composition of operating expenses and supply sources of fabric in the garment industry in Ethiopia, 2004–07

	RTW enterprises			
	Export-oriented	Tailor-turned	Others	Tailors
Composition of operating expenses				
% raw material	32.6	62.2	58.8	47.3
% labor cost	46.0	23.4	32.1	16.0
% utility and transportation	9.9	2.2	3.4	9.4
% rent	11.5	12.2	5.7	27.3
Sources of supply of fabric				
% produced domestically	43.3	6.4	44.9	9.4
% from Dubai through traders	8.5	36.7	18.0	55.9
% directly from Dubai	7.4	21.1	19.0	0
% from other countries	40.8	35.8	18.1	34.7

at the time of our survey, and the majority of the export-oriented enterprises were catering to the domestic market as well. Only a few were transacting with global value chains on a regular basis. Some others were attempting to obtain access to some global value chains by sending samples. Still others were exporting products to neighboring country markets.

According to the lower panel of Table 9.7, when the export-oriented enterprises procured materials by themselves, they used domestically produced materials more than the tailor-turned RTW enterprises and the tailors. The latter types of enterprises use expensive imported fabric to produce men's suits and women's dresses. This is why the material cost accounts for a large part of their operating expenses. For them, rent is also an important cost item, because, unlike factories, their shops must be in town, and it is more advantageous if they are located in a more crowded commercial area. If they can afford to pay high rents, they tend to prefer to be located in such an area. In our sample, 25 percent of the tailors had changed their locations by the time of our survey. The tailor-turned RTW enterprises moved their production bases to spacious areas when they extended their businesses to RTW production.

The innovative tailor-turned RTW enterprise manager was the first to develop a channel for importing material for men's suits directly from Dubai. His business grew rapidly and then he adopted the factory system, turning into an RTW enterprise. He invested substantially in equipment and introduced the two-shift system for the first time in the garment industry in the country to raise the capacity utilization rate. To match marketing with mass production, he also began TV commercials for the first time in the garment industry in the country. Following his lead, other tailors and RTW enterprises developed other channels for importing materials. According to personal interviews with him, he had no intention of going into the export garment business. He explained that he could not be successful in international business because he was not well educated.

The export-oriented enterprises have so far achieved no innovations. Instead, some of them have requested more subsidies from the government, according to a recent article.[4] Some of them complained that the quality of the domestically produced materials was too low for them to compete in the international market. In a similar vein, some others complained that it is difficult for them to compete in the international market because they had to be highly dependent on imported materials.

9.3   Estimation methods and results

Tables 9.3 and 9.5 indicate that the tailor-turned RTW enterprises are greater in employment size, more productive, and operated by more educated managers than the tailors, whereas the export-oriented enterprises are less productive than the non-subsidized enterprises despite their highly educated managers. These observations are consistent with Hypotheses 9.1 and 9.2. In this section, we would like to go beyond the comparison between enterprise types to offer stronger evidence. By using regressions, we can confirm whether export-oriented enterprises have lower productivity even after controlling for the effects of covariates. It is also interesting to examine whether labor productivity and employment sizes are positively related to managers' education levels among the tailors as well as among the RTW enterprises. We would also like to assess the impact of the experience as an import trader on productivity and employment size to test Hypothesis 9.3.

In what follows, we run the so-called reduced-form regressions in which the right-hand side variables are the manager's background attributes, listed in Table 9.3, and the years of operation. We do not claim that the variables representing background attributes are purely exogenous, because of some confounding factors, such as unobservable characteristics or disturbances correlated with some of the right-hand side variables. Since our enterprise data have four points in time, we assume that the error component consists of individual effect u_i, time effect λ_t, and idiosyncratic error ε_{it} so that the regression equation is written as

$$y_{it} = X_{it}\beta + u_i + \lambda_t + \varepsilon_{it},$$

where X_{it} is a vector of independent variables. If the individual effect, u_i, is a fixed effect, we cannot estimate the coefficients on the time-invariant variables, such as the education variable, even though we are interested in the coefficients on these variables. Therefore, we will discuss the random-effect model estimates as long as the result of the Hausman specification test suggests that they are consistent.

The estimation results concerning the tailors are reported in Table 9.8 and those concerning the RTW enterprises are reported in Table 9.9. In Table 9.8, the dependent variable is the log of the number of workers in column (1) and the log of value added per worker in column (2). As shown at the bottom of these columns, the Hausman test does not reject the consistency of the random-effect estimates. The t-statistics reported in parentheses are based on the standard errors that allow correlation within an enterprise. The manager's education level is captured by three dummy variables; that is, dummies indicating whether or not the manager is a secondary school graduate, whether or not he or she is a vocational school graduate, and whether or not he or she is a college graduate. Not a few tailors are elementary school graduates or elementary school dropouts. Compared with such uneducated tailors, secondary school graduates tend to employ a larger number of workers and have higher labor productivity, by more than 40 percent. The college graduates have even larger employment sizes, but their enterprises have lower labor productivity than the secondary school graduates' enterprises.

Although not shown in the tables, we ran regressions of other specifications as well. If the three education variables are replaced by a single variable representing the number of years of education, its estimated coefficient is 0.084 in the employment size equation and 0.066 in the productivity equation, and both are significant at the 1 percent level. The relationship between the manager's education level and labor productivity appears very different depending on which specification is used. With the years of schooling, the coefficient estimate suggests that the college graduates would have even higher productivity. We believe that the estimation with the three dummy variables is more reliable. If college graduates had very high productivity, as the coefficient on the

Table 9.8 Determinants of employment size, labor productivity, and rent payment of the tailors in the garment industry in Ethiopia[a]

	(i)	(ii)	(iii)	(iv)
	ln$N$	ln(RV/N)	ln(Initial$N$)	ln(Rent)
Secondary school dummy	0.447**	0.416*	0.586*	0.776*
	(3.52)	(2.10)	(2.13)	(2.60)
Vocational school dummy	0.275	−0.049	0.059	−0.036
	(0.79)	(−0.08)	(0.23)	(−0.04)
College dummy	1.158**	0.223	1.608*	2.090**
	(3.05)	(0.68)	(2.59)	(3.37)
Years of operation	0.018**	0.013*	−0.006	0.042**
	(3.29)	(1.79)	(−0.47)	(3.28)
Age	0.011*	0.010	0.029*	0.008
	(1.70)	(1.11)	(1.72)	(0.49)
Female dummy	0.042	0.114	0.061	0.090
	(0.33)	(0.45)	(0.22)	(0.46)
Management training dummy	0.091	−0.324	0.240	−1.348**
	(0.34)	(−0.77)	(0.46)	(−2.38)
Civil servant dummy	0.192*	0.743**	0.310	−0.070
	(2.11)	(4.46)	(1.27)	(−0.27)
Importer dummy	0.160*	1.096***	0.401**	−0.256
	(2.39)	(9.97)	(2.82)	(−1.42)
Year 2004 dummy	−0.093**	0.142**		
	(−3.02)	(3.26)		
Year 2005 dummy	−0.071**	0.060		
	(−2.98)	(1.57)		
Year 2006 dummy	−0.021*	−0.021		
	(−2.22)	(−0.84)		
Constant	−0.416	7.558**	−0.054	6.340**
	(−1.37)	(18.55)	(−0.07)	(9.34)
Number of observations	456	456	104	114
Hausman test chi squared	2.94	5.76		
p-value	0.400	0.1242		
R^2			0.144	0.245

[a]The random-effects specification is applied to the panel data columns (i) and (ii), whereas OLS is applied to cross-section data in (iii) and (iv). The dependent variable is the log of the number of production workers in column (i), the log of real value added per worker in column (ii), the log of the initial number of production workers in column (iii), and the log of rent payment in 2007 in column (iv). Years of operation and age are fixed to the values in 2007. Numbers in parentheses are t-statistics, based on cluster standard errors in columns (i) and (ii), and robust standard error in (iii) and (iv). **Significant at the 1% level, *at the 5% level. The results of the Hausman specification test indicate that the random-effects model estimates are consistent.

Table 9.9 Determinants of employment size and labor productivity of the RTW enterprises in the garment industry in Ethiopia[a]

	(i)	(ii)	(iii)	(iv)
	ln$N$	ln(RV/N)	ln$N$	ln(RV/N)
College dummy	−0.091	0.422	−0.192	0.712
	(−0.32)	(0.75)	(−0.57)	(1.14)
Export*College			0.542	−2.216**
			(0.72)	(−2.93)
Export dummy	1.075**	−0.961*	0.542	1.641*
	(2.91)	(−1.70)	(0.68)	(1.87)
Years of operation	−0.016	0.033	−0.024	0.107*
	(−1.22)	(1.05)	(−1.22)	(2.10)
Export* Years of operation			0.016	−0.136*
			(0.55)	(−2.38)
SOE dummy	1.793**	0.913	1.661**	2.018**
	(5.75)	(0.98)	(4.42)	(3.32)
Age	0.008	0.008	0.015	−0.032
	(0.53)	(0.25)	(0.99)	(−0.91)
Female dummy	−0.887*	−0.143	−0.823*	−0.272
	(−2.40)	(−0.22)	(−1.80)	(−0.36)
Management training dummy	−0.142	−0.027	−0.082	−0.070
	(−0.51)	(−0.06)	(−0.27)	(−0.14)
Civil servant dummy	0.217	−0.464	0.116	0.091
	(0.71)	(−0.94)	(0.36)	(0.18)
Importer dummy	0.471*	0.531	0.411*	0.972
	(2.22)	(0.74)	(1.77)	(1.36)
Top two dummy	2.266**	1.228**	2.267**	1.103*
	(7.46)	(3.02)	(6.98)	(2.56)
Tailor turned dummy	0.152	1.041*	0.224	0.625
	(0.35)	(1.70)	(0.51)	(1.04)
Year 2004 dummy	−0.435**	0.154	−0.437**	0.183
	(−2.74)	(0.79)	(−2.72)	(0.92)
Year 2005 dummy	−0.135	0.013	−0.137	0.044
	(−1.12)	(0.06)	(−1.13)	(0.22)
Year 2006 dummy	−0.033	−0.186	−0.038	−0.150
	(−0.37)	(−0.61)	(−0.41)	(−0.49)
Constant	3.389**	7.533**	3.171**	8.601**
	(4.32)	(4.53)	(4.06)	(5.34)
Number of observations	99	99	99	99
Hausman test chi squared	0.06	†	0.22	†
p-value	0.997		0.974	

[a]The dependent variable is the log of the number of production workers in columns (i) and (iii) and the log of real value added per worker in (ii) and (iv). Years of operation and age are fixed to their values in 2007. The results of the Hausman specification test indicate that the random-effects model estimates are consistent. †indicates that model fitted on these data fails to meet the asymptotic assumptions of the Hausman test. Numbers in parentheses are t-statistics, based on cluster standard errors. **Significant at the 1% level, *at the 5% level.

years of schooling suggests, there would be a greater number of college graduates in the tailor sample. Some of the college graduates extended their businesses to RTW. Consistently, in the weighted regression with the data combining the 130 tailors and seven tailor-turned RTW enterprises, the coefficient on the college dummy is positive and significant.[5] These results are consistent with Hypothesis 9.2.

The number of years of operation since establishment has positive and significant coefficients in both the employment and labor productivity equations, but its coefficient in the employment equation is larger and has a higher significance level. These results suggest that the tailors grow in size through the accumulation of material capital, managerial human capital, and workers' industry-specific human capital or skill. Here, material capital takes the form of rolls of cloth, better location and a larger shop, and a larger number of high-speed sewing machines. It is difficult to disentangle the effects of these different types of capital. We will return to this question soon below.

The civil servant dummy and the importer dummy have positive and highly significant coefficients in columns (i) and (ii), despite the small presence of former civil servants and former importers in the sample. The significant effect of the importer dummy is consistent with Hypothesis 9-3. These results may be interpreted as reflecting the effects of both trading experience and financial wealth. Note that most managers in the tailor sector are business owners and, if not, the manager is a child of the owner. Managers who have experience as civil servants may have accumulated financial wealth before becoming tailors. Former import traders may have had the financial ability to start tailor businesses on a larger scale than average, and their experience may help them procure high-quality material at lower costs. We will shortly examine the impact of financial ability more closely.

The coefficients on a year dummy variable indicate the difference between the situation in the year indicated and that in 2007. In column (i), the coefficients on the year dummies indicate that the employment size of the tailors expanded steadily over time more or less uniformly for all tailors regardless of the years of operation and other attributes. This must be a reflection of the booming economy of Ethiopia, especially in Addis Ababa. In column (ii), only the year 2004 dummy has a significant coefficient. Probably, this is because average labor productivity declined as employment expanded in 2005 and after following the downward-sloping average labor product curve.

Columns (iii) and (iv) report the results of regressions using the cross-section data. The dependent variable in column (iii) is the log of the initial number of workers, that is, the employment size in the first year of the enterprise's operation. We ran this regression with a view to identifying the effect of education separately from the effect of experience. The secondary school dummy and the college dummy have positive and significant coefficients in column (iii), as in column (i), and the magnitudes of these coefficients are larger in column (iii) than in column (i).[6] These results suggest that secondary and tertiary education is not helpful in the employment growth of tailors after they have started their businesses.

Note that the negligible impact of education on employment growth does not imply that education is not useful for the tailor business. In column (iv), the dependent variable is the log of rent payment in 2007. The estimation results indicate that more educated managers tend to operate their businesses in more expensive areas. For a successful tailor, it is more profitable to have a shop in a crowded, commercial area, where it is difficult to expand the size of the shop. If the tailor seeks further growth, he or she will prefer to increase the number of shops and then diversify the business. Going into the RTW business will be one option for such a tailor.

The coefficient of the years of operation in column (iii) has a very different meaning from that in column (i). In column (iii), this variable does not represent experience as a head of an enterprise, but rather the timing of establishing the enterprise. Since the coefficient is near zero, old-established and newly established enterprises do not differ in initial employment size. Age has a much larger coefficient in column (iii) than in column (i), indicating that older new entrants start larger shops but their subsequent growth is slower than for younger new entrants. Likewise, the civil servant dummy and the importer dummy have larger coefficients in column (iii) than in column (i). These results suggest that new entrants with experience as civil servants or import traders can afford to have larger shops when they start their tailor business, but their businesses do not grow as much as other tailors. It seems reasonable to infer that they can afford to install better equipment, which would lead to higher labor productivity, as indicated in column (ii), even though they are not located in high-rent areas according to column (iv). The negative and significant effect of participation in a management training program on rent is difficult to interpret.

To sum up, the effect of education on the tailor business is positive and significant, which is consistent with Hypothesis 9.2. The effect is dampened at the college level as long as the scope of analysis is limited to the tailors who stay in the tailor business. If the scope of the analysis is expanded to cover RTW businesses as well, however, the effect of higher education becomes stronger.

We turn now to the analysis of the determinants of employment size and labor productivity of RTW enterprises. The four columns in Table 9.9 present the estimates of the random-effects model and t-statistics based on standard errors that allow intragroup correlation, even though the model for the value added per worker (columns (ii) and (iv)) did not meet the asymptotic assumptions of the Hausman test. Since the education levels of RTW enterprise managers are high, the regressions do not include the secondary education dummy. Columns (iii) and (iv) include two interaction terms, whereas columns (i) and (ii) do not. One is the product of the export dummy and the college dummy, and the other is the interaction between the export dummy and the years of operation, where the export dummy indicates whether the enterprise is export-oriented. These interaction terms are included in the regressions to examine how special the export-oriented enterprises are.

In all columns, the coefficient on the college dummy is insignificant. Even if the dummy is replaced by the years of schooling, the qualitative results remain unchanged. Note, however, that the coefficient of the college dummy in the labor productivity equation is positive and that it increases from 0.4 to 0.7 when the interaction terms are inserted. We may conjecture that, given the small size of our sample, these results indicate that, among the non-subsidized enterprises, the education level of managers has a positive productivity effect. By contrast, the interaction term between the export dummy and the college dummy has a negative and highly significant coefficient, implying that the labor productivity of export-oriented enterprises managed by college graduates is lower than for those managed by the less educated. These results lend additional support to Hypothesis 9.2.

The export dummy has a positive and highly significant effect on employment in column (i) but a negative and marginally significant effect on labor productivity in column (ii). If the interaction term between this dummy and the years of operation is inserted in the regression, however, the highly significant effect of the export dummy on employment size becomes insignificant, and the negative effect of the export dummy on labor productivity becomes positive. Moreover, with the interaction terms, the insignificant effect of the years of operation becomes positive and significant at the 5 percent level. The interaction term has an insignificant effect on employment size and a negative and significant effect on labor productivity. The sum of the coefficient of the export dummy and that of the years of operation in column (iv) is negative (0.107 – 0.136) and insignificant, which clearly indicates that the subsidized enterprises do not improve labor productivity whereas the non-subsidized enterprises do. This result supports Hypothesis 9.1 and offers a contrast to the infant-industry protection argument that protected enterprises improve productivity through learning-by-doing.

The female dummy is 1 if the manager is female. Its negative and significant effect on employment size is difficult to interpret. The importer dummy has a positive coefficient in each column and is significant in the columns for employment size. These results are consistent with Hypothesis 9.3.

The SOE dummy and the top two dummy require explanation. The SOE dummy is 1 if the enterprise is formerly state-owned and 0 otherwise. Since all the former state-owned enterprises are export-oriented, the sum of the coefficients of the export dummy and this dummy indicates the difference between these enterprises and the typical RTW enterprises. The top two dummy indicates whether the enterprise is one of the two largest enterprises among the tailor-turned RTW enterprises. Thus, the top two dummy is used to control for the effects of these outliers. The estimation results indicate that the former state-owned enterprises are as large in employment as the top two enterprises but not as productive as the top two. If the top two enterprises are excluded from the sample, the estimation results as a whole are qualitatively the same as the results shown in this table.

9.4 Concluding remarks

This chapter has explored how the government's attempt to promote an industry has misfired. Because of the small sample size of the enterprises targeted by the government policy, it is difficult to offer an anatomy of why the intervention misfired. Nonetheless, by examining a case that makes a stark contrast to the successful case discussed in Chapter 8, this chapter has gained new insights into industrial development policy. In Chapter 8, we saw that the initial infusion of expertise into the international garment business brought about the sizable upward shift of the production function in the garment industry in Bangladesh in the early 1980s. This sizable technology transfer boosted the rate of returns to investments in garment factories, which invited immense investments and encouraged highly educated young people to acquire technical and managerial expertise, which was in turn followed almost immediately by the phenomenal growth of the industry, as clearly shown in Table 8.1. This dynamic process may be illustrated by a diagram such

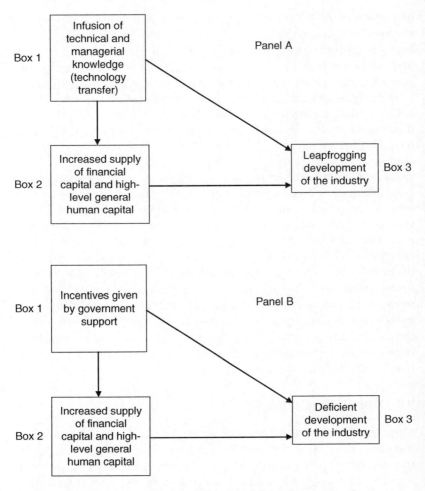

Figure 9.1 An illustration of bifurcated industrial development paths

Panel A in Figure 9.1, which shows the direct effect of technology transfer (Box 1) on the leapfrogging development of the industry (Box 3) as well as its indirect effect through its effect on the supply of financial and human capital (Box 2).

The situation of the export-oriented garment industry in Ethiopia is illustrated in Panel B. While the content of Box 1 is the infusion of technical and managerial expertise in Panel A, it is government support in Panel B. As a result of government support, wealthy people and highly educated managers were attracted to the export-oriented garment business. Thus, panels A and B share the same content in Box 2. Nonetheless, they differ greatly in the outcome, that is, Box 3. This is because in Panel B expertise in the international garment business is missing.

With the data, anecdotes, and analysis presented in Chapter 8, it was unclear whether the key to successful industrial development is held by the initial massive transfer of technical and managerial knowledge or the participation of highly educated managers in the industry. The sustained growth of the industry was a result of continual learning from abroad, which was in turn facilitated by the high level of managerial human capital. With data collected in the 2000s, it was difficult to offer direct evidence for the importance of the initial technology transfer.

It is now clear that the massive technology transfer in the beginning was vital for the development of the export-oriented garment industry in Bangladesh. Without high levels of expertise, there is no option but to fall into cut-throat competition with enterprises in other low-wage countries. Without high expertise and with the government willing to support industrial development, therefore, it is rational for the managers of subsidized enterprises to solicit further preferential treatment from the government rather than organizing learning from abroad. The industrial development promotion policy of the government is thus counterproductive unless it begins with technology transfer. Financial support will be useful only in a situation in which the target industry has already developed a sufficient pool of technical and managerial experts. If the government intends to help an industry leapfrog ahead, the support for the transfer of technology and managerial knowledge from abroad must be sustained in addition to the initial infusion of the relevant knowledge.

10
Conclusion: Towards the Design of Effective Industrial Development Policies

In order to reduce widespread and persistent poverty in developing countries, we have to develop labor-intensive industries to provide ample employment opportunities for the poor. Yet the term "industrial policy" is synonymous with "undesirable policy" for many economists and policymakers, as the policies implemented to support industrialization in the 1960s and 1970s were so unsuccessful. Such policies were highly interventionist without carefully considering market failure. In contemplating appropriate policies, it is critically important to recognize that there are many types of market failures in industrial sectors because of (1) the high transaction costs arising from imperfect contract enforcement and information asymmetry about the quality of final products, raw materials, and parts, as well as the quality and work attitude of employees, (2) spillovers of technological and managerial information from innovators to imitators, (3) underinvestment in human capital due to credit constraints and uncertainty, (4) underinvestment in public goods, such as roads, electricity, and communication systems, and (5) imperfect credit markets due to adverse selection, moral hazard, and incomplete contracts. We believe that the heart of the question is how we can reduce such market failures so as to stimulate the development of industries. The ultimate purpose of this book is to formulate effective policies to promote industrial development – we call this "industrial development policy," as distinct from "industrial policy."

We focus on industrial clusters, as most, if not all, of the labor-intensive industries in developing countries are clustered. Our basic proposition is that the relative importance of different market failures changes in the dynamic process of cluster-based industrial development.

Corresponding to such changes, appropriate policies should also change.

While asymmetric information is always a problem, the industrial cluster is effective in mitigating it because people get to know one another and information about misconduct is quickly disseminated by word of mouth within a cluster. In other words, the cluster helps markets work by reducing information asymmetry. Thus, it makes sense to support the formation of industrial clusters by constructing marketplaces to facilitate market transactions and by providing local public goods such as paved roads, electricity, and communication systems.

Due to geographical proximity, information spillover is rampant in industrial clusters. This is socially undesirable as it reduces innovation incentives. Thus, during the quality improvement phase, in which innovations are actively sought, the advantage of being in an industrial cluster tends to be eroded. For the purpose of filling the gap between the social and private benefits of innovation, government support for innovation can be justified. Since innovation requires managerial human capital, an effective way to support innovation is to invest in entrepreneurs' managerial human capital by providing appropriate training from the early stage of the quality improvement phase.

Once an enterprise succeeds in multifaceted innovations, it wants to expand the size of its operation. When the cluster is congested, it often wants to move to an industrial zone where more space with improved infrastructure is available. Thus, investing in the construction of industrial zones is an effective support policy during the quality improvement phase. Also, credit constraints are likely to be serious at this stage, when an innovative enterprise wants to expand its production capacity. It is important to note that, at this stage, it is relatively easy to distinguish between innovative and non-innovative enterprises, compared with the quantitative expansion phase, in which all enterprises appear equally small. Thus, the provision of credit becomes an effective policy measure at the quality improvement phase.

In Section 10.1 below, in order to develop a proper perspective on the nature of industrial clusters in Asia and Africa, we would like to make a brief comparison of the industrial clusters that we have studied in this and our previous books. In Section 10.2, we examine the validity of the three major hypotheses regarding the key growth drivers postulated in Chapter 1: managerial human capital, access to traders, and international knowledge transfer. In Section 10.3, we reconsider the "East Asian Model of Cluster-Based Industrial Development" or "a model of endogenous development of industrial clusters" discussed in

Section 1.2 in light of the new evidence found in this study. Finally we provide implications of this study for effective industrial development policies in Section 10.4.

10.1 Development of industrial clusters: A comparative perspective

We would like to make a brief comparison among the eight industrial clusters examined in this volume as well as with the eight industrial clusters studied in Northeast Asia by Sonobe and Otsuka (2006), in terms of the number of enterprises in a cluster, the average size of employment per enterprise, and the average years of schooling of enterprise managers. It will be shown that the comparison of these characteristics sheds light on the similarities and dissimilarities of the industrial clusters across Northeast Asia, other parts of Asia, and SSA.

10.1.1 China, Japan, and Taiwan

Table 10.1 exhibits the major characteristics of the industrial clusters in China, Japan, and Taiwan. Note that the case of the motorcycle industry in Japan was a historical study referring to the 1950s, and that some industries, namely the machine tool and printed circuit board industries, are not highly labor-intensive.[1] In what follows, we would like to point out only conspicuous differences across the eight cases.

First, the number of enterprises in the garment cluster in China, shown in the first column in Table 10.1, is large, whereas its employment size is small. While an extremely large domestic market size, the vast availability of cheap labor, and other characteristics in the Chinese economy may explain a part of these characteristics, we believe that a major reason lies in the fact that this cluster was largely at the quantity expansion phase, in which a large number of small enterprises produce similar low-quality products. Although we do not have data on the average size of employment in the case of the Japanese motorcycle industry in the early 1950s, it was likely to be relatively small, because quality competition began later, in the mid-1950s. In fact, this industry grew very fast after the mid-1950s, but only four large enterprises survived into the quality improvement phase. In all other cases, quality competition had already begun.

Second, except in the garment and electric appliance clusters in China, the schooling levels of enterprise managers are reasonably high, ranging from 11 to 16 years, which means that the majority of managers graduated from either high school or university. In these industries, the

Table 10.1 Major characteristics of industrial clusters in Northeast Asia

	Garment in Zhili, China	Garment in Bingo, Japan	Motorcycle in Hamamatsu, Japan	Motorcycle in Chongqing, China	Machine tool in Taichung, Taiwan	Electric appliance in Wenzhou, China	Printed circuit board in northern Taiwan	Printed circuit board in Jiangsu, China
Period studied	1999	1998	1952	2001	1996	2000	2003	2002
No. of enterprises	5,000	75	130	55	65	117[e]	47[e]	150
Average size of employment	17	56.8[a]	n.a.[c]	932[a]	95.6	338	1,100	70–280[f]
Average years of schooling	7.5	13.5	n.a.[c]	13.7–15.2[a,d]	13[a]	10.4	11	12–16[f]
Growth	Very high	Stagnant	Very high	Very high	Very high	Very high	High	Very high
Export	Inactive	None[b]	Active	Active	Active	None	Active	None

[a] The data are not shown in Sonobe and Otsuka (2006) but were computed from the original data.
[b] Export from subsidiaries in China to Japan is active.
[c] Not available.
[d] The first number refers to the chairman, whereas the second number refers to the general manager.
[e] The data refer to our sample, as there are no accurate data for the total number of enterprises.
[f] The first number refers to the average of the Chinese enterprises, whereas the second number refers to the average of the foreign ventures.

Source: Sonobe and Otsuka (2006).

number of enterprises is not large but the average size of employment is relatively large. The high education levels of the managers and the large sizes of enterprises are characteristics of the quality improvement phase. The average schooling levels of the managers in the garment and electric appliance clusters in China are exceptionally low, because these were originally rural industries in which a number of enterprise managers used to be farmers.[2] We expect that the average schooling levels in these two clusters will increase as quality competition intensifies.[3]

Third, the garment industry in Japan and the machine tool industry in Taiwan had relatively small employment sizes. In the former case, the enterprises are engaged mainly in designing and marketing, while establishing large production bases in China. In the latter case, the sample enterprises are assemblers relying on a large number of subcontracts with parts suppliers. So the total size of operation was larger than the employment size suggests.

Finally, we would like to point out that the majority of enterprises in Northeast Asia are located in industrial zones after moving from the congested original clusters. In other words, the current large enterprises used to be small enterprises located in indigenously developed industrial clusters and operated primarily by family labor.

10.1.2   Rest of Asia and SSA

Table 10.2 presents the summary data of the industrial clusters studied in this book. Several important findings can be made. First of all, the successful development of the garment industry in Bangladesh is remarkable; there are so many enterprises, many of them are huge, and most managers are highly educated. This industry is export-oriented, and thus the limited size of the domestic market is not a constraint on the growth of this industrial cluster. Many enterprise managers are not only educated but also intensively trained abroad. As a result, many of them are innovative. It seems to us that this industry is a good model of successful cluster-based industrial development in developing countries.

Second, in general, the clustered enterprises in SSA are small and the schooling levels of enterprise managers are low. As far as the original industrial clusters are concerned, the average employment sizes are only three to five in the garment cluster in Nairobi, six in the metalwork cluster in Nairobi, also six in the leather shoe cluster in Addis Ababa, and two in the garment cluster in Addis Ababa. Note that many of the relatively large factories, whose average employment size is 120, are located outside the indigenous clusters and are subsidized by the

Table 10.2 Major characteristics of industrial clusters in Southeast and South Asia, and sub-Saharan Africa

	Garment in Northern Vietnam	Garment in Nairobi, Kenya	Steel bar in Northern Vietnam	Metalwork in Nairobi, Kenya	Electric fittings in Sargodha, Pakistan	Leather shoe in Addis Ababa, Ethiopia	Garment in Dhaka, Bangladesh	Garment in Addis Ababa, Ethiopia
Year studied	2006	2003	2007	2006	2009	2004	2005	2007
No. of manufacturing enterprises	142[a]	750	370	150	1,200	1,000–2,000	4,100	700
Average size of employment	27	3–5[b]	10–36[c]	6–25[d]	15	6–92[e]	830–1,830[f]	2–120[g]
Average years of schooling	10.5	8.5	6.5	11–13[d]	9.4	9–15[e]	14.7–15.4[f]	9.0–14.5[g]
Growth	High	Stagnant	Pretty high	High	High	Very high	Very high	Low
Export	Active	None	None	None	None	Beginning	Very active	Inactive

[a] There are 5,000 to 6,000 household enterprises serving as subcontractors.

[b] The employment size differs across the three marketplaces.

[c] The employment size depends on the type of product.

[d] The first number refers to the average of the enterprises located in the industrial cluster, whereas the second number refers to that in the industrial zone.

[e] The first number refers to the average of the enterprises located In the industrial cluster, whereas the second number refers to that outside the cluster.

[f] The first number refers to T-shirt producers, whereas the second number refers to sweater producers.

[g] The first number refers to tailors, whereas the second number refers to ready-to-wear factories.

government. It seems clear that these industrial clusters are trapped in the quantity expansion phase.

Third, there are indications in the metalwork cluster in Nairobi and the leather shoe cluster in Addis Ababa that some enterprises managed by educated managers have moved to industrial zones. These enterprises are significantly larger than the other enterprises remaining in the original clusters. It appears that these enterprises have succeeded in innovation and have thereby enlarged the size of their enterprises. These successful enterprises look somewhat similar to those observed in Northeast Asia.

Fourth, enterprises in the garment and steel bar clusters in northern Vietnam and the electric fittings cluster in Pakistan are also small and managed by relatively uneducated managers. In contrast, the number of enterprises is relatively large, if we take into account the fact that there are thousands of household enterprises producing parts in the garment cluster in northern Vietnam. As we have seen in the previous chapters, some enterprises in these clusters have begun innovations, but the transition from the quantity expansion to the quality improvement phase is far from complete. In this respect, the problems facing the industrial clusters in Vietnam and Pakistan do not seem qualitatively very different from those facing the industrial clusters in SSA. In sum, although there are differences between Asia, represented by Vietnam and Pakistan, and SSA, represented by Kenya and Ethiopia, these are a matter of degree, but not necessarily substance.

10.2   Key growth drivers

We have postulated the following three hypotheses in Chapter 1:

Hypothesis 1: The managerial human capital of enterprise managers is the major determinant of successful multifaceted innovations.

Hypothesis 2: Traders play a critical role not only in facilitating marketing of low-quality products during the quantity expansion phase but also in assisting the production of upgraded products and supply of high-quality parts and materials, thereby improving the performance of enterprises in an industrial cluster.

Hypothesis 3: The key to successful multifaceted innovations is successful international knowledge transfer.

The purpose of this section is to examine the validity of these three hypotheses in turn, based on the results of the statistical analyses reported in this book.

10.2.1 Managerial human capital

We assume that managerial human capital is formed by formal schooling, prior experience in trading or marketing, experience as a manager, and participation in training programs. Thus, we regressed the variables representing multifaceted innovations, namely price of product as an indicator of product quality, shares of direct sales and export, and the extent of the procurement of high-quality materials, as well as the size of enterprises as an indicator of overall performance, on these indicators of managerial human capital. The regression results are summarized in Table 10.3.

The hypothesis that schooling is an important determinant of multifaceted innovations and overall enterprise performance is overwhelmingly supported by all the case studies. This hypothesis is also strongly supported by Sonobe and Otsuka (2006). According to Schultz (1975), schooling enhances the ability to deal with disequilibria. The ability to carry out innovations is deeply related to the ability to deal with disequilibria, as innovations are a major way to change the equilibria. Furthermore, the innovations in product quality, production methods, marketing, and internal management are all complementary, so in order to be successful these innovations must be adopted more or less simultaneously.[4] In all likelihood, the ability to introduce multifaceted innovations requires general human capital acquired from formal schooling. It must be pointed out that, although schooling levels of managers of large enterprises in the garment industry in Ethiopia are high, their profitability is low because of the distorted management incentives.

Marketing new and improved products and procuring appropriate new materials and parts requires human capital specific to trading. This is why industrial development is often led by managers who have been engaged in trading, particularly if the products are easy to produce but difficult to sell, such as garments and shoes (Sonobe and Otsuka, 2006). Consistently with this view, former traders play significant roles in introducing multifaceted innovations and improving the enterprise performance in five cases reported in this book (see Table 10.3). Unexpectedly, prior experience as traders is not a significant factor in the leather shoe industry in Ethiopia. We must note, however, that, although there are too few to detect statistically, former traders own and manage large and successful enterprises in this industry. It seems to us that, although trading experience is critically important, the availability of competent former traders is limited in SSA, where free marketing was suppressed by excessive market interventions by the

Table 10.3 A summary of the major determinants of multifaceted innovations and enterprise performance[a]

	Garment in Vietnam	Garment in Kenya	Steel bar in Vietnam	Metalwork in Kenya	Electric fittings in Pakistan	Leather shoe in Ethiopia	Garment in Bangladesh	Garment in Ethiopia[b]
Managerial human capital	**	**	**	**	**	**	**	– **
Schooling	**	n.a.	**	n.a.	**	n.a.	**	* **
Trading experience	*	*	**	**	**	**	**	– *
Management experience	n.a.	–	n.a.	–	n.a.	n.a.	**	– n.a.
Training program								
Acquaintance with traders	**	**	n.a.	n.a.	n.a.	n.a.	**	
International knowledge transfer	Eastern Europe	None	SOEs in Vietnam, China	FDIs in Nairobi	India, Sri Lanka, China	Italy	South Korea, Singapore, Europe, India, China	India, Mauritius

[a] *** indicates highly significant, * significant, – insignificant, and "n.a." not applicable.

[b] The symbols on the left-hand side in this column indicate the significance for the garment factories, whereas those on the right-hand side indicate the significance for the tailors.

government before the structural adjustment policies were introduced in the 1980s.

As may be expected, management experience is another important factor affecting the multifaceted innovations and performance of enterprises consistently in all the cases. It may well be that useful enterprise-specific and industry-specific knowledge has been acquired by learning-by-doing. It is, however, possible that management experience may capture the innate ability of enterprise managers to survive rather than the acquired ability to manage enterprises. Indeed, old and surviving enterprises might have invested accumulated profit in fixed capital, so that they are larger and more efficient than new enterprises.

We failed to obtain detailed information about training programs in which the managers of our sample enterprises had participated in the past, except in the case of Bangladesh. In many cases, managers responded to our questionnaire surveys that they had never participated in any training programs (see "n.a." in Table 10.3). Even when some of them said that they had participated in training programs, the dummy variable showing the participation is insignificant (see the case of the garment and metalwork industries in Kenya). This need not mean, however, that training programs are always useless. Indeed, the training received in more advanced countries has been a decisively important factor promoting innovations and enterprise performance in Bangladesh. It seems likely that well-designed, intensive, and advanced training programs are an important factor stimulating innovations and enterprise growth.

To sum up, there is no question that the managerial human capital of enterprise managers plays a critical role in cluster-based industrial development, which clearly supports Hypothesis 1. Considering that not only enterprise managers in Bangladesh but also successful enterprise managers in the leather shoe industry in Ethiopia are highly educated, the importance of formal schooling is particularly noteworthy.

10.2.2 Role of Traders

We believe that traders play the role of facilitators by bringing market information and technological knowledge into industrial clusters, in addition to providing marketing services. It is, however, difficult to identify their roles statistically, partly because all the manufacturing enterprises have access to more or less similar services of traders in their clusters, and partly because busy traders are reluctant to disclose data on their activities to outsiders. We are, however, fortunate to be able to detect their roles in our three case studies.

In the garment cluster in northern Vietnam, whether enterprise managers have relatives who are overseas Vietnamese traders affects the quality and export share of their products and the performance of their enterprises. In the garment cluster in Nairobi, enterprises that have attracted petty traders produce a large quantity of a small number of products in relatively large workshops, which results in superior overall performance of the enterprises. In the garment cluster in Bangladesh, entrepreneurs who are well-trained but do not have access to capital choose to become traders, who transact with enterprises managed by inexperienced entrepreneurs. In this way, traders contribute to the expansion of production by providing relevant information to manufacturers in this cluster. Moreover, long-term contracts with outside traders have become common among producers attempting to improve the quality of their products in the steel bar cluster in Vietnam and the electric fittings cluster in Pakistan.

Taking into account the finding that former traders manage their manufacturing enterprises successfully, it seems clear that the knowledge of marketing is an integral component of managerial human capital. This view is consistent with the results of our informal interviews with enterprise managers, who stress that how to sell the improved products at higher prices is a major issue in enterprise management. These arguments support Hypothesis 2.

10.2.3 International knowledge transfers

For researchers who have studied industrial development in East Asia, it is obvious that learning from abroad is critically important in improving the performance of enterprises. Hamada et al., (2010) argue that the Japanese economy grew miraculously in the 1960s because of effective learning from advanced countries. There is ample anecdotal evidence to support such an argument from our case studies. For example, at present successful enterprise managers in the garment industries in Vietnam and Bangladesh often visit China to learn improved technology and management practices. Also, leading enterprise managers in the leather shoe cluster in Ethiopia often visit Italy to learn designs, production systems, and marketing. It is also worth noting that, in the metalwork cluster in Nairobi, managers with work experience at foreign ventures, such as Indian companies, tend to operate larger enterprises and produce higher-quality products than those who have never worked for foreign ventures in this industry. Also, enterprises in Asia commonly use machines imported from China and their managers learn how to operate the machines from Chinese mechanics, which facilitates the transfer of production technology from China to other countries.

It is important to note that the impact of learning from abroad is found to be statistically significant in our study of the garment enterprises in Bangladesh; managers who were trained abroad perform significantly better than other managers. This is an important finding in view of the usual difficulties in quantifying such effects. Although we do not have other statistical evidence, Hypothesis 3 seems consistent with our empirical observations.

We would also like to point out that it is important to learn not only technological but also managerial knowledge from abroad. Once new production technology is introduced, how to sell the new products, control quality, and manage workers become crucial management issues. Therefore, as with multifaceted innovations, learning from abroad must be multifaceted if it is to be successful.

10.3 A model of endogenous development of industrial clusters reconsidered

In describing the model of endogenous development of industrial clusters in Section 1.2, we took it for granted that (1) innovations are stimulated by the declining profitability of producing low-quality products due to the rapid entry of new imitating enterprises during the quantity expansion phase, (2) the quantity expansion phase is followed by the quality improvement phase, and (3) clustered enterprises tend to stay in the clusters throughout the quality improvement phase. These points need to be re-examined because the China shock also triggered efforts to innovate, the garment cluster in Bangladesh skipped the quantity expansion phase, and some progressive enterprises actually left congested industrial clusters even in SSA.

10.3.1 Role of the China shock

When the price of low-quality products is declining in the quantity expansion phase, the enterprise has the option of either continuing to produce low-quality products, even though the profitability of doing so will decline, or attempting to introduce innovations to restore profitability. According to the model of endogenous development, declining profitability stimulates innovations. While the price may decline endogenously, it may also decline for exogenous reasons. The question is whether the exogenous price reduction brought about by the China shock also induces the effort to innovate by the entrepreneurs who suffer from this shock.

The answer seems to be in the affirmative, judging from the reactions of enterprises to the China shock in the leather shoe industry in Ethiopia and the electric fittings industry in Pakistan. Regardless of the causes of the price reduction, enterprises seem to face the same options: they may continue to produce low-quality products or improve the quality of their products through innovations.[5] The latter option becomes preferable as the former option becomes less profitable over time.

Furthermore, Nadvi (1999a) reports that producers of surgical instruments in Pakistan were forced to improve the quality of their products when the US banned the import of low-quality surgical instruments for sanitary reasons. Similarly, Tewari (1999) finds that the collapse of the Soviet Union, which had a high demand for low-quality, low-priced products, stimulated garment enterprises in India to improve the quality of products in order to market their products in North America and Europe, where only high-quality products are in demand. Thus, not only declining prices internally generated by market forces, but also exogenous shocks, seem to stimulate incentives to innovate for the survival of the enterprises.

Yet, according to our frequent follow-up visits to the garment clusters in Nairobi, this cluster has seriously suffered from the China shock; the number of stalls has been declining and the composition of products has shifted from regular clothes to native costumes and bags, which China does not export to Kenya. In this cluster, the endowment of managerial human capital is meager and learning from abroad is completely lacking. It seems that the China shock cannot be overcome without sufficient managerial human capital and learning from abroad.

10.3.2   Possibility of leapfrogging

Is it possible to leapfrog over the quantity expansion phase and to begin industrialization from the quality improvement phase with exports? Since the development of the garment industry in Bangladesh began with the production of high-quality exportable products, the answer is yes. Yet it is exceedingly important to recognize that this was possible because of the large-scale training of highly educated and competent workers with potential entrepreneurial talent in more advanced countries, such as South Korea and Singapore. In other words, there was sufficient investment in managerial human capital, with a view to acquiring advanced technological and managerial knowledge from abroad.

It will not be easy to attract many competent young entrepreneurs before industrialization begins. Also there is the question of who provides the training. The Daewoo Corporation of South Korea trained 130

Bangladeshi workers for 8 months, which was obviously a mistake from the viewpoint of this private company, as all of them left their jobs. To the extent that training provides not only firm-specific information but also industry-specific knowledge, and to the extent that trainees are mobile, it will not pay for foreign companies to invest in the managerial human capital of native employees. A similar story was reported from the case of the printed circuit board industry in Taiwan, in which almost all the first-generation Taiwanese managers were spin-offs from American or Japanese joint ventures (Sonobe and Otsuka, 2006).

The Ethiopian government also attempted leapfrogging in the garment industry by subsidizing newly established large export-oriented enterprises and locating them in the industrial zones. This was, however, unsuccessful, as there was no serious attempt to strengthen the managerial human capital of the managers of those subsidized enterprises.

The lesson we should learn from the experience of the garment industry in Bangladesh is that, if we provide appropriate training programs, it is possible to improve the quality of products and the efficiency of marketing and internal management. The case of Bangladesh seems to provide *prima facie* evidence of the importance of investing in managerial human capital and learning from abroad by means of training programs.

10.3.3 Relocation

Although our empirical knowledge is insufficient, our studies suggest that the relocation of innovative enterprises away from industrial clusters often takes place once the enterprises have succeeded in multifaceted innovations. Here we have to note that the pioneering enterprises tend to be located in the center of the cluster, which is most congested, and that they tend to be innovative, whereas latecomers or imitators are located on the periphery and are usually less innovative. The relocation takes place partly because the innovative enterprises require larger factory space, which cannot be found in the congested cluster, and partly because they want to avoid imitation by non-innovative enterprises in the cluster. The relocation is short-distance if subcontracting to parts suppliers and transactions with traders are important for the efficient management of the innovative enterprises, or if the local government sets up a spacious industrial zone nearby. The relocation will be long-distance if the major motivations to move are to expand the scale of production to a significant extent and to escape from imitation completely.

As we mentioned earlier, most innovative enterprises in Asia are located in industrial zones, having moved from the original clusters. We have also observed that some high-performing enterprises in the metalwork cluster in Nairobi and the leather shoe cluster in Addis Ababa have also moved to industrial zones. These observations suggest that the advantages of the industrial clusters are outweighed by the disadvantages at a certain stage of the quality improvement phase. To the extent that information spillovers are still rampant in the quality improvement phase, the role of industrial clusters will be eroded.[6] This point, however, needs further research in future.

10.4   Strategy for cluster development

In this final section, we attempt to draw implications from our study for designing effective cluster development policies.

10.4.1   Training for entrepreneurs

The most important policy is to provide training programs to strengthen the managerial human capital of enterprise managers with a view to introducing advanced technological and managerial knowledge from advanced countries. Needless to say, the imported technology and management practices must be "appropriate," avoiding excessively capital-using and knowledge-intensive production systems, in which low-wage developing countries do not have a comparative advantage. It is also advisable to institutionalize the training system by setting up vocational schools and by inviting foreign experts in management and engineering.

Following the Bangladeshi model, such training can be offered to initiate a new industry, even though choosing an appropriate industry, inviting appropriate trainees, and teaching appropriate subjects are not easy tasks by any means. A less risky choice is to provide the training program to the stagnant clusters, where many enterprise managers are eager to introduce innovations to increase the profitability of their businesses.

In order to confirm or disconfirm the effectiveness of such training programs, we have carried out experimental projects offering 3- to 4-week training programs to randomly selected managers in our samples in the metalwork clusters in Nairobi, Kenya, and Kumasi, Ghana, and the leather shoe and garment clusters in Addis Ababa, Ethiopia. We are now planning to offer 2-month training programs in the garment cluster in Dar es Salaam, Tanzania, the metalwork cluster in Addis

Ababa, and the two industrial clusters in Vietnam discussed in Chapters 2 and 4, in collaboration with the World Bank. Since it takes time for such training programs to have an impact on the efficiency of management, we plan to collect data in the future to rigorously assess the impacts of the training programs. We hope to be able to assess the true impacts of the management training programs in a number of different settings in the near future.

In the long run, increasing the educational levels of potential entrepreneurs will also become important. This, however, is not necessarily a part of industrial development policies, as schooling has many other purposes.

10.4.2 Investment in infrastructure

There are at least two types of investment in infrastructure to promote the development of industrial clusters. The first is designed to facilitate the formation of industrial clusters. Constructing marketplaces to facilitate market transactions (which has been actively implemented in Zhejiang province in China as well as in the garment industries in Nairobi), demarcating industrial areas (which was done in the metalwork cluster in Nairobi), offering favorable income tax treatment (which has seldom been implemented except in China), and providing basic infrastructures such as roads and electricity are the major examples of policies to support the formation of industrial clusters.

The construction of industrial zones for innovative enterprises is a critically important policy to assist the development of the industrial cluster in the quality improvement phase. As was seen in the case of the garment industry in Ethiopia, the provision of space in the industrial zone to new enterprises is a risky option, as it is not clear whether the supported enterprises are indeed innovative and promising enterprises. A better policy is to accept the enterprises in the industrial clusters that have proved successful in improving enterprise management.

10.4.3 Provision of subsidized credit

To our knowledge, credit is not a major constraint on enterprise growth until quality competition is intensified. Without exception, initial capital is raised from relatives and friends in addition to the entrepreneur's own funds. Since the optimum size of operation is small in the quantity expansion phase, the capital requirement is also small. Furthermore, due to the division of labor among manufacturing enterprises in the cluster, the capital requirement for new enterprises tends to be small (e.g., Ruan and Zhang, 2009). Furthermore, providing subsidized credit to promising enterprises is difficult in the quantity expansion phase because the majority of enterprises are small and produce similar low-quality products. Thus, the adverse selection problem of subsiding non-innovative enterprises cannot be avoided if the credit policy is implemented in the quantity expansion phase.

It is, thus, timely to provide subsidized credit to innovative enterprises once innovative activities become common. In order to increase the size of production, demand for credit by innovative enterprises becomes high. It is also relatively easy to distinguish between innovative and non-innovative enterprises at this stage. Therefore, we advocate subsidized credit policies for innovative enterprises in the quality improvement phase of cluster-based industrial development.

10.4.4   Randomized and natural experiments

Our study provides strong evidence to justify the support of the formation of industrial clusters in the quantity expansion phase, the formation of managerial human capital in the quantity expansion phase, and the provision of space and subsidized credit at appropriate stages of the quality improvement phase. As effectiveness, however, has yet to be proved, no recommendation is rigorous and totally convincing. In order to assess the effectiveness of the training programs for the formation of managerial human capital, randomized experiments in which training is offered to the managers of randomly selected enterprises would be appropriate, and are already underway, as was mentioned earlier. In order to assess the effectiveness of policies of constructing industrial zones and providing subsidized credit, randomized experiments may not be feasible. In such cases, an opportunity for a "natural" experiment should be sought in order to examine the causal effects of the intervention. To conduct natural experiments, we hope to collaborate with local governments and aid agencies in the industrial clusters when we have completed the case studies.

By combining randomized and natural experiments, truly effective industrial development policies will be established. That is the remaining issue we have to address.

Notes

1 Introduction: The Scope and Significance of the Study

1. Syverson (2010) assigns the origin of the literature on the role of managerial capital to Walker (1887). Afterwards, Kaldor (1934), Lucas (1978), and Rosen (1982) constructed theoretical models incorporating entrepreneurs' managerial ability and know-how as a factor reflecting the difference in productivity across firms, but an elaborate, particularly empirical, examination into their importance had never been done until recent years.
2. In the pioneering study of industrial clusters by Marshall (1920), inter-enterprise transactions and information spillovers are considered to be important sources of agglomeration economies, in addition to the formation of a skilled labor market. Yet, the roles of innovations and managerial human capital are not recognized.
3. As will be emphasized in this study, the role of traders in the development of industrial clusters is critically important, even though it is not generally acknowledged in the literature.
4. Since new production may require a number of materials and parts, an urbanized location is preferred to initiate the new business. See Jacobs (1969, 1984) for a discussion of "the urbanization economies" arising from the diversity of industries.
5. We visited Nairobi (Kenya), Kampala (Uganda), Arusha and Dar es Salaam (Tanzania), Addis Ababa (Ethiopia), and Kumasi (Ghana), in order to find informal industrial clusters.

2 Overseas Vietnamese Traders in a Garment Cluster in Vietnam

This chapter draws on Nam et al., (2010).

1. Hatay is a province next to Hanoi (the capital city). The commune is the smallest administrative unit in Vietnam. One commune often consists of several small villages. Laphu is, therefore, a relatively large village.
2. Many of these *Vietkieu* were born in Laphu, went to Russia and Eastern Europe in the late 1980s to work, and stayed there. They mainly worked in factories, but some started small trading businesses, of which garment trading was the most common, among others, since it did not require much capital to start with.
3. Registered enterprises are registered under the Law of Enterprise of Vietnam (VietLaw, 2005). The difference between registered and unregistered enterprises is that the former have the rights to import and export directly; have foreign currency accounts; and have to sign labor contracts with workers as

well as having to pay health and unemployment insurance to hired workers. The administrative procedure is not complicated and the minimum initial capital required is small, but many large enterprises have not registered.
Two important advantages of being registered are having a better reputation
and being allowed to import material from, and export products directly
to, foreign countries. Unregistered workshops, however, can enjoy lower
income tax and do not have to pay insurance to workers. Therefore, both
types of enterprises coexist in Laphu.

4. A few subcontractors buy material from, and sell parts to, the market by
   themselves.
5. We dropped these observations in 2000 for the consistency of the analysis,
   because subcontractors do not produce finished products.
6. Primary school (1st to 5th grade) is compulsory in Vietnam. Lower secondary school is from 6th to 9th grade; upper secondary school is from 10th to
   12th; and undergraduate is from 13th to 16th.
7. Some products have already been exported to high-income countries such
   as the USA and Germany. The main exported products were, however, caps.
   In the traditional export markets of Laphu, competition from Chinese and
   Turkish products became fiercer over time.
8. Essentially the same conclusions can be derived by the reduced-form regression analyses (Nam et al., 2010).
9. The F-tests on the instruments in the first stage regression presented at
   the bottom of Table 2.11 show high predictive power of these instrumental variables. The results of the over-identification test indicate that all
   the aforementioned predetermined variables can be valid instrumentals
   (Wooldridge, 2002), providing confidence in the validity of our identifying
   variables.

3   Petty Traders in a Garment Cluster in Kenya

This chapter draws on Akoten and Otsuka (2007).

1. Our definition of tailor and mini-manufacturer, which is not based on sales
   transactions with traders, differs slightly from that of McCormick et al.,
   (1997). They perceive tailors as those who make garments to order, while
   mini-manufacturers are defined as those who use a scaled-down version of
   mass production technology.
2. The survey dealt with firms that were established in or before 1995. From
   SEM, 16 firms did not meet this criterion and were dropped from the survey.
   One firm was also dropped because it had not undertaken production from
   January 2003 to the time of the survey but was still selling its old stock of
   garments, while three others refused to cooperate. From URB, six did not
   meet the above criterion, while two did not cooperate. SUB had 20 cases
   that failed the criterion.
3. This is the largest marketplace in Kenya, not only for imported garments but
   also for other products.
4. Profit is calculated for each firm for the month of April 2003, which is considered an average month, so that it is multiplied by 12 to arrive at the current year profit.

5. Following Caves et al., (1982) and Rao et al., (1995), the relative TFP index (based on the Törnqvist index) is expressed as

$$\ln\left(\frac{TFP_j}{\overline{TFP}}\right) = \ln\left(\frac{Q_j}{\overline{Q}}\right) - \sum_{i=1}^{n}\frac{1}{n}(\overline{s}_i + s_{ij})\ln\left(\frac{X_{ij}}{\overline{X}_i}\right), \quad \text{where } s_{ij} = \frac{P_{ij}X_{ij}}{\sum_{j=1}^{m}P_{ij}X_{ij}} \text{ is}$$

the value share of input i ($i=1,..,n$) for firm j ($j=1,...,m$). TFP_j, Q_j, s_{ij}, P_{ij}, and X_{ij} are, respectively, the total factor productivity index, output, cost share of input i, price and quantity of input i for firm j, while the variables with a bar on top represent the average of each of these variables for all firms, hence representing the variables for a hypothetical "average" firm. Thus, multiplying the exponential of the right hand side of the above equation by 100 gives the relative TFP index of firm j as compared with that of an "average" firm in percentage terms.

6. Although there is no way to confirm the accuracy of the employment data in 1995, the respondents seem to remember the size of their operations before the massive importation of garment products began in the mid-1990s. For rough confirmation, the average employment in 1990 was 4.7 and that obtained by McCormick et al., (1997: 1,099) in 1989 for similar firms was 4.2, suggesting that the data do not suffer from serious recall errors and are thus reliable. Needless to say, the current size of enterprises cannot be used as an explanatory variable in the regression analysis, as it is endogenous.

7. According to the *Daily Nation* on the internet, the crime rate tends to be high in Gikomba and other densely populated suburbs. This is likely to hamper investment in better technologies. (http://www.nationaudio.com/News/DailyNation/Today/News/Special%20Report6654.html), accessed on January 26, 2004.

8. Following Evans (1987), we tried including their quadratic and interaction terms as well, but an F-test to check their joint significance was rejected. So, we did not consider the interaction terms in the analyses. For brevity, we refer to natural logarithm as logs in subsequent sections.

9. The results in this and the subsequent tables have low (pseudo) R-squared because of too much noise in the individual level cross-section data. At the aggregate level (or time series data), this noise cancels out so that high levels of R-squared can be attained. Thus, unlike time series data, in cross-section data the important result is not (pseudo) R-squared but the significance of independent variables, singly and jointly.

10. Marginal effect is the partial effect of the regressor (evaluated at the mean values) conditional on the dependent variable being positive. It is obtained by multiplying the coefficient of the regressor by an appropriate adjustment factor.

11. Elsewhere, Fafchamps and Minten (2001) show that better connected traders in Madagascar have larger sales than those with fewer connections, while a study on sub-Saharan African countries by Ramachandran and Shah (1999) shows empirically that firms owned by Asian and European managers with a higher ratio of relatives (parents) in the same business grow faster than those owned by African managers.

12. See Akoten et al., (2006) for the determinants and consequences of informal credit (rotating saving and credit associations) in the garment clusters under study.

13. In all cases, moral hazards and information asymmetry are mitigated through strong community ties and long-term contractual relationships.

4 The Product Ladder in the Steel Bar Industry in Vietnam

This chapter draws on Nam et al., (2009).

1. Even though a few large rolling mills operated their own workshops to produce cast billets themselves, they used all the billets to produce finished steel products and did not sell them to other enterprises.
2. In the village, there are small household enterprises that further process wire rods into miscellaneous products, such as nails and spikes; traders of charcoal and industrial gases; owners of trucks for rent; and machine repair shops. We, however, did not include these households and traders in our sample.
3. Value added is defined as sales revenue minus material and utility costs.
4. This is also consistent with our Hypothesis 2 postulated in Chapter 1.
5. The regression without the inverse Mills ratio, which is not reported in this table, shows that the bias is upward.
6. The estimation without the inverse Mills ratio, which is not shown in this table, indicates that the bias is downward.

5 The Move to the Formal Sector in the Metalwork Industry in Kenya

This chapter draws on Sonobe et al., (2010).

1. See Figure 3.1 for the location of Kariobangi, which is designated as "SUB."
2. The literal translation of *Jua Kali* is the hot sun, and this word refers to informal-sector artisans because they work outside under the hot sun. See King (1996) for detailed descriptions of the activities and history of the *Jua Kali* sector in Kenya.
3. Those enterprises on the other side of the main roads that surround the Kariobangi Light Industries are excluded from this number as well as our sample.
4. In Nairobi, there are other *Jua Kali* clusters, including the Kamukunji metalwork cluster, of which the activities and history are described by Kinyanjui (2007).
5. For the parts suppliers, the most important type of customers are metal product fabricators in the cluster, but sales to individuals account for a quarter of their revenues, because they accept repair work orders from individuals and sell simple car repair parts to individuals.
6. The data shown in Table 5.5 exclude the hardware shops and miscellaneous service providers, since they have low percentages of marketing to quality-conscious buyers by nature of their lines of trade.
7. The lower portion of Table 5.5 also excludes the hardware shops and miscellaneous service providers. The hardware shops procure steel materials from Mombasa. Hence their percentages of direct procurement are much higher

than in other types of businesses. Some of the miscellaneous services providers are recycle businesses, whose direct purchase is difficult to define.
8. Note that, if we include the leavers in the regression analysis, our conclusions are strengthened rather than weakened.

6 The Coping Strategy of the Electrical Fittings Industry in Pakistan

This chapter draws on the first draft of the PhD dissertation of Babur Wasim, entitled "Cluster-Based Industrial Development: The Case of the Electrical Fittings Cluster in Sargodha, Pakistan," submitted to the National Graduate Institute for Policy Studies, where the authors serve as members of Mr Wasim's PhD thesis committee. We would like to express our sincere appreciation for his contribution.

1. We do not include the subcontracting workshops in the analysis in this chapter because the decisions on design and specification, raw material procurement, and marketing of finished products are made only by the company owners.
2. Sialkot is known as a major producer of surgical instruments and soccer balls (Nadvi, 1999a, 1999b, 2008). Gujarat and Gujranwara are clusters of enterprises producing plastic products, metal products, machines, and electric appliances (Nabi, 1988; Caniëls and Romijn, 2003).
3. FBS had no list, whereas SMEDA had a list of only 31 firms.
4. There was a large factory in Karachi named PPI, established before the partition, which was the main source of electrical fittings and accessories in the country before the start of the electrical fittings industry in Sargodha. Even government offices used to buy electrical fittings from this factory (UNIDO, 2006).
5. The first factory was closed down in the late 1970s when the son of the pioneer emigrated from Pakistan.
6. SMEDA estimates that Chinese imports account for 30 percent of domestic consumption. Although our interviewees listed China's market share as varying from 20 to 50 percent, they consistently claimed that China's market share has been declining in recent years.
7. The coefficients in size and growth functions are related to each other, as explained in the discussions about equations (6.3) and (6.4). However, the relationships among the estimated coefficients in Table 6.9 are not exact, as slightly different samples were used to estimate the size and growth functions due to new entry.

7 The V-Shaped Growth in the Leather Shoe Industry in Ethiopia

This chapter draws on Sonobe et al., (2009).

1. See Bigsten and Söderbom (2006) for a recent review of the literature on industrial development in sub-Saharan Africa.

2. Leather shoes are footwear with outer soles of rubber, plastics, leather or composition leather and uppers of leather, that is, footwear classified as HS Code 6403.
3. Armenians also established a modern leather tannery in the 1920s in Addis Ababa.
4. Nadvi (1999a) and Schmitz (1995) argue that improvements in quality and efficiency are associated with improvements in long-term supplier–manufacturer relations.
5. Tikur Abbay employed 500 workers in 2000 and 280 in 2004. Anbessa employed 750 workers in 2000 and 660 in 2004. While Anbessa had a larger labor force than Tikur Abbay, the value added of the latter was nearly four times as large as that of the former.
6. The average price is the US dollar value of imports or exports divided by the number of pairs imported or exported. Throughout the paper, nominal values in Ethiopian Birr are converted into US dollar values by using the exchange rate data taken from IMF (2007).
7. We cannot find the wage earnings in the leather shoe industry in China, which accounts for about 40 percent of products of the leather industry.
8. Value added is defined here as sales revenue minus the cost of intermediate inputs such as leather, soles, and accessories, as the cost of energy and water was negligible.
9. Some of the second-generation entrepreneurs were born outside Addis Ababa, because their fathers were initially farmers and then became migrant workers employed in the leather shoe industry in Addis Ababa.
10. Lika (1997) describes the operation of leather shoe enterprises in Addis Ababa and the working conditions of their workers based on survey data of 82 enterprises.
11. According to Table 3 of Gunning and Mengistae (2001), enterprises in the leather products industry in Ethiopia grew by 28 percent over the 5-year period from 1989 to 1993, whereas other industries recorded negative growth.
12. We compare prices of men's shoes rather than those of ladies' and children's shoes because most sample enterprises produce men's shoes.
13. An appropriate price index in Ethiopia for leather shoes to be used to obtain real prices is unavailable. To compare shoe prices between 2000 and 2004, nominal prices in Ethiopian Birr were converted into US dollar equivalents using the average exchange rate in each year. The data on exchange rate were taken from IMF (2007).
14. Consistent with these observations, Stokke (2008) exemplifies the increasing importance of education in technology adoption.
15. The corresponding growth rates for the SOEs were –20.5 percent in the first period and –7.2 percent in the second period.
16. Mengistae (2006) corrects for the attrition bias arising from the use of the sample consisting only of surviving enterprises.

8 International Knowledge Transfer in a Garment Cluster in Bangladesh

This chapter draws on the PhD dissertation of Khondker Abdul Mottaleb, entitled "Human Capital and Industrial Development: The Case of the Garment

Industry in Bangladesh," submitted to the National Graduate Institute for Policy Studies, where the authors served as members of Mottaleb's PhD thesis committee. We would like to express sincere appreciation for his contribution.

1. The Greater Dhaka area consists of Dhaka and the two neighboring districts, Narayanganji and Gazipur. Narayanganji was traditionally the center of the production of hosiery and now has many T-shirt factories. Gazipur is a newly developed cluster of garment factories, especially those producing sweaters.

2. To be more precise, those whom we label T-shirt producers are the producers of T-shirts, polo shirts, and other knitwear items produced by using the so-called circular machines. Those whom we label sweater producers are the producers of sweaters, cardigans, and other knitwear items produced by using the so-called flat knit machines.

3. Since all the sample enterprises keep records, the recall data on financial variables are accurate.

4. The percentage of regular workers in the total number of workers is about 60 percent in the T-shirt sector and a little less than 40 percent in the sweater sector, according to our data. Operators of large machines tend to be regular workers and to be paid on a time-rate basis. Part of the reason why the T-shirt sector has a higher percentage of regular workers is that the sector is more capital-intensive.

5. Two of the foreign trading houses are from South Korea, one from Sri Lanka, one from India, and one from Italy.

6. They are more highly educated than their counterparts in the case studies of the garment, electric appliance, machine tool, and motorcycle industries in East Asia conducted by Sonobe and Otsuka (2006).

7. In these 2SLS regressions, it is practically impossible to predict which exogenous variables serve as instrumental variables. Thus we select instrumental variables based on two criteria. One is that they should have significant effects on the endogenous variable in the first stage. The other criterion for the valid instruments is that they should have no direct effects on the dependent variable of the second-stage regression. These criteria are checked by means of the first-stage F test and the over-identification test. In addition to the ordinary 2SLS, we will also employ the instrumental variable Generalized Method of Moments (IVGMM), which is a statistically more efficient estimator in the presence of heteroskedasticity (Wooldridge, 2001).

8. The results are very similar, which indicates that heteroskedasticity is not serious. The instruments used are all the exogenous variables other than the years of operation and the year dummies.

9 Misfired Promotion of the Export-Oriented Garment Industry in Ethiopia

1. Ethiopia became eligible for apparel benefits in August 2001.

2. This paragraph is based on our interview with the Textile & Leather Industry Department of the Ministry of Trade and Industry conducted on November 7, 2007 at the Ministry.

3. The survey was financially supported by the Ethiopian Development Research Institute and the 21st Century COE Program of the National

Graduate Institute for Policy Studies. The data set is available from the authors upon request.

4. Issayas Mukuria, "Garment Makers Gripe to Government about Bottlenecks," *Addis Fortune*, 8(393), November 11, 2007.

5. A weighted regression was applied because the data of the tailor-turned RTW enterprises were taken from the census whereas the data of the tailors were taken from the random sample.

6. While their significance levels are lower than in column (i), this does not affect our argument, since the lower significance levels simply result from the much smaller sample size in column (iii).

10   Conclusion: Towards the Design of Effective Industrial Development Policies

1. Yet we believe that the basic pattern of the development of these industries is not so different from that of other cluster-based industries.

2. Actually there are three different clusters in the printed circuit board industry in Jiangsu province in China. Although we do not have accurate data, there are a large number of small enterprises managed by relatively uneducated managers in a village-based rural cluster in this industry.

3. Indeed, in the electric appliance industry in China, small enterprises managed by uneducated managers tended to be absorbed by large enterprises managed by educated managers.

4. It is somewhat surprising that such complementarity was not recognized by Schumpeter (1912), when he enumerated the different types of innovations.

5. Other options are to close the business and to shift to a product mix that suffers less from the China shock.

6. According to Rabellotti (1999) and Schmitz (1999), information spillovers among producers lose significance in the quality improvement phase, because of the development of the exclusive subcontracting system. If this is the case, the advantage of being in the industrial cluster may be maintained.

References

Adelman, M.A. (1955) "Concept and Statistical Measurement of Vertical Integration," in G.J. Stigler (ed.), *Business Concentration and Price Policy* (Princeton, NJ: Princeton University Press).

Akerlof, G.A. (1970) "The Market for 'Lemons': Quality Uncertainty and the Market Mechanism," *Quarterly Journal of Economics*, 84(3), 488–500.

Akoten, J.E., and Otsuka, K. (2007) "From Tailors to Mini-Manufacturers: The Role of Traders in the Performance of Garment Enterprises in Kenya," *Journal of African Economies*, 16(4), 564–95.

Akoten, J.E., Sawada, Y., and Otsuka, K. (2006) "The Determinants of Credit Access and Its Impacts on Micro and Small Enterprises: The Case of Garment Producers in Kenya," *Economic Development and Cultural Change*, 54(4), 927–44.

Arellano, M., and Bond, S. (1991) "Some Tests of Specification for Panel Data: Monte Carlo Evidence and an Application to Employment Equations," *Review of Economic Studies*, 58(2), 277–97.

Arrow, K.J. (1962) "The Economic Implications of Learning by Doing," *Review of Economic Studies*, 29(3), 155–73.

Arrow, K.J. (1985) "Economic Development: The Present State of the Art," in K.J. Arrow (ed.), *Collected Papers of Kenneth J. Arrow, Volume 6: Applied Economics* (Cambridge, MA: Harvard University Press), reprinted from Papers of the East-West Communication Institute, No.14, 1975.

Bangladesh, Export Promotion Bureau (2005) *Export from Bangladesh 1972–73 to 2004–2005* (Dhaka: Export Promotion Bureau).

Bangladesh Garment Manufacturers and Exporters Association (BGMEA) (various years) *BGMEA Members Directory* (Dhaka: BGMEA).

Bangladesh Knitwear Manufacturers and Exporters Association (BKMEA) (2005) *BKMEA Members Directory 2005* (Dhaka: BKMEA).

Barr, A. (2000) "Social Capital and Technical Information Flows in the Ghanaian Manufacturing Sector," *Oxford Economic Papers*, 52(3), 539–59.

Barro, R.J., and Sala-i-Martin, X. (1992) "Convergence," *Journal of Political Economy*, 100(2), 223–51.

Bazan, L., and Navas-Aleman, L. (2004) "The Underground Revolution in the Sinos Valley: A Comparison of Upgrading in Global and National Value Chains," in H. Schmitz (ed.), *Local Enterprises in the Global Economy* (Cheltenham, UK: Edward Elgar).

Beck, T., Demirgüç-Kunt, A., and Honohan, P. (2009) "Access to Financial Services: Measurement, Impact, and Policies," *World Bank Research Observer*, 24(1), 119–45.

Becker, G.S., and Murphy, K.M. (1992) "The Division of Labor, Coordination Costs, and Knowledge," *Quarterly Journal of Economics*, 107(4), 1137–60.

Bhagwati, J. (1982) "Directly Unproductive, Profit-Seeking Activities," *Journal of Political Economy*, 90(5), 988–1002.

Bigsten, A., and Gebreeyesus, M. (2007) "The Small, the Young, and the Productive: Determinants of Manufacturing Firm Growth in Ethiopia," *Economic Development and Cultural Change*, 55(4), 813–40.

Bigsten, A., and Söderbom, M. (2006) "What Have We Learned from a Decade of Manufacturing Enterprise Surveys in Africa?," *World Bank Research Observer*, 21(2), 241–65.

Bigsten, A., Collier, P., Dercon, S., Fafchamps, M., Gauthier, B., Gunning, J.W., Oduro, A., Oostendorp, R., Patillo, C., Söderbom, M., Teal, F., and Zeufack, A. (2000) "Contract Flexibility and Dispute Resolution in African Manufacturing," *Journal of Development Studies*, 36(4), 1–37.

Bigsten, A., Collier, P., Dercon, S., Fafchamps, M., Gauthier, B., Gunning, J.W., Oduro, A., Oostendorp, R., Patillo, C., Söderbom, M., Teal, F., and Zeufack, A. (2004) "Do African Manufacturing Firms Learn from Exporting?," *Journal of Development Studies*, 40(3), 115–41.

Bigsten, A., Kimuyu, P., and Lundvall, K. (2004) "What to Do with the Informal Sector?," *Development Policy Review*, 22(6), 701.

Bloom, N., and Van Reenen, J. (2007) "Measuring and Explaining Management Practices Across Firms and Countries," *Quarterly Journal of Economics*, 122(4), 1341–409.

Bloom, N., and Van Reenen, J. (2010) "Why Do Management Practices Differ across Firms and Countries?," *Journal of Economic Perspectives*, 24(1), 203–24.

Bruhn, M., Karlan, D., and Schoar, A. (2010) "What Capital is Missing in Developing Countries?," *American Economic Review*, 100(2), 629–33.

Burki, A., and Terrell, D. (1998) "Measuring Production Efficiency of Small Firms in Pakistan," *World Development*, 26(1), 155–69.

Caniëls, M.C.J., and Romijn, H.A. (2003) "Agglomeration Advantages and Capability Building in Industrial Clusters: The Missing Link," *Journal of Development Studies*, 39(3), 129–54.

Caves, D.W., Christensen, L.R., and Diewert, W.E. (1982) "Multilateral Comparisons of Output, Input, and Productivity Using Superlative Index Numbers," *Economic Journal*, 92(365), 73–86.

Central Bureau of Statistics (CBS), International Center for Economic Growth (ICEG), and K-Rep Holdings Ltd. (1999) *National Micro and Small Enterprise Baseline Survey 1999: Survey Results* (Nairobi: CBS, ICEG, and K-Rep Holdings Ltd).

China, National Bureau of Statistics (various years) *China Labor Statistical Yearbook* (Beijing: China Statistics Press).

China, National Bureau of Statistics (2005) *China Statistical Yearbook* (Beijing: China Statistics Press).

Collier, P., and Gunning, J.W. (1999) "Explaining African Economic Performance," *Journal of Economic Literature*, 37(1), 64–111.

Crespo, N., and Fontoura, M.P. (2007) "Determinant Factors of FDI Spillovers – What Do We Really Know?," *World Development*, 35(3), 410–25.

Daniels, L., and Mead, D.C. (1998) "The Contribution of Small Enterprises to Household and National Income in Kenya," *Economic Development and Cultural Change*, 47(1), 45–71.

David, C.C., and Otsuka, K. (1994) *Modern Rice Technology and Income Distribution in Asia* (Boulder: Lynne Rienner).

Davidson, R., and MacKinnon, J.G. (1993) *Estimation and Inference in Econometrics* (Oxford: Oxford University Press).

DiGregorio, M.R. (2001) "Iron Works: Excavating Alternative Futures in a Northern Vietnamese Craft Village," PhD dissertation, University of California, Los Angeles.

Ding, K. (2007) "Domestic Market-based Industrial Cluster Development in Modern China," IDS Discussion Paper No.88, Institute of Developing Economies, Japan External Trade Organization.

Easterly, W. (2002) *The Elusive Quest for Growth: Economists' Adventures and Misadventures in the Tropics* (Massachusetts: MIT Press).

Evans, D.S. (1987) "Tests of Alternative Theories of Firm Growth," *Journal of Political Economy*, 95(4), 657–74.

Fafchamps, M. (2004) *Market Institutions in Sub-Saharan Africa: Theory and Evidence* (Cambridge, MA: MIT Press).

Fafchamps, M., and Minten, B. (2001) "Social Capital and Agricultural Trade," *American Journal of Agricultural Economics*, 83(3), 680–5.

Fafchamps, M., and Söderbom, M. (2006) "Wages and Labor Management in African Manufacturing," *Journal of Human Resources*, 41(2), 346–79.

Fisman, R. (2001) "Trade Credit and Productive Efficiency in Developing Countries," *World Development*, 29(2), 311–21.

Gereffi, G. (1999) "International Trade and Industrial Upgrading in the Apparel Commodity Chain," *Journal of International Economics*, 48(1), 37–70.

Giuliani, E., Pietrobelli, C., and Rabellotti, R. (2005) "Upgrading in Global Value Chains: Lessons from Latin American Clusters," *World Development*, 33(4), 549–73.

Gunning, J.W., and Mengistae, T. (2001) "Determinants of African Manufacturing Investment: The Microeconomic Evidence," *Journal of African Economies*, 10(Suppl. 2), 48–80.

Hamada, K., Otsuka, K., Ranis, G., and Togo, K. (2010) forthcoming *The Miraculous Growth and Stagnation: Lessons from the Postwar Japanese Development Experience* (London: Routledge).

Hart, O., and Moore, J. (1990) "Property Rights and the Nature of the Firm," *Journal of Political Economy*, 98(6), 1119–58.

Hayami, Y. (1998) "Toward an Alternative Path of Economic Development: An Introduction," in Y. Hayami (ed.), *Toward the Rural-Based Development of Commerce and Industry: Selected Experiences from East Asia* (Washington, DC: World Bank Economic Development Institute).

Hayami, Y. (2006) "Communities and Markets for Rural Development under Globalization: A Perspective from Villages in Asia," Discussion Paper Series on International Studies 2006–08–02, Foundation for Advanced Studies on International Development.

Hayami, Y., and Godo, Y. (2005) *Development Economics: From the Poverty to the Wealth of Nations*, 3rd edn (Oxford: Oxford University Press).

Hayami, Y., and Kawagoe, T. (1993) *The Agrarian Origins of Commerce and Industry: A Study of Peasant Marketing in Indonesia* (New York: St Martin's Press).

Heston, A., and Sicular, T. (2008) "China and Development Economics," in L. Brandt and T.G. Rawski (eds), *China's Great Economic Transformation* (New York: Cambridge University Press).

Hong, C.-M., and Gee, S. (1993) "National Systems Supporting Technical Advance in Industry: The case of Taiwan," in R.R. Nelson (ed.), *National Innovation Systems: A Comparative Analysis* (Oxford: Oxford University Press).

Hoq, M. (2004) "Knitwear Industry in Bangladesh: An Untold Story," in Bangladesh Knitwear Manufacturers and Exporters Association (BKMEA) (ed.), *Explore the Galore of Bangladesh Knitwear 1st Bangladesh Knitwear Exhibition* (Dhaka: BKMEA).

Huang, Y., and Bocchi, A.M. (eds) (2008) *Reshaping Economic Geography in East Asia* (Washington, DC: World Bank).

Humphrey, J., and Schmitz, H. (1996) "The Triple C Approach to Local Industrial Policy," *World Development*, 24(12), 1859–77.

Humphrey, J., and Schmitz, H. (1998) "Trust and Inter-Firm Relations in Developing and Transition Economies," *Journal of Development Studies*, 34(4), 32–61.

Hymer, S., and Resnick, S. (1969) "A Model of an Agrarian Economy with Nonagricultural Activities," *American Economic Review*, 59(4), 493–506.

Iddrisu, A., and Sonobe, T. (2007) "Human Capital and Industrial Development: A Case Study of an Auto Repair and Metalworking Cluster in Ghana," mimeo, Foundation for Advanced Studies on International Development.

International Monetary Fund (IMF) (2007) World Economic Outlook Database, available at http://www.imf.org/external/pubs/ft/weo/2007/01/data/index.htm accessed on June 22, 2007.

Itoh, M., and Tanimoto, M. (1998) "Rural Entrepreneurs in the Cotton-Weaving Industry of Japan," in Y. Hayami (ed.), *Toward the Rural-Based Development of Commerce and Industry: Selected Experiences from East Asia* (Washington, DC: World Bank Economic Development Institute).

Jacobs, J. (1969) *The Economy of Cities* (New York: Vintage).

Jacobs, J. (1984) *The Wealth of Nations: Principles of Economic Life* (New York: Vintage).

Japan International Cooperation Agency (JICA) (2004) *The Study on Artisan Craft Development Plan for Rural Industrialization in The Socialist Republic of Vietnam* (Hanoi: JICA).

Kaldor, N. (1934) "The Equilibrium of the Firm," *Economic Journal*, 44 (173), 60–76.

Karlan, D., and Morduch, J. (2009) "Access to Finance," in D. Rodrik and M. Rosenzweig (eds), *Handbook of Development Economics, Volume 5* (Amsterdam: North Holland).

Khan, S. (2004) "Textile and Clothing Sector in Bangladesh: Post MFA Challenges and Action Plan," mimeo, Bangladesh Ministry of Commerce and WTO Cell.

Kikuchi, M. (1998) "Export-Oriented Garment Industries in the Rural Philippines," in Y. Hayami (ed.), *Toward the Rural-Based Development of Commerce and Industry: Selected Experiences from East Asia* (Washington, DC: World Bank Economic Development Institute).

King, K. (1996) *Jua Kali Kenya: Change & Development in an Informal Economy, 1970–95* (London: James Currey; Nairobi: East African Education Publisher; and Athens: Ohio University Press).

Kinyanjui, N. (2007) "The Kamkunji metalwork cluster in Kenya," in D.Z. Zeng (ed.), *Knowledge, Technology, and Cluster-Based Growth in Africa* (Washington, DC: World Bank).

Klein, B., and Leffler, K. (1981) "The Role of Market Forces in Assuring Contractual Performance," *Journal of Political Economy*, 89(4), 615–41.

Knorringa, P. (1999) "Agra: An Old Cluster Facing the New Competition," *World Development*, 27(9), 1, 587–1, 604.

Krugman, P. (1991) *Geography and Trade* (Cambridge, MA: MIT Press).

Lazerson, M. (1995) "A New Phoenix: Modern Putting-Out in the Modena Knitwear Industry," *Administrative Science Quarterly*, 40(1), 34–59.

Levy, B. (1991) "Transaction Costs, the Size of Firms and Industrial Policy," *Journal of Development Economics*, 34(1/2), 151–78.

Lika, T. (1997) "Employment and Income in the Urban Informal Sector: A Case Study of Informal Leather Shoe Making Enterprises in Wereda 5, Addis Ababa," MA thesis, Addis Ababa University.

Liu, D., and Otsuka, K. (1998) "Township-Village Enterprises in the Garment Sector of China," in Y. Hayami (ed.), *Toward the Rural-Based Development of Commerce and Industry: Selected Experiences from East Asia* (Washington, DC: World Bank Economic Development Institute).

Lucas, R.E. (1978) "On the Size Distribution of Business Firms," *Bell Journal of Economics*, 9(2), 508–23.

Marshall, A. (1920) *Principles of Economics* (London: Macmillan, now Palgrave Macmillan).

McCormick, D. (1999) "African Enterprise Clusters and Industrialization: Theory and Reality," *World Development*, 27(9), 1531–51.

McCormick, D., and Kinyanjui, M.N. (2000) "Toward a Practical Understanding of Enterprise Clusters in Kenya," Final Report Submitted to International Centre for Economic Growth, University of Nairobi.

McCormick, D., Kinyanjui, M.N., and Ongile, G. (1994) "Networks, Markets, and Growth in Nairobi's Garment Industry," Final Report to International Centre for Economic Growth, University of Nairobi.

McCormick, D., Kinyanjui, M.N., and Ongile, G. (1997) "Growth and Barriers to Growth Among Nairobi's Small and Medium-Sized Garment Producers," *World Development*, 25(7), 1095–1110.

McPherson, M. (1996) "Growth of Micro and Small Enterprises in Southern Africa," *Journal of Development Economics*, 48(2), 253–77.

Mengistae, T. (2001) "Indigenous Ethnicity and Entrepreneurial Success in Africa: Some Evidence from Ethiopia," Policy Research Working Paper 2534, World Bank.

Mengistae, T. (2006) "Competition and Entrepreneurs' Human Capital in Small Business Longevity and Growth," *Journal of Development Studies*, 42(5), 812–36.

Mlachila, M., and Yang, Y. (2004) "The End of Textiles Quotas: A Case Study of the Impact on Bangladesh," IMF Working Paper No.WP/04/108, International Monetary Fund.

Mottaleb, K.A. (2007) "Human Capital and Industrial Development: The Case of the Knitwear Garment Industry in Bangladesh," PhD dissertation, National Graduate Institute for Policy Studies.

Murakami, N., Liu, D., and Otsuka, K. (1994) "Technical and Allocative Efficiency among Socialist Enterprises: The Case of the Garment Industry in China," *Journal of Comparative Economics*, 19(3), 410–33.

Murakami, N., Liu, D., and Otsuka, K. (1996) "Market Reform, Division of Labor, and Increasing Advantages of Small-scale Enterprises: The Case of The Machine Tool Industry in China," *Journal of Comparative Economics*, 23(3), 256–77.

Nabi, E. (1988) *Entrepreneurs and Markets in Early Industrialization: A Case Study from Pakistan* (San Francisco, CA: ICS Press).

Nadvi, K. (1996) "Small Firms Districts in Pakistan," DPhil thesis, University of Sussex.

Nadvi, K. (1999a) "Collective Efficiency and Collective Failure: The Response of the Sialkot Surgical Instrument Cluster to Global Quality Pressures," *World Development*, 27(9), 1605–26.

Nadvi, K. (1999b) "Shifting Ties: Social Networks in the Surgical Instrument Cluster of Sialkot, Pakistan," *Development and Change*, 30(1), 141–75.

Nadvi, K. (2008) "Global Standards, Global Governance and the Organization of Global Value Chains," *Journal of Economic Geography*, 8(3), 323–43.

Nam, V.H., Sonobe, T., and Otsuka, K. (2009) "An Inquiry into the Transformation Process of Village-based Industrial Clusters: The Case of an Iron and Steel Cluster in Northern Vietnam," *Journal of Comparative Economics*, 37(4), 568–81.

Nam, V.H., Sonobe, T., and Otsuka, K. (2010) "An Inquiry into the Development Process of Village Industries: The Case of a Knitwear Cluster in Northern Vietnam," *Journal of Development Studies*, 46(2), 312–30.

Otsuka, K., Estudillo, J.P., and Sawada, Y. (2009) *Rural Poverty and Income Dynamics in Asia and Africa* (London: Routledge).

Piore, M.J., and Sabel, C.F. (1984) *The Second Industrial Divide: Possibilities for Prosperity* (New York: Basic Books).

Quddus, M., and Rashid, S. (2000) *Entrepreneurs and Economic Development: The Remarkable Story of Garment Exports from Bangladesh* (Dhaka: University Press Limited).

Rabellotti, R. (1995) "Is There an 'Industrial District Model'? Footwear Districts in Italy and Mexico Compared," *World Development*, 23(1), 29–41.

Rabellotti, R. (1999) "Recovery of Mexican Cluster: Devaluation Bonanza or Collective Efficiency," *World Development*, 27 (9), 1571–85.

Rahman, M. (2004) "Surviving in a Quota Free World: Will Bangladesh Make it?," Dialogue Reports No. 72, Centre for Policy Dialogue.

Rahman, M. (2005) "Bangladesh After MFA Phase Out," *South Asian Journal*, 8 (April–June), available at http://www.southasianmedia.net/Magazine/journal/8_phases_out.htm accessed on August 3, 2007.

Ramachandran, V., and Shah, M.K. (1999) "Minority Entrepreneurs and Firm Performance in Sub-Saharan Africa," *Journal of Development Studies*, 36(2), 71–87.

Ranis, G., and Stewart, F. (1993) "Rural Nonagricultural Activities in Development," *Journal of Development Economics*, 40(1), 75–101.

Rao, D.S.P., Selvanathan, E.A., and Pilat, D. (1995) "Generalized Theil-Törnqvist Indices with Applications to International Comparisons of Prices and Real Output," *Review of Economics and Statistics*, 77(2), 352–60.

Rhee, Y.W. (1990) "The Catalyst Model of Development: Lessons from Bangladesh's Success with Garment Exports," *World Development*, 18(2), 333–16.

Rivers, D., and Vuong, Q.H. (1988) "Limited Information Estimators and Exogeneity Tests for Simultaneous Probit Models," *Journal of Econometrics*, 39(3), 347–66.

Romer, P.M. (1986) "Increasing Returns and Long-Run Growth," *Journal of Political Economy*, 94(5), 1002–37.

Romer, P.M. (1990a) "Are Nonconvexities Important for Understanding Growth?," *American Economic Review*, 80(1), 97–103.

Romer, P.M. (1990b) "Endogenous Technological Change," *Journal of Political Economy*, 98(5), S71–102.

Rosen, S. (1982) "Authority, Control, and the Distribution of Earnings," *Bell Journal of Economics*, 13(2), 311–23.

Ruan, J., and Zhang, X. (2009) "Finance and Cluster–Based Industrial Development in China," *Economic Development and Cultural Change*, 58(1), 143–64.

Saxena, S.B., and Wiebe, F. (2005) *The Phase-out of the Multi-fiber Agreement: Policy Options and Opportunities for Asia* (San Francisco: Asia Foundation).

Schmitz, H. (1982) "Growth Constraints on Small-Scale Manufacturing in Developing Countries: A Critical Review," *World Development*, 10(6), 429–50.

Schmitz, H. (1995) "Small Shoemakers and Fordist Giants: Tale of a Supercluster," *World Development*, 23(1), 9–28.

Schmitz, H. (1999) "Global Competition and Local Cooperation: Success and Failure in the Sinos Valley, Brazil," *World Development*, 27 (9), 1627–50.

Schmitz, H. (ed.) (2004) *Local Enterprises in the Global Economy, Issues of Governance and Upgrading* (Cheltenham, UK: Edward Elgar).

Schmitz, H. (2005) *Value Chain Analysis for Policy Makers and Practitioners* (Geneva: International Labor Office).

Schmitz, H., and Knorringa, P. (2000) "Learning from Global Buyers," *Journal of Development Studies*, 37(2), 177–205.

Schmitz, H., and Nadvi, K. (1999) "Clustering and Industrialization: Introduction," *World Development*, 27(9), 1503–14.

Schultz, T.W. (1975) "The Value of the Ability to Deal with Disequilibria," *Journal of Economic Literature*, 13(3), 827–46.

Schumpeter, J.A. (1912) *The Theory of Economic Development: An Inquiry into Profits, Capital, Interest, and the Business Cycle* (London: Oxford University Press).

Schumpeter, J.A. (1950) *Capitalism, Socialism and Democracy* (New York: Rand McNally).

Siddiqi, H.G.A. (2005) *The Readymade Garment Industry of Bangladesh* (Dhaka: University Press Limited).

Sluwaegen, L., and Goedhuys, M. (2002) "Growth of Firms in Developing Countries: Evidence from Côte d'Ivoire," *Journal of Development Economics*, 68(1), 117–35.

Smith, R., and Blundell, R. (1986) "An Exogeneity Test for a Simultaneous Equation Tobit Model with an Application to Labor Supply," *Econometrica*, 54(3), 679–85.

Sonobe, T., and Briones, R.M. (2001) "Role of Urban-Rural Subcontracting in Rural Industrialization: A Case Study of the Export-oriented Garment and Metal Craft Industries in the Philippines," mimeo, Tokyo Metropolitan University.

Sonobe, T., and Otsuka, K. (2006) *Cluster-Based Industrial Development: An East Asian Model* (New York: Palgrave Macmillan).

Sonobe, T., Hu, D., and Otsuka, K. (2002) "Process of Cluster Formation in China: A Case Study of a Garment Town," *Journal of Development Studies*, 39(1), 118–39.

Sonobe, T., Kawakami, M., and Otsuka, K. (2003) "Changing Roles of Innovation and Imitation in Industrial Development: The Case of the Machine Tool Industry in Taiwan," *Economic Development and Cultural Change*, 52(1), 103–28.

Sonobe, T., Hu, D., and Otsuka, K. (2004) "From Inferior to Superior Products: An Inquiry into the Wenzhou Model of Industrial Development in China," *Journal of Comparative Economics*, 32(3), 542–63.

Sonobe, T., Hu, D., and Otsuka, K. (2006) "Industrial Development in the Inland Region of China: A Case Study of the Motorcycle Industry," *Journal of Comparative Economics*, 34(4), 818–38.

Sonobe, T., Akoten, J.E., and Otsuka, K. (2009) "An Exploration into the Successful Development of the Leather-Shoe Industry in Ethiopia," *Review of Development Economics*, 13(4), 719–36.

Sonobe, T., Akoten, J.E., and Otsuka, K. (2010, forthcoming) "The Growth Process of Informal Enterprises in Sub-Saharan Africa: A Case Study of a Metalworking Cluster in Nairobi," *Small Business Economics*.

Stigler, G.J. (1951) "The Division of Labor is Limited by the Extent of the Market," *Journal of Political Economy*, 59(3), 185–93.

Stokke, H.E. (2008) "Productivity Growth and Organizational Learning," *Review of Development Economics*, 12(4), 764–78.

Syverson, C. (2010, forthcoming) "What determines productivity?," *Journal of Economic Literature*.

Tewari, M. (1999) "Successful Adjustment in Indian Industry: The Case of Ludhiana's Woolen Knitwear Cluster," *World Development*, 27(9), 1651–71.

Tybout, J.R. (2000) "Manufacturing Firms in Developing Countries: How Well Do They Do, and Why?," *Journal of Economic Literature*, 38(1), 11–44.

United Nations Industrial Development Organization (UNIDO) (2006) *Diagnostic Report of Electrical Fittings Cluster Sargodha* (Islamabad: UNIDO).

United States International Trade Commission (USITC) (2007) *Sub-Saharan Africa: Factors Affecting Trade Patterns of Selected Industries: First Annual Report* (Washington DC: USITC).

VietLaw (2005) available at http://www.luatvietnam.vn

Vietnam, General Statistics Office (2005) available at http://www.gso.gov.vn accessed on September 25, 2007.

Villoria, N.B. (2009) "China and the Manufacturing Terms-of-Trade of African Exporters," *Journal of African Economies*, 18 (5), 781–823.

Walker, F.A. (1887) "The Source of Business Profits," *Quarterly Journal of Economics*, 1(3), 265–88.

Weijland, H. (1999) "Microenterprise Clusters in Rural Indonesia: Industrial Seedbed and Policy Target," *World Development*, 27(9), 1515–30.

Williamson, O.E. (1985) *The Economic Institutions of Capitalism: Firms, Markets, Relational Contracting* (New York: Free Press).

Wooldridge, J.M. (2001) "Applications of Generalized Method of Moments Estimation," *Journal of Economic Perspective*, 15(4), 87–100.

Wooldridge, J.M. (2002) *Econometric Analysis of Cross Section and Panel Data* (Cambridge: MIT Press).

World Trade Organization (WTO) (2007) International Trade Statistics, available at http://www.wto.org/ english/res_e/statis_e/statis_e.htm accessed on August 23, 2007.

Yamamura, E., Sonobe, T., and Otsuka, K. (2003) "Human Capital, Cluster Formation, and International Relocation: The Case of the Garment Industry in Japan, 1968–98," *Journal of Economic Geography*, 3(1), 37–56.

Zafar, A. (2007) "The Growing Relatonship between China and Sub-Saharan Africa: Macroeconomic, Trade, Investment, and Aid Links," *World Bank Research Observer*, 22 (1), 103–130.

Author Index

Subject Index